DIGNITY
BY
FIRE

Dismantling Arizona's
Anti-Immigrant Machine

Randy Parraz

Printed in the United States of America

ISBN Hardcover: 978-1-7376954-1-7

*To all the families who suffered unnecessarily and unjustly
under the reign of Senate President Russell Pearce,
Sheriff Joe Arpaio, and Governor Jan Brewer…*

*To my father, John Parraz, whose life's work as a public servant
continues to inspire me some forty-two years after his tragic death…*

*To my mother, Inez Parraz, whose sheroism, commitment,
and devotion to her family and children during some of our
darkest moments provided the foundation for my success…*

*To my life partner, Lilia Alvarez, who provides the spiritual and moral
pillars for our family as we strive each day to serve our community…and*

*To my children—Natalia, Mikabella, and Leonel—in the hope that
this story serves as an example of the bold, courageous, and visionary
leadership that this world needs and they may someday provide.*

Table of Contents

Foreword

"The arc of the moral universe is long, but it bends towards justice," words first spoken by abolitionist minister Theodore Parker in 1856, repeated by Martin Luther King Jr., and popularized by Barack Obama. *However, justice is not inevitable, and at certain points in the arc, action is required to keep it bending.* One of those points of action took place in Arizona in 2011. As varied a group of citizens as has ever been assembled—Republican and Democrat precinct committeepersons, progressive Democrats, Mormon housewives, labor activists, conservative lawyers, immigration advocates—took matters into their own hands in what would become the first ever recall of a senate president in the 235-year history of the United States.

Arizona in 2010 was not a hospitable place for civil rights. Sheriff Joe Arpaio had enjoyed a two-decades-long reign of terror building his "America's toughest sheriff" image at the expense of immigrants, minorities, and inmates in his inhumane "Tent City" jail. Arpaio had a willing accomplice in Maricopa County Attorney Andrew Thomas, who ran almost exclusively on an anti-immigrant platform and would eventually be disbarred for his unethical tactics. When Senate Bill 1070—the broadest and strictest anti-immigrant measure in recent US history—passed in 2010, Arizona Governor Jan Brewer gleefully signed the bill into law, despite warnings that the law unfairly and unconstitutionally targeted Latinos and immigrants.

Astride all of this was the man whom the New York Times would later call "the most powerful politician in Arizona"—Senate President Russell Pearce. Pearce was the author and champion of SB1070 and other similarly regressive legislation, mainly targeted at immigrants. He had served in the Arizona legislature for years as a far right-wing outlier, but by 2010 he had bullied his way into the position of senate president. Concerned by Pearce's almost single-minded focus on immigration issues, an opposition group was born. Citizens for a Better Arizona put the new senate president on notice that his actions were being watched to ensure that the legislature focused on issues important to every Arizonan—health care, education, job creation, and public safety. Instead, it quickly became clear Pearce was preparing to take his unique brand of nativism mainstream while attempting to purge the legislature of representatives unwilling to go along.

When Randy Parraz came up with the idea of recalling Senator Pearce and asked me to be the chairman of the recall committee, I didn't hesitate in saying "yes." Randy and I came from very different backgrounds—he a progressive Democrat, Latino, community organizer, Harvard-educated, union activist and me a conservative, White, Mormon, lifelong Republican, attorney, and business owner. However, we shared a concern for the reactionary and toxic state of politics in Arizona at the time. The recall movement was initially met with almost universal skepticism. Most argued that Pearce was simply too powerful, too well-funded, and too entrenched in the most conservative legislative district in the state. Many well-intentioned politicians tried to dissuade us from going forward with the recall, arguing that it would only serve to consolidate Pearce's power and embolden him to take more drastic positions. Threats of physical violence and damage to our businesses and reputations became commonplace. Pearce himself boasted that he was 16–0 in elections and that he "welcomed" the chance to improve on that record.

Pearce didn't realize the brand of reactionary politics he, Arpaio, Brewer, and Thomas represented was wearing thin on Arizonans. The recall was an idea whose time had come, but even the organizers would be astounded at the diverse support it received. One of the memorable moments for me came while working in the Citizens for a Better Arizona office, preparing to canvass a neighborhood in Pearce's district. I saw Liana Clarkson, who was a Republican precinct committeeperson, Mormon, mother, and grandmother, preparing mailers alongside Dan O'Neal, who was at the time the chairman of the Progressive Democrats of Arizona, approaching seventy years of age, and an atheist!

That experience was not unique, and we witnessed others like it almost daily for ten months. When Pearce lost the special recall election to someone who had never run for office, none of us realized the magnitude of change that followed.

The effect on Arizona politics in the aftermath of the recall was palpable. The movement put extremist politicians on notice and created room to maneuver for more moderate leaders. I don't think even Randy or I realized the full impact of what the recall accomplished until we had a private meeting several months later with a legislative leader of Pearce's party. He congratulated us on the recall and reminded us that Pearce had been the main opponent to expanding Medicaid coverage in the state. He told us that as a result of removing Pearce, 250,000 more Arizonans now had healthcare. This would not have been possible had Pearce remained senate president.

The recall today remains a part of the civics instruction in Arizona schools—an example of the power of everyday citizens to hold their leaders accountable. I learned many things from participating in this important part of Arizona's history, but two stick out. First, when people from divergent backgrounds put their differences aside and work together towards a common goal, all political problems can be solved. And second, there is no limit to what can be accomplished when no one cares who gets the credit (an axiom made famous by Ronald Reagan). We experienced that in the recall when hundreds of Arizonans took a stand and worked together without regard for who would benefit most or get credit.

However, every conflagration requires an initial spark, and for this one, I give credit to my friend—Randy Parraz.

Chad Snow
Chairman, Citizens for a Better Arizona

CHAPTER 1

Fire

There's a certain kind of fire that no water could put out.
~ Dr. Martin Luther King Jr.

Inspiration for this book's title came from Dr. Martin Luther King Jr.'s "I've Been to the Mountaintop" speech of April 3, 1968, at Mason Temple in Memphis, Tennessee, the night before his assassination. When referencing Birmingham Sheriff Bull Connor's use of fire hoses to beat back the nonviolent forces of children marching in the streets for justice, King mentioned the idea of "transphysics" and that "there was a certain kind of fire that no water could put out." No matter how much water Bull Conner dumped on these children, it would never touch the fire of righteousness that burned eternally in the hearts and minds of those who were fighting for a better future. Nothing demands the healing power of this fire more than when the most vulnerable among us are stripped of their *dignity*—their sense of self-worth, respect and honor. The word dignity comes from the Latin *dignus*, meaning worthy. The fight in Birmingham was not just about ending segregation or the right to vote. It was about dignity—about Blacks being *worthy* of equal justice under the law and *worthy* of the right to vote.

We all have "it" inside of us, the kind of fire no water can put out. The kind of fire that shapes who we are and inspires what we do. When

I was a child, my grandmother, Mamá Mary, spoke to me of a certain flame I had inside that made me special. In Catholic school, I learned about God, the story of the burning bush, and the fire of the Holy Spirit. In these instances, fire did not consume, destroy and devour all that crossed its path. This kind of fire inspired, motivated, and emboldened one to press forward—to lead, speak, and act in pursuit of some higher calling. It is this kind of fire that inspires us to reclaim our dignity when others, because of their differences, are judged and treated as less than human.

By age eleven, I still had not connected to my fire; I had not experienced any real sense of struggle, loss, or financial hardship. My father, John Parraz, was a sergeant with the Sacramento County Sheriff's Office; my mother, Inez Parraz, was an administrative assistant at JCPenney. They provided a middle-class lifestyle for my two brothers and me. My parents owned their home and we each had our own bedrooms. Despite the costs of private education, my parents sent all three of us to St. Charles Borromeo Catholic school. Although we began each school year wearing new clothes, lay-away was our norm, where clothes, once selected, were held until my mom could pay the entire bill weeks later.

In spring 1979, only four months before my twelfth birthday, this all changed. I had never heard an expression of such pain and pure agony in my life. The cries coming from the next room sounded almost like a wounded animal gasping for air. My mother wailed loudly and cried out, "Please let him be alive! Please tell me that he is in the hospital!"

I did not know what to do. I laid there in a sleeping bag emotionally scared and physically paralyzed. My mind flooded with questions: *What's causing her so much pain? How come my tíos [uncles and aunts] are not crying? When is my father going to arrive? Did something happen to Mama Mary and Tata Mike?*

As I laid there, I recalled the cold and somber embrace I felt just minutes earlier when my *tíos* arrived. When the door opened, I jumped up and embraced them with a hug filled with excitement and anticipation of the special day that was about to unfold. However, as I looked at them, I could see only sadness and sympathy in their eyes. As they walked past my brothers and me, I had no idea of the severity of the tragedy that now fell on their shoulders to deliver to their sister and her sons.

My mother, brothers, and I had arrived in Visalia, California, on a Friday to be part of a huge family celebration—the fiftieth wedding anniversary of my grandparents, Mamá Mary and Tata Mike. My maternal grandfather, Miguel Navarrete, was born in Coyame, Chihuahua, Mexico.[1] He immigrated to the US with his parents during the Mexican Revolution. My maternal grandmother, Maria Reyes, was born in Cuatrocienegas, Coahuila, Mexico. Both of my maternal grandparents immigrated to the US with their families when they were young.

Visalia was about three hours from our home in Sacramento. My mother left work early so we could arrive at the evening rehearsal dinner. Like my father, she, too, was rising in her career and blazing a path right before this tragedy struck. She had left her job at JCPenney to become a computer technician for a new company called TRW. Now, when she walked into JCPenney, it was to fix electronic cash registers, not to keep track of administrative records. As part of their affirmative action program, TRW recruited my mother and sent her to New Jersey for three weeks of intense computer training, where she did remarkably well among those in her cohort.

My father planned to join us Saturday morning after finishing up some work-related meetings. He was recently appointed to serve in the newly created position of minority affairs liaison for Sacramento County Sheriff Duane Lowe. As with most public officials with political responsibilities, my father did not have a typical nine-to-five job.

---

[1] My grandfather was part Tarahumara, an indigenous people from the state of Chihuahua, Mexico, known for their long-distance running ability.

Within minutes, my *tíos* came out of the room and asked us to join my mother. As we entered the room, I could see my mother on her knees, sobbing hysterically. My *tíos* asked us to kneel beside her with our arms around each other—holding tight and waiting for the very moment that would make this day—March 31, 1979—the worst day of our lives. My *tío* asked my mother to tell us what had happened. Instead, she began to hyperventilate, unable to speak. Nor could she hold herself upright, so my *tíos* positioned themselves on each side of her for support.

At this point, I knew something terrible had happened to my father. Still, I gazed downward and told myself repeatedly: *My dad is going to be OK.*

My *tío* tried again, "Inez, you need to tell them. They need to hear it from you." My mother wept louder, still unable to put more than two words together. Finally, after three tries, my *tío* put his arm on our shoulders and said, "Your father has been in an accident."

An accident? Thoughts coursed through my mind: *Tell me he is in the hospital. Tell me we can go visit him. Tell me he is alive.* My heart beat so fast, my body was shaking.

"Your father is no longer with us." My *tío* continued to talk, but my mind had blocked out everything. Part of me felt embarrassed because no tears of sadness rolled down my face. At that moment, my mind and body went into deep denial and survival mode. I refused to accept this news. There had to be some other explanation for my father's delay.

So, what was to be a joyous wedding anniversary celebration instantaneously turned into preparing for a funeral. Still in denial, I was fully present for the grieving and celebrating of my father's life. He had been hit by a car and died instantly. Two weeks later, after the funeral and after everyone returned home, I looked out the window in my bedroom and noticed my father's car missing from the spot where he had always parked it. The reality of his death and his absence from our lives had finally sunk in—he was gone.

Questions raced through my mind: *Who would protect us? Who would lead our family forward? Who would help us? What was expected of me? How could I help my mother? How could I honor my father?*

At that moment, I accepted his death and, in doing so, felt a deep burning sensation in my chest—a sensation that moved me way beyond tears and dropped me to my knees. As I knelt, I prayed. I silently told my father I would never take drugs, and I would commit myself to school and get straight As—no matter what.

My father's life example and his tragic death ignited my fire.

John Parraz was not just a deputy sheriff. My father was one of two co-founders of the National Latino Peace Officers Association, an organization founded in the 1970s to combat discrimination in recruiting, hiring, and retaining Latino officers. One of seven children, he grew up in Corcoran, California; his parents, Carlos and Dolores Parraz, migrated from West Texas to California during the Great Depression. My paternal grandfather Carlos was born in Pecos, Texas, and my paternal grandmother Dolores was born in a small Texas town called La Mesa. They both worked in the fields, where Carlos had a reputation of being the fastest cotton picker around. My father earned his bachelor's degree in criminal justice by going to night school *after* he was married and supporting three young boys.

In our household, the word MAGA meant something completely different than it does today. It was not a presidential slogan; it stood for the Mexican American Golf Association. My father held various MAGA leadership positions while building a political base to perhaps run for office, maybe sheriff in a neighboring county. My father's term of endearment for me was "*güero güerinche*," the light-skinned one. Because of my light hair and fair complexion, which differed from his black hair and brown complexion, he always joked that I was not his son. My father had just begun to live a life full of promise when his life was tragically cut short.

If he could accomplish so much before his fortieth birthday, surely, I could honor him and his legacy by doing my part. The fire ignited by my father's death fueled my drive through high school, college, and graduate school. After passing the California State Bar, it inspired my decision to move to Dallas and pursue a career as a community organizer to help people build power to solve problems. And that fire fueled many efforts to challenge people in positions of authority who had abused their power by attacking some of our most vulnerable communities.

My journey as a student activist, community organizer, and workers' rights advocate spanned three decades. From college sit-ins to civil disobedience actions for workers on strike to organizing campaigns to support issues and candidates for working families, my exposure to various approaches to social change was extensive.

After graduate school, I traveled to India to study Gandhi's teachings of nonviolence. While in Calcutta, I met Mother Teresa and volunteered with Missionaries of Charity to serve the poorest of the poor in Calcutta. After witnessing Mother Teresa's approach to service, my commitment deepened to advocate on behalf of the "have-nots."

My life as an organizer took me to Dallas, Washington, DC, and northern and southern California. By 2002, after spending six years with the National AFL-CIO, I was offered the position of AFL-CIO state director for Arizona. Besides a family vacation trip to the Grand Canyon as a child, I knew very little about Arizona. I took the job more as an opportunity for a fresh start and a new challenge but with no particular desire to live in Arizona. For the next two years, my primary assignment involved coordinating a statewide process to rethink, restructure, and rebuild the labor movement in Arizona. By 2004, I grew impatient and frustrated with the AFL-CIO's structural limitations when it came to initiating and driving a national campaign to organize millions of unrepresented workers. The emphasis on politics and the inability to hold leaders accountable for moving an agenda that would attract and inspire a new generation of workers forced me to rethink my career. In short, I felt our strategies did not match the urgency of the situation, like showing up to a house fire with a water pistol instead of a massive fire truck. I abruptly resigned from the AFL-CIO in June of 2004 and returned with my family to Southern California. Even though I did not have a job lined up, and with a spouse and two daughters to support, I knew I could not stay a day longer. It was time to go. Within a year, I was still only employed part-time and in the middle of a full-blown divorce.

Over the next few years, I bounced from one project to another. By 2006, though, I accepted an opportunity to serve as executive director of the Voter Registration and Education Project (VREP), a nonprofit organization that worked closely with the California Latino Legislative Caucus to educate, mobilize and engage Latino voters. However, my stint with VREP did not last long. Just as my professional career regained its footing, my personal life continued to unravel.

In the spring of 2007, as our divorce was being finalized, my wife decided to move back to Scottsdale, Arizona, with our daughters, Natalia, seven, and Mikabella, five. I remained in Sacramento and made a commitment to fly to Phoenix every other weekend to visit my daughters. I underestimated the emotional impact of this new arrangement, especially when we said goodbye at the airport. The look in their eyes as tears ran down their cheeks and the sounds of them crying as they asked me to stay pierced my heart. Those images and sounds would stay with me from that moment until I returned two weeks later.

What had I done? Had I made the right decision to allow them to relocate to Scottsdale? How much longer could I do this? What might happen if or when I can't come to see them every two weeks?

After only a month of this new arrangement, I knew in my heart that I could no longer continue to work and live in Sacramento. In June, I resigned from VREP and prepared to move back to Arizona. Upon my return to Arizona, the Laborers' International Union of North America hired me to serve as the political director for a groundbreaking campaign to organize immigrant workers in residential construction. At the time, I knew very little about a sheriff named Joe Arpaio and a state senator named Russell Pearce—and of course, they had never heard of me.

During the next two years, the harassment and persistent attacks on these workers by Arpaio and his deputies escalated along with the rising tide of anti-immigrant sentiment throughout Arizona and the country. Arpaio, the self-proclaimed "toughest sheriff in the country" was known for forcing inmates to wear pink underwear and creating a so-called Tent City.[2] He was also the most-sued sheriff in the country—the defendant in more than 2,000 lawsuits—as he constantly abused his power to intimidate, harass, and punish his enemies. As attacks against immigrants became increasingly popular politically, Arpaio exploited this by launching crime sweeps in Latino neighborhoods and worksite raids on businesses with a predominantly Latino immigrant workforce.

By the spring of 2010, Arizona's anti-immigrant movement pushed the Arizona legislature to pass the most radical anti-immigrant bill in the country—Senate Bill 1070. Its author, State Senator Russell Pearce, ascended to power on a platform of hate, bigotry, and anti-immigrant rhetoric that culminated with the passage of Arizona's "Show me your papers" law. Pearce and Arpaio joined forces to harass, lock up and deport every "illegal" in the state. With the passage of SB 1070, law enforcement officers statewide had the authority to stop anyone who looked "reasonably suspicious" and ask for proof of citizenship.

The passage of SB 1070 triggered a tremendous reaction from groups of all backgrounds who denounced the law as anti-immigrant, racist, divisive, unnecessary, punitive, and mean-spirited. Despite calls

---

[2] Tent City was an outside jail that consisted of military-type tents. It was dismantled after Sheriff Arpaio was defeated in the 2016 election.

to boycott Arizona, protests at the Capitol, civil disobedience, prayer vigils, and mass marches, Pearce emerged unscathed and emboldened.

Like many progressives in Arizona, I, too, had my SB 1070 moment. When Governor Jan Brewer signed the bill into law, I declared my candidacy for US Senate the very next week to run against incumbent John McCain. As the only Latino candidate in the country running for the senate, I thought my campaign could serve as a call to action and spark a movement for thousands of Latino activists and other progressives. Unfortunately, my candidacy never garnered enough support to make it out of the primary. Although my mom will tell you I came in fourth, the reality is I placed last among three other contenders.

Seven months after the passage of SB 1070, Pearce's ascension continued. Within days of being reelected to the state senate, his colleagues rewarded his racist, xenophobic, and anti-immigrant conduct by selecting him as the next president of Arizona's state senate. When the legislative session opened on January 10, 2011, Pearce appeared to be invincible. His credentials included senate president, Tea Party president, and some even referred to him as the *de facto* governor (Brewer's signing of SB 1070 cemented her reelection). Buoyed by his power, Pearce's legislative assault against immigrants was just getting started. By March, he had introduced another round of anti-immigrant bills that far surpassed the impact and reach of SB 1070.

My internal fire dictated that the de-humanizing of immigrants had to stop. The extreme attacks on education, teachers, women, workers, unions, even the Constitution—all had to stop. Reluctant to wait Pearce out, a small group of citizens and I decided to pick a fight and launch an unprecedented grassroots movement to remove him from office. If we won, the legislative agenda would be reset, especially when it came to anti-immigrant laws. But if we lost, Pearce and his allies would be emboldened to ramp up their rhetoric, attacks, and extreme brand of politics, especially when it came to immigration.

Just ten months later, in November 2011, Pearce made a different type of history. *He became the first sitting president of a state senate in US history to be recalled and removed from office.* Pearce was done. He went from being one of the most powerful politicians in Arizona to being dethroned.

What follows is a story about how a very small number of ordinary Arizonans banded together to set in motion a series of events that ultimately led to Pearce's downfall. From the time the recall effort surfaced to Pearce's final defeat in the 2012 Republican primary, Arizonans had never before witnessed a political narrative of this magnitude.

Pearce's rhetoric and tactics made some Republicans nervous, but no Republican in their right mind would initiate a recall against one of their own, let alone a senate president. No matter how much Pearce's actions infuriated Democrats, no Democrat could defeat Pearce in a special recall election. Neither party, then, was about to wage a recall effort against Pearce. In short, no current institution—political, business or nonprofit—saw any gain in initiating such a public attack on the senate president.

When we announced the recall, people laughed.

When we collected signatures, people said, "You are wasting your time."

When we turned in the signatures petitioning for a recall, people said, "You don't have a candidate."

When the candidate finally emerged, people said, "He doesn't have a chance."

When we defeated Pearce by double digits, people said, "Pearce will simply reclaim his seat nine months later in the 2012 Republican primary."

Some nine months later, when we defeated Pearce—again, by double digits—people finally acknowledged he was politically done.

The decision to launch the Pearce recall grew out of our belief in ordinary grassroots Democrats and Republicans, liberals and conservatives—that they too would share our concern that Pearce was just too extreme for Arizona. To recall and remove him from office, Republicans *needed* Democrats, and Democrats *needed* Republicans. Republicans needed Democrats to spearhead the collection of signatures to recall Pearce and initiate a special recall election. And Democrats needed Republicans to identify and recruit the right type of Republican candidate to challenge Pearce.

Now in 2021, with the nation so bitterly divided, the story of the Pearce recall provides a compelling example of how both Republicans and Democrats, sometimes secretly and other times in the open, can, should and must work together to rid politics of individuals who are too extreme, too divisive and too destructive. For some politicians, the decision by activists and other leaders to wait them out until the next election has immediate, damaging, and sometimes irreversible consequences. Pearce's hateful rhetoric and racist behavior encouraged others to do the same.

When we initiated the recall, nothing was certain about the outcome. I'm reminded of Victor Hugo's statement, "There is nothing more powerful than an idea whose time has come." After one hundred years of Arizona political history, in 2011, the time had come for Russell Pearce to be the first—the first president of the senate and legislator removed from office by citizens fighting for a better Arizona.

CHAPTER 2

Unchecked Hate

Hate is too great a burden to bear. It injures the hater more than it injures the hated.

~ Coretta Scott King

For many in the progressive movement, Pearce's SB 1070 hit us like a wild brushfire, incapable of being contained. However, we shouldn't have been blindsided by Pearce's assault against immigrants in 2010. He had been pushing extreme bills on immigration since he entered the Arizona House of Representatives in 2001. Pearce was the former chief deputy to Sheriff Arpaio and the architect of the infamous Tent City. He took a hard line on those who broke the law—especially when it involved border issues.

Early in his career as a legislator, many of Pearce's extreme bills did not make it out of committee, even though Republicans controlled both houses. From the moment he entered politics, Pearce set out to redefine what it meant to be Republican and conservative in Arizona. The process of criminalizing undocumented immigrants started slowly and began to build with each legislative session. In 2002, he introduced a bill calling for the Arizona National Guard to control the southern border and engage in agreements with other entities to stop illegal crossings. The bill failed. Pearce authored another bill seeking more federal resources for border security. It failed.

In 2003, Pearce introduced his first voter identification bill, requiring proof of citizenship for all voters, to keep "illegals" from voting. The bill failed. He then turned his attention to hospitals and introduced a bill that would require health care professionals to notify the US Department of Immigration and Naturalization Service of any undocumented patients—designed to keep them from receiving any taxpayer-funded benefits. It failed.

When it came to "Dreamers," the children of undocumented parents who were brought to the US without the permission of the government, Pearce took pleasure in limiting their educational opportunities in Arizona.[1] He authored a bill that required universities and community colleges to bar admittance to undocumented students and report the legal status of all students every semester to the Arizona Board of Regents and US Attorney General's office. This bill was held in committee.

By 2004, the Pearce anti-immigrant train gained momentum. He sponsored a bill to deny undocumented students the ability to be classified as in-state students. If he could not bar Dreamers from entering state colleges, then he wanted to squeeze them out financially by raising their costs for pursuing a college degree. Pearce did not stop there. He then filed a bill that mandated the state to verify citizenship for every driver when issuing driver's licenses. The bill required all drivers to show proof that their presence in the US was "authorized."

Pearce used the "us" (citizens) versus "them" (illegals) framework to drive his anti-immigrant agenda. According to him, the illegal immigration "crisis" was akin to, as he put it, "injecting yourself with cancer cells

---

[1] The term "DREAM" as it refers to "Dreamers" means individuals who qualify for relief under the Development, Relief, and Education for Alien Minors (DREAM) Act. The bill has yet to pass both houses of Congress.

to see what will happen. It's like importing leper colonies and hope we don't catch leprosy."

John Loredo, a fourth-generation Arizonan served in the legislature from 1996 until 2004. He was elected to serve as the Democratic Minority Leader in 2002. Loredo found Pearce and his views highly offensive from the moment Pearce was elected to the house. Loredo led the effort to kill every one of Pearce's anti-immigrant bills before they even reached the floor. Although Loredo could not kill Pearce's bills on his own, he could rely on an anti-Pearce Republican Caucus of about fifteen members who would, when necessary, crossover and help block Pearce's extremist agenda.

Before Loredo left the legislature in late 2004, he spoke to business leaders at the Arizona Chamber of Commerce. As he took the podium, he turned to Benito Almanza, president of Bank of America, and said softly, "I am going to rip into Russell Pearce." Such personal attacks rarely happened at these public functions. As he ended his speech, Loredo warned business leaders about Pearce, "You better stop him. You better stop him now. Because I am telling you after he is done coming after us, he is coming after you. When he does, you will be in trouble."

Indeed, in the next few years, Pearce, using candidates more like himself, targeted some of the more moderate, pro-business Republicans so he could impose his extremist agenda on the legislature. In 2005, Pearce and his Republican allies finally broke through and managed to get a bill to the governor's desk that authorized all peace officers to function as Immigration and Naturalization Service agents and investigate, apprehend, detain, and remove aliens. Democratic Governor Janet Napolitano vetoed the bill, but the criminalization of undocumented immigrants ratcheted up with each passing year.

To support Pearce's desire to deport thousands of undocumented immigrants, Pearce and his allies funded private prisons built and operated by the Correction Corporation of America to warehouse all those suspected of being "illegal." The legislature even passed a concurrent resolution whereby all illegal aliens detained for unlawful entry could be denied bail and detained indefinitely, thereby creating a new pool of customers—undocumented immigrants—for these prisons. This resolution eventually became law.

In addition to these bills, Pearce relentlessly recycled bills he'd filed in prior years, especially the one that barred Dreamers from being classified as "in-state" residents for tuition purposes and receiving any government assistance for post-secondary education. In 2006 alone, Pearce and his anti-immigrant colleagues introduced twenty-five bills related to immigration, the border, and other areas of everyday living that impacted undocumented immigrants.

When Pearce could not get his bills passed in the legislature, he turned to the ballot and statewide propositions. From 2004 through 2007, Pearce successfully pushed ballot initiatives that required voter identification to cast a ballot, named English as the official language, banned in-state tuition and financial aid to undocumented college students, and prohibited businesses from knowingly or intentionally hiring undocumented workers (also known as "employer sanctions" or E-Verify). They all passed.

Before Pearce arrived in the legislature, there was no employer sanctions law or human smuggling law. With the passage of employer sanctions in 2007, Pearce provided Arpaio the legal framework to conduct arbitrary and discriminatory raids against businesses that employed Latino immigrants. When I interviewed Arpaio by phone, he told me, "That's when I started my push on illegal immigration, anybody here in the country (illegally) should be arrested and deported. I didn't have the laws before. I had the 287 (g) program[2] that gave me authority. I

---

[2] The 287 g program allowed the director of Immigration and Customs Enforcement (ICE) to enter into agreements with state and local law enforcement agencies to perform limited law enforcement functions.

commend him (Pearce) for pushing these laws. I had both the state and federal laws on my side."

These victories for Pearce culminated in the passage of SB 1070 in 2010. It broadened Arpaio's legal authority to identify, detain, and deport "unauthorized aliens."[3] The law also required "aliens" aged eighteen and older to carry documents at all times, made it a state crime to be in Arizona without papers, legalized the "reasonable suspicion" standard for law enforcement officers to stop and ask for someone's papers, and criminalized the harboring, transportation, and employment of an unauthorized alien. Anyone who knowingly invited an undocumented person into their homes, hired them to babysit their kids, cut their lawns, or clean their homes were considered criminals.

Arpaio, usually the one to take credit for anything that involved rounding up undocumented immigrants, deferred to Pearce when it came to SB 1070. Arpaio praised Pearce's determination and vision: "He came up with SB 1070. Pearce was the one driving all of the anti-immigrant work. The governor took four or five days to sign the bill, but it was really Pearce who started this thing. Pearce should have got the credit not Brewer. Pearce was first with the anti-immigrant rhetoric."

And then Arpaio, who was quick to cash in on the anti-immigrant fervor building in Arizona and across the country, continued his worksite raids and illegal profiling of Latino citizens and immigrants. By November 2010, Arpaio and his deputies had racked up close to forty worksite raids that did little to punish employers but cruelly and unnecessarily caused unimaginable harm to undocumented immigrants caught up in the raids.

Despite Pearce's track record, the extremism of SB 1070 caught the progressive movement by surprise. As someone relatively new to Arizona, I didn't sense much urgency from various leaders. What I kept

---

[3] "Unauthorized aliens" is the legal term used in the original text of SB 1070.

hearing in progressive circles went something like: "These types of bills don't usually make it out of committee. If they do, then the business community will step in. If they don't step in, then the governor will surely veto such an anti-immigrant, anti-Latino bill."

Unfortunately, these leaders underestimated how Republicans valued and respected the Latino community—not the immigrant community—but Latinos who were in positions of power and influence. Chicanos Por La Causa (CPLC), one of the largest community-based organizations in the country, invited Governor Jan Brewer to speak at their annual dinner just days before she was scheduled to sign SB 1070. Brewer had yet to indicate her position on the bill before speaking to the predominantly Latino audience. Before she took the stage, CPLC chairwoman Erica Gonzalez-Melendez, made it clear where the group stood on SB 1070: "The eyes of our state and the eyes of our nation are upon you," she said. "What sits before you on your desk is the most hateful piece of legislation directed at Latinos in the recent history of our state."

Her comments drew huge applause. Gonzalez-Melendez continued, "This law would further open the door to racial profiling of all Latinos in our state and would create a culture of fear and mistrust ... This law only panders to the racist fearmongers of our state ... Governor, we ask, actually, we respectfully demand, that you veto Senate Bill 1070."

The crowd responded with a standing ovation and began to chant "Veto! Veto! Veto!" Despite the crowd's chants, Brewer gave her remarks as planned and refused to share with the group where she stood on SB 1070.

The leadership at CPLC chose to engage Brewer rather than isolate her, hoping that by letting her speak at the dinner, she would not then turn her back on them and sign SB 1070. But other events conspired against those opposed to the bill. The murder of rancher Rob Krentz along the Arizona-Mexican border a month earlier by someone suspected of being "illegal," coupled with Brewer's need to squash any Republican challengers in the upcoming Republican primary, left little room for her to maneuver.

On April 23, 2010, after ten days of protests, rallies, meetings, and candlelight vigils—Brewer turned her back on the Latino community and signed the bill. It catapulted Arizona into the national debate on immigration. Arizona became ground zero in the fight to challenge and roll back any current and future attacks against immigrants and their families.

With the stroke of her pen, Brewer accomplished two objectives. First, she cemented her victory in the 2010 Republican primary. Within weeks of signing the bill, all Brewer's challengers withdrew from the race. Pearce's SB 1070 was the perfect gift for a vulnerable and weak governor in need of some intervention to solidify her path to victory in November. Some would argue that without SB 1070, Brewer would not have survived the Republican primary. And second, Brewer's signing categorized a whole class of people—brown people in this case—as being "reasonably suspicious" by their mere presence in the state.

Brewer had succeeded Governor Janet Napolitano, who had been appointed by President Barack Obama as secretary of homeland security in 2009. Most agreed Napolitano would have vetoed SB 1070.

Pearce's success was the culmination of almost a decade's worth of anti-immigrant dogma, attacks, and half-truths intended to scapegoat Latinos and immigrants for all that was wrong in Arizona, a sentiment that seemed to be catching on.

Eager to capitalize on this, Pearce spent the summer challenging the legality of the Constitution's guarantee of birthright citizenship. With little concern about the limits of state's rights, Pearce proposed denying citizenship to children born in this country to "illegal" immigrants—as if the *United Counties of Arizona* trumped the authority of the United States of America. To further fire up his base, Pearce referred to these children as "anchor babies" whose birth in the United States allowed their parents and family members to access all sorts of public benefits.

To close out 2010, Pearce authored and pushed one more statewide proposition attacking people of color: the Arizona Civil Rights Amendment. This proposition banned all affirmative action programs in Arizona administered by government agencies at all levels—state, county, city and school districts. Despite opposition from numerous organizations and elected officials, the ban on affirmative action passed with 60 percent of the vote or a margin of more than 300,000 votes.

During his first decade in the legislature, Pearce, similar to President Trump, did not hold back on what he thought about immigrants, Mexicans, and, of course, all those "illegals." Here are just a few examples of Pearce's hate-filled beliefs taken from his statements and emails discovered in a request for public information filed by the Arizona ACLU:

What's coming across that border today are gang members, child molesters, drug runners, human smugglers, three out of ten have a criminal record.

Can we maintain our social fabric as a nation with Spanish fighting English for dominance? ... It's like importing thousands of Islamic jihadists and hope they adapt to the American Dream.

We create cultural and linguistic apartheid by creating a slave class of workers unassimilated while growing in numbers and antagonistic strength. This condition creates a perfect formula for rioting and violence that will tear our nation to pieces! Ask Paris, France!

Battles commence as Mexican nationalists struggle to infuse their men into American government and strengthen control over their strongholds. One look at Los Angeles with its Mexican-American mayor shows you Vicente Fox's general Varigossa (correct spelling is Villaraigosa) *commanding an American city.*

They create enclaves of separate groups that shall balkanize our nation into fractured nightmares of social unrest and poverty.

Corruption is the mechanism by which Mexico operates. Its people spawn more corruption wherever they go because it is their only known way of life.

Tough, nasty illegals and their advocates grow in such numbers that law and order will not subdue them. They run us out of our cities and states. They conquer our language and our schools. They render havoc and chaos in our schools.

The illegal aliens in the United States have a crime rate that's two-and-a-half times that of non-illegal aliens. In particular, their children are going to make a huge additional crime problem in the U.S.

I'm racist because I don't want to be taxed to pay for a prison population comprised of mainly Hispanics, Latinos, Mexicans or whatever else you wish to call them. ... I'm a racist because I believe the News Media has a duty to tell us the names and race of criminals. ... I'm a racist because I object to having to pay higher sales tax and property tax to build more schools for the illegitimate children of illegal aliens. ... I'm a racist because I dislike having to push one for English and/or listening to a message in Spanish.

Pearce also associated with White supremacists such as JT Ready, described by the Southern Poverty Law Center as a neo-Nazi. In the early 2000s, Pearce sponsored Ready to join the Mormon Church of Latter-day Saints; he later ordained Ready as an elder with the church. In 2007, Pearce shared a stage with Ready at a rally on the Capitol grounds and applauded many of Ready's anti-immigrant and nativist statements. As Ready's White supremacist views were exposed, Pearce was forced to distance himself from Ready publicly. In 2012, Ready murdered his girlfriend and three members of her family, including a sixteen-month-old girl, before turning the gun on himself. They say the company a person keeps says a lot about the character of a woman or man. Though extreme, this was not atypical of the company Pearce kept.

When Pearce took his seat as senate president in January 2011, John Loredo viewed the proceedings from the balcony. The former legislator found Pearce's rise to power extremely difficult to accept. "When I left in 2004, this guy was nothing," Loredo said. "And now he is senate president. We can't mess around with this anymore. We need to build for 2012. This is bad. Now he has the authority to come right at us." With no legislative or executive branch backstop in sight, Pearce was ready and eager to continue the work of demonizing and scapegoating immigrants and their families.

Given Loredo's experience as a legislator and political operative, I asked him to meet me in November 2010 to share the idea of recalling Pearce. Although Loredo desperately wanted Pearce out of office, he found the psychology of initiating this public fight at this particular moment a bit challenging. "We just lost eleven seats and now you want to take on the president of the senate," he said. "We can't even win our own races."

I reminded him that for now we did not have to worry about finding a candidate. We just had to focus on collecting 7,756 signatures, and maybe, just maybe, we could make Pearce the first senate president to be recalled. In Arizona, if 25 percent of the total number of voters in a particular legislative district who voted in the previous election sign a petition to recall a state legislature, then that elected official must run again in a special election to hold onto their position. Loredo liked the idea but needed more time to get his affiliates and other national allies, such as Public Campaign, interested in taking on such a fight.

Time was not on our side. Pearce did not struggle, fight, and campaign for ten years to become senate president just to maintain the status quo. He was about to launch one of the most aggressive anti-immigrant legislative offensives in Arizona's history, and we needed a strategy to stop him. The next election was two years away—way too long to wait.

We needed put a stop to the hate that was about to be unleashed … again.

CHAPTER 3

Threshold for Injustice

When someone shows you who they are, believe them the first time.
~ Maya Angelou

The weekend after the November 2, 2010, election felt like a funeral. Very little had changed in Arizona. Governor Brewer won reelection by double digits. Sheriff Arpaio's reelection campaign was still two years away, and State Senator Russell crushed his opponents by a 20 percentage-point margin of victory. Could it get any worse?

Like most political junkies, I enjoyed watching the Sunday morning talk shows at the local and national levels. For me, the shows immediately following elections were always must-see TV. As I sat on the couch watching the Sunday morning news show *Sunday Square Off*, NBC's local equivalent to *Meet the Press*, Pearce was the main guest. My first thought was: *Why is Russell Pearce on "Sunday Square Off" after the election?* It was no surprise that he would be reelected.

Then, host Brahm Resnik asked, "As president of the senate, how…" and before he finished the question, I jumped up from the couch and yelled, "Oh hell no! Are you kidding me? President of the senate?"

After each election, senators of the majority party meet to elect the person to serve as senate president. Most voters do not follow such legislative moves, but Pearce's election by his colleagues to serve as senate president was breaking news.

I moved closer. Had I heard that correctly? President of the senate?

My heart rate spiked. My stomach turned. I could not believe it. The message was clear: if you push policies that attack the Latino community, you'll be rewarded. Politicians typically change their behavior when there are real, swift, and hard-hitting consequences to their actions. During the seven months following the enactment of SB 1070, all the tactics to protest, confront, and persuade Senator Pearce to end his assault against immigrants and their families failed. He was reelected with 56 percent of the vote, and he now controlled the state's legislative agenda with a veto-proof majority in the Senate. With the reelection of Governor Jan Brewer, whose victory was in large part a direct result of her unwavering support for Pearce's bill, Pearce could now count on her total support of his extreme agenda.

And now Pearce was being congratulated, recognized, and featured on this show in his new leadership role. He had reached a level of power and influence few would have predicted. Early on in his political career, he represented a minority within his own party. Many of his extreme and anti-immigrant bills never even made it out of committee—committees controlled by Republicans. Now, a decade later, Pearce had other Tea Party legislators and a very thankful governor to do his bidding.

I redirected my attention to the interview and stood there with my mouth wide open, still shocked about what I had just heard and eager to learn more about Pearce's agenda as the new senate president. When Pearce sought his colleagues' votes for president, Resnik asked, had he pledged not to sponsor bills related to immigration or that challenged the Fourteenth Amendment's guarantee of citizenship to any person born in the US?

Pearce gave a strong no: "What we agreed to was ... as the president of the senate ... you know, I'm not gonna run a lot of bills. My job is to help move the agenda forward. The Fourteenth Amendment is gonna be run by other folks."

Pearce did not support the Fourteenth Amendment. He intended to introduce a bill to deny citizenship to any person born in the US whose parents were "illegal."

Resnik pressed Pearce on this: "Did Senator-elect John McComish and the others just misunderstand you? Because it was their clear understanding that there is going to be no immigration legislation this year."

"No, there wasn't," Pearce responded. "That's just absolutely not true. There was no deal cut. What there was is comments by me that I'd like other folks to carry as much of this legislation as possible."

As I listened to Pearce back off his pledge to *not* introduce immigration legislation, I could tell he was already planning to take his anti-immigrant agenda to a new level when the 2011 legislative session started in January.

The conversation turned to health care for the poor and Arizona's Health Care Cost Containment System Administration (AHCCCS), Arizona's Medicaid program. Pearce had been a harsh critic of any type of federal program or state mandate to expand health care for those most in need.

Resnik then asked Pearce if he was willing to turn down billions of dollars of federal aid even if that meant forcing upwards of one million Arizonans who get health care through AHCCCS to "fend for themselves."

Pearce refused to retreat or back down from his pledge to not take federal dollars to help poor Arizonans maintain their health care coverage. "What I'm saying is you sometimes can't afford to take the federal money. It's like going to Dillard's, you don't have any money, but it's a great sale. So, I'm gonna buy it, but I have no money. The federal money comes with strings. No more are we going to have our hands tied by the federal government to do what's right for Arizona. I don't think we'll take the money."

Resnik pressed Pearce about what will happen to individuals kicked off of the health care program. Pearce said, "They'll probably be OK."

At the time of this interview, one in five Arizonans relied on the state's Medicaid system for health care, while some 18,000 children had been cut from KidsCare—the version of the program for children. Likening the decision whether to provide health care for poor families and children in need to someone buying designer items he cannot afford at Dillard's department store revealed Pearce's profound dislike for any government program to help the poor.

Resnik ended the show by asking Pearce about a potential run for governor.

He did not hesitate to plant that seed. "In the end, it's the game you play. You never slam doors shut."

His words, "You never slam doors shut," echoed in my ears. How could someone as mean-spirited, hateful, divisive, racist, and bigoted as Pearce be rewarded with one of the most powerful positions in the state? What did this say about Arizona? About the millions of people who simply sat back and watched Pearce's ascendancy without any major objection? About me, as an Arizona resident, sitting back as Pearce was about to walk into the next legislative session as the senate president? Because he had just been reelected, one word came to mind: *Recall*.

We could not just wait him out. We had to force him out. Fortunately, Arizona was one of nineteen states that allowed its citizens to recall state officials.

Although familiar with the term, I had never initiated a recall. My only experience occurred during my time with the AFL-CIO. In 2003, an effort was launched to recall California Governor Gray Davis. I was assigned to help mobilize our union members in Southern California to defeat the recall campaign. Once Arnold Schwarzenegger declared his candidacy, it was game over. A wealthy, popular movie star with a tough-guy image and global name identity—who also happened to be married to a Kennedy—made our job mission impossible. As we knocked on doors and made phone calls to our members, we struggled to break through the political noise. On many of those calls, I felt more like a salesman peddling vacuum cleaners and encyclopedias than an organizer reminding our members why it was in their economic self-interests to vote against the recall.

Once the interview ended, I moved to the kitchen table and opened my laptop. I did a quick internet search with the words "Arizona recall." Within seconds I was on my way to becoming an expert. On Ballotpedia it said: "A recall can be filed against any public officer on any grounds. The recall may not be filed until after the elected official has been in office in his or her first term for at least six months." However, this six-month limit did not apply to state legislators. For state legislators, a recall petition could be initiated just five days after the start of the legislative session following their election.

Based on this, we could not legally launch a recall against Pearce for roughly another seventy days, the period of time from November 7, 2010, to five days after the opening of the January 2011 legislative session. Launching a recall would send a powerful message that people in Arizona were willing to fight back and legislators like Pearce must be held accountable.

I continued my research, downloading the secretary of state's guide for initiatives, referendums, and recalls. I still did not know what a recall entailed or what it would cost. As I read through the guide, the mechanics of launching a recall seemed straightforward and doable. We needed to gather signatures from registered voters in the district Pearce represented. Pearce's district, Legislative District 18 (LD 18), stretched from the west to east parts of the southern half of the city of Mesa. To recall Pearce, we needed 25 percent of the voters from LD 18 who participated in the 2010 election to sign the recall petition.

In this case, 31,023 people voted in Pearce's LD 18 race—which meant we needed 7,756 signatures to recall Pearce. I typed up a quick summary of the information:

- Eligible to be recalled anytime five days after legislative session begins on January 10, 2011
- Need 25 percent of total voter turnout from past election
- Total signatures needed = 7,756
- 120 days to collect and submit the signatures (roughly sixty-five signatures a day)

None of this seemed out of reach. I clicked on the voter registration counts to get a sense of the universe of voters by party. As the numbers popped up on the screen, I about fell off my chair. It read, "Registered Republicans—26,616. Registered Democrats—18,345. Registered Other—21,616." I felt a jolt of energy surge through my body. I had worked on numerous political campaigns and was very familiar with voter lists, the voter file, targeted universes, and precinct walks. I could not believe that we had a universe of 39,961 registered Democrats and "Other" voters from which to collect 7,756 valid signatures.[1] And because the voter file—a database accessible to the public that contains the voting history of each registered voter—could be easily purchased, we had access to the names, addresses, and in some cases, phone numbers of close to 40,000 registered voters in LD 18. We could take our petition directly to voters' homes and avoid the awkwardness of standing out in front of stores and on street corners. If only one out of every four voters we talked to signed the petition we'd easily surpass 7,756 signatures.

---

[1] During the petition gathering process, not all signatures are valid. Signatures can be deemed "not valid" for a number of legitimate reasons, including but not limited to: voter lives outside of district, citizen is not registered, signature is illegible, signature does not match the signature on file, etc. It is not uncommon for petitions submitted for final review to have a validity rate ranging from 55—65 percent.

I paced back and forth, talking out loud, "120 days … 7,756 signatures … universe of 40,000 voters." Not only did this seem doable, it sounded almost too easy. Curious about past recall elections, I did another search about successful recalls in Arizona. Wow! Nothing. I pressed the search button again. Nothing. Other than a recall effort against a corrupt governor—who eventually resigned before the recall could move forward—*no legislator had ever been recalled in Arizona.*

I then expanded my search to include any recall of a senate president anywhere in the nation. Nothing. Although state senators had been recalled as far back as 1913, there was no record of any successful campaign to recall a sitting senate president. A recall would be a lot of things, but if we decided to move forward, it would definitely *not* be easy.

The more I thought about it, the more it made sense. When someone becomes senate president, these conclusions can be drawn: their party is in charge; they have the support of fellow senators; they have power and influence within their state political party; if a special recall election was held, no one in their own party would challenge them; and they'd be allowed to maintain their position of power throughout the entire recall process. So, while signatures were being gathered, they could use whatever means they had as senate president to go after their adversaries. Also, for the most part, senate presidents were usually individuals who can work well with others—and who can be influenced or restrained by corporate and other special interest groups.

I made a few more notes then closed my laptop. I sat there trying to sort out the emotions that were stirring inside. My mind reverberated with the phrase "threshold for injustice," a phrase I had used many times when I ran for office. I came across it while reading stories about the civil rights movement. The term "threshold for injustice" refers to a tipping point, an accumulation of past injustices that cause someone to be outraged enough to shift from being a private citizen to a public actor. The threshold for injustice manifests the moment one feels compelled to stand up, speak out, or take action. In that moment, an internal transformation occurs that unleashes the courage, energy, and determination to pursue the pathway towards justice relentlessly. Each individual has their own threshold for injustice. However, many injustices continue because most people's thresholds are way too high.

Pearce's election as senate president was my "threshold for injustice" moment. In a matter of minutes, all my other professional interests faded. I knew I could not rest until Pearce was unseated.

I spent the next few weeks reaching out to a broad range of leaders to gauge their interests in the idea of recalling Pearce. These people became my informal Pearce Recall Exploratory Committee. I spoke with labor leaders, state senators, Democratic party operatives, and other individuals deeply involved in progressive politics. People liked the idea but thought it stood little chance—too many risks, minimal reward. Even if we succeeded in getting the signatures, we would never be able to recruit the right candidate. No sane Republican would dare challenge Pearce in a special recall election. And because Pearce could easily defeat any Democratic challenger, the whole recall process appeared to be a Don Quixote-like adventure tilting at windmills. Others believed that such a strategy could make things worse. Still, the idea of the recall gave me a new sense of purpose and urgency.

One of my most interesting meetings occurred with Ken Chapman, executive director of the Maricopa County Democratic Party (MCDP). I knew Ken from my run for US Senate, and I had heard he was bringing an Obama-style approach to politics by emphasizing base-building and voter mobilization in the field with people from all walks of life. We stayed in touch after my campaign; I liked the way he talked about movement politics.

Organizing 101 dictates that with each new campaign you ask two fundamental questions: First, what do you want, what change do you seek? Second, who or what do you need to make it happen? Once answered, the campaign can identify and mobilize the resources needed to win. I needed a strong ally in the MCDP. I needed help with voter lists, identifying Democratic activists in LD 18, and a strong ally to ensure no Democrat would challenge Pearce in a special recall election.

Since Ken's main objective as the county's Democratic leader was to identify, recruit, train, and support Democratic candidates for office—recalling Pearce was not part of his 2011 strategic plan. However, as an organizer and private citizen, he could not pass up the chance to take out Pearce. Ken was born in the Midwest but came to Arizona at age five with his mother for Arizona's hot, dry climate. She had a lung disease, and doctors advised her that places like Arizona could help her condition. Ken came from a biracial family—Black father, White mother, which can be a challenge on many fronts.

"I kind of grew up with a weird racial identity because my sister is darker than I am," he said. "Obviously I passed (as White), and so when it's my mom, my sister, and me, my sister was adopted. And when it was my dad, my sister, and me, I was adopted. It was the only way the world worked at that time."

When Ken's parents divorced, he stayed with his mother and grandparents in Arizona. His mother's lung condition worsened. As she struggled with her health, Ken painfully watched a broken and corrupt health care system kick his mother off her health insurance coverage because she had met her lifetime cap. She died shortly after that.

It was during this dark and difficult time that Ken's friend bought him a copy of Obama's book *The Audacity of Hope*. "I saw Obama in 2004 on TV and started reading his book. Obama was talking about fixing health care, but he talked about it using the very same language my mom used." Ken joined Obama's presidential campaign in 2007.

Against that backdrop, Ken saw Pearce as a threat to immigrants and their families and a threat to every poor family and child in need of health insurance.

Ken and I perceived the crisis of having Pearce as president of the senate from a similar vantage point. The majority of the political players took the traditional and predictable approach to this new development. It went something like this, "Let's start preparing for 2012. We'll recruit better candidates. We'll debate Pearce and his allies on the legislative floor and in the press (nothing like an angry press release to stop the damage). The Republicans will overplay their hand. And as a result of our efforts, voters will see that the Democrats are the better party and we will win."

Before our meeting, Ken said no one had been talking about taking the fight to Pearce or the Republicans in any significant way. Like other activists, Ken was tired of politics as usual. He felt we needed to shake things up.

After the 2010 election, Ken remembered how it felt, "We got our asses handed to us. And I actually remember a couple of days after the election when you actually get to reflect. Bernie Bergmann, my deputy director, and I were actually sitting on the tailgate of my truck and contemplating the universe and politics and we're talking about how what we needed was a new hope—something to believe in. Something to look forward to that wasn't rooted in the politics of the past."

Ken viewed the Pearce recall as an act of redemption.

"In 2010," he said, "we had a handful of legislative and statewide Democratic candidates pushing a narrative that SB 1070 did not go far enough. Our chairperson, Ann Wallack, had taken a very public stance against SB 1070, so we had internal divisions within our own Democratic political family about what our message should be post-SB 1070."

All the Democratic candidates who either embraced SB 1070 or ran to the right of it lost. "They sold out the party," Ken said. "They sold out our values. They sold out the community, and they got slaughtered. We needed something different. We needed something new."

On the day we met in person, Ken entered the conference room with a grin on his face—the rumors about recalling Pearce were already spreading. When I started to explain why we needed to recall Pearce, Ken interrupted, "Before we go any further, I just want to make it clear that I am here as a private citizen and am not functioning in my official capacity as executive director for the Maricopa County Democratic Party. That being said, I think this could actually catch fire. What can I do to help?"

I explained that a successful outcome meant spending the next ten months working on a campaign that would elect a moderate Republican to replace Pearce. I emphasized our need to send a message to Pearce, the Republican Party, and other anti-immigrant politicians around the country that this type of behavior would not go unpunished. And with Pearce's track record, we simply could not wait him out.

Ken agreed with the strategy from the outset. "This is the perfect time to go on the offensive," he said. "This will give our volunteers in LD 18 a chance to talk to voters face-to-face about something they can do right now, something no other voter can do in any other district—sign a recall petition to get rid of the likes of Pearce. We can talk to them about issues well beyond immigration, issues like Pearce's never-ending appetite to cut funding for public education and health care for those most in need."

He also understood that we had to run a Republican to divide the Republican vote so our Democratic base could come in and deliver the knock-out blow. The special recall election, if done correctly, meant getting thousands of Democrats to embrace an "anyone but Pearce" approach to getting him out of office—even if that meant voting for a Republican.

Something special happened when I said, "Arizona is one of the few states that has the ability to recall elected officials. This has never been done, but no one is more deserving of being recalled than Russell Pearce." Boom! At that moment Ken's mind exploded with all the possibilities that came with such a campaign.

"YES!" he shouted.

For Ken, the Pearce recall would also be an opportunity to get back at all those in the Democratic Party who'd made the wrong call in 2010 when it came to immigration and SB 1070. The recall provided a clear and visible mechanism to basically ask Democrats where they stood on Pearce and his racist agenda. In addition, the recall provided a counternarrative to those who took the "lay down and die" mentality following the disastrous election results. "There were donors and politicos that left politics after 2010," Ken said. "They literally picked up and moved. They played the game and lost. They were done."

Two weeks later, we met again to discuss what to call the recall committee. This time, Ken brought Bernie Bergmann, his deputy director. We spent about thirty minutes brainstorming ideas. From "Arizona United" to "We Are Arizona" and about thirty other variations, we threw them all up on the wall. We needed a name that would be inviting, all-encompassing, and somewhat aspirational. We debated whether to include the word "citizen" and whether to make the name geography-specific to the voters in Mesa, or broader, to include all Arizona. Our focus came down to Citizens for something—"Citizens for Justice," "Citizens for Change," "Citizens United," "Citizens Against Hate."

Finally, Ken said, "Pearce is about to unleash a whole bunch of bad bills that will impact the entire state. We should call the recall committee 'Citizens for a Better Arizona.' We need citizens to sign the recall petition so we can have a better Arizona."

I liked it—simple, clear, and to the point. I ran the name by a few more people, and it didn't set off any alarms.

I called Ken the next day. "Everyone I have spoken with likes 'Citizens for a Better Arizona.' Now let's go make Citizens for a Better Arizona the new hope in Mesa and for the entire state of Arizona!"

Next, I had to process all the feedback, opinions, and perspectives from my one-on-one meetings. In October, following my loss for US

Senate, I needed a break from the intensity of Arizona politics. I booked a December trip to Rome for my partner, Lilia, and me.

Had I known then that by December, I would be consumed devising a strategy to recall the newly elected senate president, our trip to Rome probably would never have occurred. In hindsight, I can now say it happened at the right time and in the right city. The backdrop of Rome—its history, architecture, grandeur, culture, and cuisine—inspired our decision to move forward and served as the launching pad for our very first public action to challenge Pearce's power, authority, and position.

CHAPTER 4

When History Calls ... Answer!

History is not a burden on the memory
but an illumination of the soul.

~ Lord Acton

By the time Lilia and I left for Rome, I had met with more than twenty leaders, potential funders, and volunteers about recalling Russell Pearce. Most of them could not mask their skepticism and outright opposition to the idea—and these were progressives. Some even laughed.

When we landed in Rome, I began to doubt whether the Pearce recall was "the call" I had to answer. Since June 2008, I had been immersed in the effort to hold Sheriff Arpaio accountable for his discriminatory and abusive ways. Part of me wanted to continue that fight once we returned from Rome. However, Arpaio was not up for reelection until 2012. We needed a major victory sooner; we needed one now.

Rome in December can be brutal with its wind, cold, rain, and ice. The integration of this city's ancient touchstones with modern-day living made each day of our trip an adventure. We walked for miles down narrow, winding streets, taking in all that Rome offered—the architecture, statues, artwork, people, and food. Midway through our vacation, we made our way to the Colosseum.

When I was a candidate for US Senate and needed someone to run our field campaign in Maricopa County and Yuma counties, I called one of my colleagues, Dana Kennedy, and asked her if she knew of anyone who would be up for the challenge.

Without hesitation, she said, "Lilia Alvarez."

The daughter of farmworkers and a graduate of the Head Start program, Lilia had just completed her first year of law school. She was the first person in her family to graduate from high school, college and pursue a graduate degree. Dana described her as intelligent, kind, passionate, extremely hardworking, and well-spoken.

Based on Dana's glowing recommendation, I called Lilia and attempted to hire her immediately. It took a couple of calls to recruit her since she was already employed in Yuma doing legal work. Eventually, she said yes and joined our team. Impressed by her professionalism, maturity, spirituality, and commitment to serve others, I asked Lilia, after the election, if she would be open to being in a relationship with me. She said yes. Three and a half months later, there we were—together in Rome.

On this particular afternoon, the weather took a turn—cool but not cold, a bit overcast but no rain or wind. While walking the grounds of the Colosseum, Lilia and I talked about my next move. She still had another year and a half to complete law school; her immediate next steps were clear. After walking around the arena, we settled in a little nook near its floor overlooking the hypogeum—the area underneath the floor where gladiators, slaves, animals, and prisoners awaited their fate.

Lilia sensed my inability to relax. She asked, "So have you decided?"

"Decided what?"

"We are not going to be able to enjoy our vacation until you come to terms with all that is stirring inside you. You know what I am talking about. Are you going to continue hammering on Sheriff Arpaio or pursue the recall of Russell Pearce?"

"I don't know," I said. "I'm torn. I feel that all the work we have done to challenge Arpaio—all the actions, events, and meetings—needs to continue. I don't just want to walk away when we have him seriously concerned about what we may do next."

"Who says you have to walk away from the Arpaio fight?" Lilia asked. "Pearce is one of Arpaio's biggest allies, and let's not forget Pearce introduced SB 1070 to give Arpaio legal cover for his illegal traffic stops and worksite raids. Taking on Pearce would be part of the overall strategy to undercutting Arpaio's support. Plus, Arpaio's reelection isn't until 2012."

My mind started processing all the data. The recall Pearce strategy, if successful, would allow us to build an organization with the capacity, resources and reach to challenge Arpaio's hold on power in 2012.

"That's true," I said. "However, I also feel that by going after Pearce we may unite the right in ways that could make it even more difficult for us to take them on in 2012. As senate president, Pearce can use his position to raise money, recruit candidates, and I hate to say it, even pass laws to punish organizations and groups aligned with our cause. Some people in our Democratic and progressive circles will likely perceive this as an act of desperation by a failed US Senate candidate doing whatever it takes to grab headlines and remain relevant."

"Yes, but you know that simply is not true," she said. "You have done the research and from what you have told me this is actually doable. I am speaking about the signature-gathering part of the recall. I am still unsure about the candidate part, but I feel confident that if you get the signatures someone will run—the right someone will step forward. And besides, this is too righteous of a cause to pass up."

As Lilia continued to make the case for pursuing Pearce over Arpaio, a voice in my head kept asking: *What are you afraid of? Why are you reluctant to commit?*

As I leaned against the ancient stone wall, I knew the answer. I wanted my next campaign to be something that had a higher probability of success than recalling the president of the senate or running for US Senate. My fragile ego kept undercutting my ability to commit and channel all my creative energies to this effort. Knowing that this had never been done before gave me pause. The negative thoughts kept running through my head: *What if volunteers don't show up? What if no one donates to the recall? What if people slam their doors in our face? What if I fail—again?*

After a brief moment of silence, I said to Lilia, "If I decide to do this it will consume most of my time during the week and on weekends."

"I understand."

"If I decide to do this, I will need your help—especially when it comes to recruiting volunteers and asking people for money."

"I understand."

"If I decide to do this, we are going to make a lot of the traditional 'power people' uncomfortable because this will be way outside their experience. Many of them will not take me and the recall seriously."

"I understand. But you don't need everyone's support. You just need the right people. Right here, at this moment, what feels right? Listen to your heart. What speaks to your passion? Arpaio or Pearce? Don't think, just go with what you feel! Arpaio or Pearce?"

Standing there in the Colosseum, a place where gladiators fought to the death, where Christians were fed to the lions, and where prisoners awaited their executions, I felt a jolt of energy electrify my body. I looked at Lilia and blurted out, "Recall Pearce. Let's do it!"

The "call" I received in November during Pearce's appearance on *Sunday Square Off* had been answered.

Speaking those words out loud washed away any remnants of uncertainty, doubt, and indecisiveness. As we made our way back to the hotel, I felt like a kid on Christmas morning. I couldn't wait to get back to Arizona, but we still had a few more days to enjoy Rome. For the rest of the afternoon and into the evening, Lilia and I continued to talk through the strategy. We both realized we couldn't wait until our return to Arizona to get started. We needed to launch the plan now.

Lilia suggested that we set up a Facebook event for January 10, the first day of the legislative session. That gave us only twenty-five days to get people to turn out at the Capitol. Because we had not formed a recall committee, we asked our Facebook friends to join us at the Capitol to launch Citizens for a Better Arizona, a newly formed coalition to hold Senate President Pearce accountable. By the time we boarded the plane for Arizona, more than one hundred people had signed up. As we landed, the number swelled to more than 150.

With a touch of inspiration and a dose of technology, the first phase of the Russell Pearce recall movement had been launched in Arizona.

From Rome.

CHAPTER 5

Gracias, Sheriff Arpaio

Fear makes come true that which one is afraid of.
~ Viktor Frankl

Energized by my decision in Rome to make the Pearce recall happen, I was still uncertain how to execute the plan. In a few short weeks, we'd need to submit paperwork to create the committee and file the recall petition. We did not want to file the recall petition five days after the session began. We wanted to appear reasonable and fair and give Pearce a chance in his new position to tone down his rhetoric and actions, especially when it came to immigration. We also needed time to bring together the other pieces of our strategy: talking to voters in LD 18, finding a chairman for our recall committee, identifying a voter in Pearce's district to file the recall petition, and locking down commitments of at least $10,000 from potential donors by the end of January.

Meanwhile, we needed to set the agenda, speakers, and other details for our January 10 kickoff. Most importantly, the campaign still needed a leader—our main spokesperson. Someone who would broaden our political base, interview well on camera, help with fundraising, and give the recall effort more legitimacy.

It definitely could not be me. As a progressive community and labor organizer, a Democrat, and a Scottsdale resident, I did not meet the criteria.

Our wish list included someone who was:

- Caucasian/White
- Male
- Republican
- Mormon
- A business owner
- A good communicator, quick on their feet and camera ready
- Fluent in English and Spanish
- Supportive of the Latino community and immigrant families.

In about five seconds, I had my list of one: Chad Snow. He was a Republican and a Mormon who grew up on the west side of Phoenix. His parents, a Catholic father and a Mormon mother, shared socially progressive values. In the Snow household, if someone made a derogatory comment about another person's color Chad's mom would say, "Under our skin, we are all pink." Chad spent two years as a Mormon missionary in Spain and became fluent in Spanish. He was a lawyer and founding partner of the law firm of Snow and Carpio (now known as Snow, Carpio, and Weekley). When it came to live interviews, Chad was calm, confident, well-spoken, and personable. For most of his adult life, Chad steered clear of politics, protests, and campaigns. However, with the rise of such extremists as Pearce and Arpaio, and with a growing list of Latino clients he cared deeply about, Chad became increasingly frustrated and eager to do something.

While driving to Chad's office to make the "big ask," I flashed back to the unlikely series of events that brought together such an unlikely pair—a liberal, progressive, labor and community organizer and a conservative, Republican, Mormon business owner. Credit Sheriff Joe Arpaio.

In spring 2008, I helped organize a community activist group, Maricopa Citizens for Safety and Accountability (MCSA), to expose

Arpaio's abusive practices and policies. His use of fear and intimidation against his enemies caused many established groups to avoid taking on the sheriff in public. The perception of Arpaio and his allies as being above the law was real—creating a problem when we needed to organize some sort of opposition. The citizens' group provided cover to people who wanted to speak out against Arpaio, while protecting their organizations from retaliation by Arpaio and his deputies.

In this group's early days, we focused on safety and accountability, not immigration. In a county where Republican voters outnumbered Democrats by close to 200,000, we needed a message that would resonate more with moderate voters. Instead of taking Sheriff Arpaio head-on over immigration, an issue that worked to his benefit, we focused on his policies, practices, and abuses of power that had cost the county hundreds of millions of dollars. The bi-monthly meetings of the Maricopa County Board of Supervisors became our new platform to press our concerns and coordinate our actions.

By the fall, MCSA had established itself as a persistent and effective adversary to Sheriff Arpaio and his department. Because four of the five county board members were Republicans and Arpaio supporters, our demands were met with stiff resistance. Throughout the summer, we attended their board meetings, each time making one simple request: to place our issues on the formal agenda. As we escalated our pressure, Arpaio amped up the intimidation. One day, he stationed more than fifty deputies and detention officers just outside the building where the board of supervisors met. On another occasion, Arpaio had our supporters arrested for clapping during a meeting. Instead of scaring our supporters, it emboldened them and provided another example of how Arpaio misused taxpayer dollars to pursue his own agenda.

At the September 28 meeting, Arpaio took it a step further. This time we interrupted the meeting by holding up anti-Arpaio signs and speaking out. When directed, participants would stand, hold up a sign, make a brief statement, and sit down—our version of the Whac-A-Mole game. Our signs read, "Unsafe Communities," "No Justice," "$40,000,000 Wasted," "People Matter," "Corruption," and "Safety First." Because no one stood up and talked for more than six seconds, security officers had a difficult time reaching each person to give them a warning or ask them to leave. Because board members had refused to place our issues on the agenda, we were not going to let them hold their meeting without a protest.

Before the meeting, we'd agreed that no one would do anything that might lead to an arrest; we would cooperate with the sheriff deputies and other law enforcement officers even if it meant leaving the meeting when instructed to do so. Civil disobedience was not to be deployed. Everything went as planned ... until they asked *me* to leave.

As the supervisors discussed the first agenda item, Corrine, one of our supporters, shouted, "Under Sheriff Arpaio's watch there have been uninvestigated rapes."

Next, Charles weighed in from the back of the auditorium, "Under Sheriff Arpaio's watch, over $40 million in legal payouts." Sheriff's deputies and court security began to scurry around the packed auditorium, trying to identify the speakers.

From another part of the room, Ray stood up and shouted: "Under Arpaio, murderers have been able to run free in our streets."

Seconds later, I stood up and spoke directly to Chairman Andrew Kunasek, "Are you going to put this on the agenda for October 15 to talk about this issue?" Before I could finish my next sentence, the head of court security grabbed my arm and turned me toward the back of the room.

"Time to leave, Randy," he said as he began to escort me from the auditorium.

I complied. As I walked towards the exit, everyone raised their signs, and other supporters continued to stand and speak out. Mission accomplished. Or so I thought.

Outside the building, a few supporters had gathered about twenty-five feet from the entrance. The group included Ray Ybarra, Corinne Horowitz, Ivan Brickman, and Charles Smith. They also had been asked to leave. As we waited, more sheriff's deputies exited the building and took positions very close to ours. This seemed odd since more than eighty of our supporters remained inside with fewer than ten of us outside. Why would so many officers be outside when all the action was inside?

Within minutes, four sheriff deputies approached me and ordered me to leave. "Randy, you have been asked to leave the area," one said. "You cannot stand in front of the building. You need to move to the sidewalk." The sidewalk was another hundred feet or so away from the building.

"I was asked to leave the meeting and I left," I said. "What's the problem?"

Another deputy jumped in, "You have trespassed. You need to move to the sidewalk or you will be arrested."

"I was told to leave the meeting. Give me a break. Why do I have to move away from the building?"

Not sure who was in charge, I continued to ask questions. Suddenly one of the deputies said, "Step down or be arrested."

Before I could respond to that order, Deputy Chief David Trombi walked behind the deputies and uttered sternly, "He's a 42. He's a 42."

Unaware of what that meant, I turned to leave. Immediately, one of the deputies grabbed my left forearm and said, "You are under arrest."

"For what?"

"Trespass." He then reached for my other arm.

Still thinking I had a chance to avoid the arrest, I made one final plea, "I am walking away. I am leaving."

What they were saying didn't quite register. I kept trying to leave. One of our supporters, Ivan, whispered in my ear, "They are going to charge you with resisting arrest if you don't completely surrender now."

And at that moment, another deputy said, "Too late now." He then pulled my arms and hands behind my back and handcuffed me.

After three months of continued pressure on Sheriff Arpaio and his office, he had responded: he would do whatever it took to defend his reputation and record.

The deputies paraded me back into the building and down a hallway adjacent to the supervisors' meeting area so everyone still present could see that they had placed me under arrest. We then took an elevator to the garage level, and when the door opened, I could not believe what I saw. Lined up along the wall were some twenty-five to thirty sheriff's officers in full riot gear—helmets, shields, boots, and batons—ready to take on a group of about eighty unarmed, peaceful citizens attending a board of supervisors meeting. A row of tables stood across from the deputies, apparently to process all the protesters they expected to arrest. I could sense their satisfaction when they saw me—and their disappointment when they realized it was *only* me.

They sat me down at the booking table and started to process the paperwork. "What am I being charged with?" I asked.

"Criminal trespass and disorderly conduct."

"For standing in front of a public building?"

"No, for refusing to leave the meeting."

It was apparent this officer did not witness what happened. I did leave the meeting. He was just executing the plan as instructed.

"I left the meeting. I was standing outside when the deputy asked me to go to the sidewalk. You know this is wrong."

He stayed quiet. I then had to turn over my belongings—cell phone, wallet, belt, and shoelaces.

As an organizer for many causes, I had been arrested on other occasions. In most instances, disorderly conduct and trespass charges usually resulted in a "cite and release." They remove people from the protest area, issue citations, and then release them. As the main organizer for the action and the father of two daughters who needed to be picked up after school, I had no desire to spend any time in jail.

I asked, "Officer, will I be free to leave once you write up the citation?"

"No. You will be booked, and your arraignment will be later today."

Meanwhile, Arpaio decided to show up at the meeting and ramp up his rhetoric. When the meeting reconvened, he reminded board members he alone was in charge of his budget and warned them to leave it alone. "This is my money!" he declared. The four Republican members of the board of supervisors sat there in silence. No one objected to what had just unfolded.

As the booking process came to an end, I expected to go to a holding cell with other alleged criminals until my arraignment. Again, I was wrong. The booking officer instructed me to do something I had never experienced. "Randy, please stand and place your hands in front of you and spread your legs slightly apart."

At this point, I didn't know what to expect. Maybe an intrusive pat down? Or a body search? Another officer approached from behind and dropped a chain to the floor by my ankles. The officer then handcuffed my hands in front of me and then placed leg shackles around each ankle.

In utter disbelief, I asked, "Do you always place individuals charged with trespass and disorderly conduct in leg shackles and handcuffs?"

"Never," one deputy said.

"Then why are you doing it to me?"

"Just following orders."

This confirmed my suspicion that this was an orchestrated crackdown to punish and silence our group. Deputies were ordered to arrest and detain me, and they complied. They were ordered to leg shackle and handcuff me, and they complied. Never before had officers been told to impose such treatment on someone charged with criminal trespass and disorderly conduct.

And, still, they complied.

They were not done. I was led on a long walk through the garage with heavily armed deputies on each side of me and behind me. From the moment the deputies approached me outside the supervisors' building, someone was assigned to videotape my every move. Because of the leg shackles, my stride was limited. Forced to walk in a stutter-step kind of way to avoid falling, my pace was slow. It was surreal, walking in my dark navy suit, handcuffed and leg-shackled, with four armed deputies surrounding me.

We finally arrived at a cell, which was more like a cement bunker—no windows, toilet, or anything else—just an overhead yellow light that made a buzzing sound. They undid the handcuffs and leg shackles and left the room military-style—each placing an arm on the shoulder of the guard in front of them as they moved backwards out the door—as if I were some sort of terrorist.

I did not understand why they placed me in a high-security cell, considering what they had charged me with. I paced about the cell to pass the time. My mind raced with constant questions: *How long am I going to be in this cell? Who is going to pick up the girls after school? What time is it? How long are they going to keep me here? What about my phone call? Is anyone doing anything to get me out of here?*

After about ten minutes of this, a certain calmness set in as well as the realization that I would be there for a while. It was extremely quiet, nothing but the buzzing of the light fixture above me. It felt like being locked up in a bomb shelter—completely cut off from the world.

To pass the time, I replayed everything that happened that morning to recall it all at a later date in detail. I flashed back to a class I'd taken in law school when someone asked who had the most power over a person in their day-to-day life.

Someone said, "Congress."

Someone else said, "Banks."

Another said, "The Supreme Court."

Finally, the professor weighed in. "Officers with a badge and a gun. They are the only ones, in a matter of seconds, who can strip you of your freedom or take your life."

The moment the deputy sheriff placed his hands on me, I became a criminal. I couldn't do anything to fight back without making the situation worse.

After almost two hours, the door opened. I was being moved to another cell. Again, I was handcuffed. Now my escort included three deputies—two uniformed men and one in plainclothes (no name badge)—leading me through numerous hallways and offices. As we walked through the jail, I turned to the deputy in plainclothes. "Do you always treat individuals charged with trespass and disorderly conduct this way?"

He replied with a grin, "No, but Randy, you are high profile."

I did not know then that this deputy in plainclothes was David Letourneau, captain of the sheriff's bomb squad and SWAT Team. Think about that: Arpaio assigned this man to monitor our activities.[1] How could this sheriff get away with illegally arresting citizens, politicians, or judges? How could he get away with so many lawsuits and legal settlements that cost the taxpayers millions of dollars? Or refuse to investigate more than four hundred sex crimes because he was too busy chasing "illegals" along the highway? Or conduct random worksite raids targeting undocumented immigrants? Arpaio's tactics of fear and intimidation had given him a free pass to do as he wished without any

---

[1] The next morning after my arrest, we held a press conference in front of the board of supervisors building. Guess who showed up in a black leather jacket, wearing dark sunglasses? None other than Captain Letourneau. It felt like a scene out of some mobster flick. He stood there motionless as my attorneys and I spoke to the media, and when we asked him his name and title, he refused to answer. I recognized him that morning only because of the "high profile" comment he made to me in jail the day before.

real challenge from the very institutions established to do so. The list of politicians, business leaders, and county attorneys with the courage to challenge Arpaio's authority was short. That list also lacked depth, power, and influence. This had to change.

After about what seemed to be a five-minute walk through the jail, the deputies uncuffed me and placed me in another holding cell. From what I could tell, a decision had been made to keep me isolated for the duration of my arrest. This cell was a bit of an upgrade. It had a toilet, sink, and phone on the wall. The phone turned out to be a mixed blessing. Yes, I could make a call, but when the person answered, they would first hear a recording that went something like this, "This is a call from the Maricopa County Jail. Will you accept the charges?"

The other challenge was that the collect call option only worked for landlines. So here I was in jail, no Blackberry (cell phone), no phone numbers I could look up, and the only landline number I knew was that of my ex-wife. I imagined how my call to her would be received: "I know this is my week to take care of the girls, but I am in jail. Can you please pick up the girls after school today?" This awkward conversation never happened. Because she was at work, the call went unanswered.

Hours passed, and I still had no contact with the outside world.

A bag of food dropped through a slot in the door. I settled in for a longer wait. They had no intention of getting me out in time for lunch or dinner. I looked inside the clear plastic bag—green bologna on moldy bread and a rotten tangerine—and tossed it in the trash. As the hours passed, I continued to pace back and forth. Unlike my first cell, where the thickness of the walls made it impossible to hear anything else, I now heard everything: loud thumping sounds made by inmates being slammed up against the walls, distant voices yelling and cursing in the hallway.

I kept telling myself: *It's almost over. Just another thirty minutes. Just another thirty minutes. Just another thirty minutes.*

After about five hours, the door opened. I was escorted by two deputies to where other inmates were lined up to go before the judge. This time they did not handcuff me. As I joined the line (still wearing my suit) with other inmates wearing black-and-white-striped prisoner uniforms, they started to joke amongst themselves.

"Who is this VIP? Where's my suit?"

"Yeah, where can I get a suit like that?"

The guards told everyone to keep quiet and walk single file down the hallway. We entered a brightly lit room with rows of metal benches. We were instructed to sit and wait for our names to be called.

After about thirty minutes, the judge called my name. I stood up and walked to the bench. Before I could say a word, she said, "Your attorneys are waiting to meet with you in the back. Please meet with them, and then I'll call you back up here once you are ready to give your plea."

Attorneys? What attorneys? We made no arrangements for legal representation because our plan did not involve civil disobedience. I had intended to simply plead "not guilty" and wait to be released.

I walked to a small room where I was greeted by two men. A tall, White, blond-haired, slender gentleman extended his hand and said, "My name is Chad Snow, and this is my partner, Alex Carpio. We were sitting in the audience at the meeting today. I can't believe what happened. We are attorneys and we are here to represent you."

Chad explained he had been following our work against Arpaio in the news and shared our view that Arpaio had gone too far. A lifelong Republican, Chad had voted for Arpaio. But the worksite raids, costly lawsuits, racial profiling, and abuses of power had moved Chad, for the first time, to attend his first meeting of the board of supervisors.

"Look at me," he said. "I am White, blond, taller, and in better shape than you, and they actually thought I was you."

I smiled. "What do you mean?"

"After they escorted you out, one of the deputies came to where we were sitting in the audience and tapped me on my shoulder. He looked at me and said, 'Come with me.' I had no idea why he wanted to speak to me, but I knew he had no right to pull me out of the meeting. So, when I stood up, I held up one of the signs you guys passed out and flashed it to the crowd. The deputy then escorted me to the hallway just outside the auditorium, asked me to place my hands behind my back, and then proceeded to handcuff me."

This treatment stunned Chad. He had never been handcuffed nor even part of any protest. An active Mormon, Chad believed in other ways to resolve disputes. When he flashed one of our signs, it was probably the first act of public protest in his life.

"What did you do?" I asked.

"I asked him if I was under arrest, and if so, for what charge? I then told them I was an attorney and asked for each of their names. Shortly thereafter, another deputy comes by and says, 'That's not him' and they immediately uncuffed me and walked me out of the building. That's when I saw you coming back in the building, handcuffed with a whole bunch of deputies around you."

We laughed at the absurdity of us both being targeted by Arpaio—me for standing in front of a building and Chad, literally for sitting in the audience.

Before I left the room to enter my formal not guilty plea, we stood up. Chad put his arm around my shoulder and with a look of astonishment and disbelief, said, "I don't know how they mistook me for you. I am so much better looking than you."

Although Chad's partner Alex handled my case, Chad and I became friends. But had it not been for our shared interest in holding Sheriff Arpaio accountable, our paths never would have crossed. And we would not have developed the friendship, trust, and respect necessary to take on someone as powerful as Arpaio or, later, Senate President Russell Pearce.

Sometimes when you pressure your adversary, they'll do something that ends up helping your cause.

Arpaio's decision to crack down on our protest sowed the seeds for the recall of Pearce some two years later. Over time, I came to appreciate the experience of being arrested, shackled, jailed, and treated as a high-profile prisoner. Some twenty-eight months after my arrest, I knew Chad Snow was just the person to chair Citizens for a Better Arizona.

As I pulled into the parking lot at Chad's office building, I reviewed the reasons why Chad needed to be our chairman. I expected a long and difficult conversation. I knew that this could adversely affect his wife, children, and his law practice, and it could also cause some friction within the Mormon Church.

When I opened the door to Chad's office, I felt prepared but uneasy. I ran the numbers and talking points through my head again—we needed only 7,756 signatures. We had 40,000 Democrat and independent voters to solicit. We only needed to raise $40,000. Chad would just have to speak at a few events (not true but I was prepared to use it).

Going into this conversation, I still had no answer for the "Do you have a candidate?" question. As I walked towards Chad's office, more questions surfaced: *What if he says no? Who is my plan B person? There is no plan B person. Stay focused on plan A.*

I entered his office, and Chad sensed my uneasiness.

After we greeted each other and joked around for a few minutes, I revealed the real reason for my visit. "I have something to share with you that I think can be a game-changer for Arizona without us having to wait until the 2012 election. I've looked at the numbers and did some research on Pearce and his district. I think we can take him out."

Chad, a bit surprised, smiled and asked, "What do you mean take him out? Pearce owns that seat."

"I think we can recall Pearce and take him out of office. We can't allow him to preside over the senate. Imagine all the damage he can do in two years." I paused, expecting to get a lot of clarifying questions. None came.

Instead, Chad responded, "I like it. Sounds good to me. You know you can count on me to help out. Do you need some office space or money?"

These were the least of my concerns. I needed much more—a whole lot more. "Chad I need you to be our chairman. I need you to ..." Before I could finish, Chad jumped up and said, "Let's go kick his ass! I'm all in! Yes, I will be the chairman and do whatever else you need me to do."

Shocked at how quickly he agreed, I asked, "Don't you need to discuss this with Rachel and how this may impact your family? You'll be one of the main faces of our campaign and the press will be all over this. This is going to be a very big deal." I figured this was a good time to stop talking.

"Don't worry about it. Rachel will be fine. This is a righteous cause and we are on the right side." I stood up, thanked him for doing this, and we hugged it out.

Unlike my other conversations with hardcore progressive activists and Democratic Party operatives, Chad never even asked if we had a candidate. As someone who represented many Latino clients with work-related injuries, Chad had seen firsthand how Pearce's policies affected families and hurt good people. From Chad's perspective, Pearce's pursued an anti-immigrant agenda for very cynical reasons.

"As a member of the LDS Church," Chad said, "when you see one of your own acting badly, you want to do whatever you can to correct it or at least put the message out there that not all Mormons are like Pearce."

With Chad now in place as our chairman, I could now focus on putting the other pieces of the recall together.

As I drove home, an immense feeling of gratitude came over me. I flashed back to the first time I met Chad in Arpaio's jail. I smiled, took a deep breath, and yelled, "Thank you, Sheriff Arpaio! Your boy Pearce is about to go down!"

CHAPTER 6

Three Calls

*If you know you are right, stay the course even though
the whole world seems to be against you…*
~ Ralph Waldo Emerson

Our January 10 kickoff was just around the corner. With Chad Snow in place as chairman of Citizens for a Better Arizona, we could focus on our opening day action of the Arizona 2011 legislative session. By January 4, more than 175 people had signed up for our event at the Capitol. Our message could not focus solely on SB 1070 and Pearce's attacks on undocumented immigrants. We needed to craft a message that spoke to a broader constituency. To mainstream our message, we needed a slate of speakers who would cover other issues. We needed to make this about jobs, safety, and doing what was right for Arizona taxpayers.

We needed a call to action—something for people to do besides listen to people at a press event. The action also had to be designed to buy me some time to pull together other parts of the campaign before the recall could be officially launched. To accomplish both objectives, we appointed a delegation to deliver to Pearce's office a "21-Day Notice" from Citizens for a Better Arizona. We also drafted a letter inviting Pearce to a town hall meeting in his district at a date and time of his choosing before January 31.

When the legislature reconvened, we wanted our message to be moderate and our demands reasonable.

On the Saturday before the kickoff, the Arizona Dream Act Coalition asked me to do a workshop on organizing at Arizona State University. About midway through it, people were distracted by incoming messages on their phones.

I checked, too, and couldn't believe the headline: Congresswoman Gabby Giffords had been shot and murdered at a political event in Tucson. The story went on to say that multiple people had been shot and murdered, including a child. We all looked at one another, completely stunned. How could this happen? What had happened? Shortly after these headlines hit, we later learned the reports about Giffords were inaccurate. She was still alive, barely, and fighting for her life. Before we continued our workshop, we brought everyone together and addressed what had just happened. We also stood in silence to honor all those who had been struck down by the gunman.

As I drove home from the workshop, I did not think for a second to postpone our launch of Citizens for a Better Arizona. Tea Party activists would still be at the Capitol in full force and we needed to counter their message. But leaders in the Democratic Party were thinking otherwise.

First thing Monday morning on the day of our kickoff, Ken Chapman was instructed to jump on a conference call with other party leaders. On the call were State Senator Kyrsten Sinema, Senate Minority Leader David Schapira, State Senator David Lujan, House Minority Leader Chad Campbell, State Democratic Party Chairman Andre Cherney, State Democratic Party Executive Director Luis Heredia, and Maricopa County Democratic Chairwoman Ann Wallack.

Given the impressive roll call of attendees, Ken's interest peaked. Ken recalled the highlights of the conference call: "So, Sinema is leading the call early on the morning of the first day of the legislative session. She is filled with piss and vinegar. She starts off, 'Fuck this and fuck that. Randy is a wild card. He is fucking all this up. The recall is never going to work. This is the Randy show. To do this on the first day is disrespectful to Gabby and we need to have a different message.'"

Then, Ken said, House Minority Leader Campbell chimed in.

"Campbell said something like 'This (Pearce recall) is going to make things worse for Dems in the legislature. This is bad for the party, and it will be bad for our candidates in the future. It will make winning in 2012 impossible,'" Ken said. "From Campbell's perspective, we as Democrats had to prove that we too can be tough on immigration."

Throughout most of the 2010 legislative session, Sinema and Campbell spearheaded the strategy for Democrats on how to best respond to SB 1070 as it made its way through the legislature. In the past, such bills were vetoed by then-Governor Janet Napolitano, a Democrat. However, with Napolitano gone and Brewer now in the governor's office, everything changed. In 2010, SB 1070 finally had a political path to victory—a Republican-controlled House and Senate and a Republican governor. Democratic leaders struggled to define and deploy the right strategy against SB 1070. To avoid having their vote on SB 1070 used against them in future elections, some did not cast a vote while others casted a "no vote"—knowing full well there was nothing they could do to stop the bill from reaching the governor's desk. With Pearce now sworn in as the new senate president, the last thing Sinema and Campbell wanted was another public fight on anything related to immigration.

After Campbell finished his overview, one of the state party representatives chimed in with what became the official position, "The state party is not going to touch this. Somebody needs to talk to Randy to get him to stop doing this."

Then the attention turned to Ken and the Maricopa County Democratic Party (MCDP). The voice over the phone phrased it like this, "OK, so the MCDP is not going to do anything on this right? Isn't that right Ken?"

Ken paused. He had to be careful how he responded. We had met numerous times about recalling Pearce, discussed what to name the recall committee, and agreed that the overall strategy of going after Pearce was the right thing to do. Before Ken jumped on that call, he was already all in to recall Pearce.

Ken parsed his words carefully. "If the press conference happens, we are going to show up. So far, the people I have spoken to are really excited about this, and Randy hasn't been whatever problem you think he is."

Before the call ended, Sinema agreed to call me to make sure, at the very least, I would not launch Citizens for a Better Arizona on the first day of the legislative session.

After Ken hung up, it seemed really odd to him that this group of elected officials was trying to control someone they had already described as a hot head and uncontrollable. "Yet somehow," he said, "they thought that a phone call from some random person who doesn't even know you personally and who is not involved in the recall effort is somehow going to make a difference. At this moment, we had no party infrastructure. We had just gotten decimated in the election. Somehow thinking that there was some control was a bit comical."

What Ken did not share on that call was that he had already agreed to bring the podium we would use at the Capitol. Now, he had to sneak the podium out of the state Democratic Party's office and into his truck. Lucky for us, Ken successfully maneuvered the podium into his truck without anyone taking notice. When we showed up for the event a few hours later, the podium was positioned perfectly.

Fresh off the morning call with her Democratic colleagues on the morning of the first day of the legislative session in 2011, Kyrsten Sinema was about to shake things up even more. A few hours before our launch of Citizens for a Better Arizona I received not one, not two, but three unexpected calls from heavy hitters in Democratic Party politics suggesting I postpone and or cancel the launch of Citizens for a Better Arizona.

Call number one.

A very calm and sweet-sounding voice said, "Hello Randy. This is Kyrsten Sinema. How are you?"

"I am fine Kyrsten. What's up?"

"I hear you are planning on doing a press event later this morning."

"Well, it's not just a press event, it's an action that involves the press …" Before I could elaborate, she cut me off.

"I just want to let you know that we met and decided that no one is going to do press today. I have canceled all my press engagements. So, you should cancel your event as well."

At this point I'm not sure who "we" was but assumed it was other Democratic elected officials and party leaders.

"Kyrsten I am not understanding your request. I don't work for you or the Democratic Party. We know the Tea Party is going to be out there talking to the press. We need to counter their message …" She cut me off again.

Raising her voice, and in a demanding tone, she continued, "Randy I am not asking you. I am telling you to cancel your event. If you hold your event, you will be disrespecting Gabby and her entire family."

Although I knew of Congresswoman Giffords, I'd never met her or her family. Our event had nothing to do with that shooting, and the Republican leadership chose not to postpone the opening day of the legislature. The emotional hooks Sinema thought she could use on me by invoking the Giffords tragedy did not work.

"You seem to have been misinformed about the purpose of our event. We are not recalling Pearce today. We are announcing the formation of a new coalition called Citizens for a Better Arizona to hold Senate President Pearce accountable and to call for an end to his extreme brand of politics. We are not going to cancel the event."

Sinema was now yelling, "Randy, if you don't cancel this event …"

I hung up. Although Sinema and I knew each other, there was no political friendship or alliance of any kind. There was no point in me staying on the phone, especially since I still had a lot of preparation to do for the noon launch.

Unfortunately, I was unaware of how determined Sinema and the rest of the Democratic Party leaders were to derail the launch of Citizens for a Better Arizona.

Call number two.

Within minutes of hanging up on Sinema, I received a call from Stan Chavira, the political director for the United Food and Commercial Workers Union Local 99. UFCW 99 is the largest private-sector union in Arizona and a huge player in Democratic circles.

Stan began the call in his usual friendly and warm way, "Hey, bro, what's going on? We hear you have an event planned for later this morning at the Capitol."

"Yes. We are launching our coalition, Citizens for a Better Arizona to hold Senate President Pearce accountable for his extremist agenda. I mentioned this to you guys a few weeks back."

"Yes, I remember. We need you to do us a favor. Can you push back your kickoff a couple of days?"

"What do you mean, 'push it back'? Stan, there is only *one* first day of the legislative session. If we don't launch today, we will lose some of our momentum."

"Look," he clarified, "we don't want you to cancel your event. Just postpone it a couple of days."

Thinking this was an informal chat and unaware of what was really going on, I continued to emphasize the importance of holding the event on day one. As I was in mid-sentence explaining again why we could not cancel the event, someone else on the call yelled, "Cancel the fucking event. We hardly ever ask you for anything. We need you to do this for us. Cancel the event!" The call then dropped.

I did not realize that Jim McLaughlin, president of Local 99, was also on the call. I had known Jim since 2002 when I became the state director for the National AFL-CIO in Arizona and Jim had just become the president of UFCW. He was one of my biggest political allies, and he had come through for me on several special projects and campaigns. And it was Jim and UFCW that recruited, encouraged, and financially supported me to run for the US Senate. Jim was someone I wanted on my side. Although Sinema failed to get me to cancel the event, she or someone else on that Democratic leadership call had correctly identified the very person who could get me to change my mind.

For the first time that morning, I considered canceling. Jim and Stan had called me while driving to Tucson to help their members at the Safeway store where Gabby Giffords and others had been shot and murdered. They were literally in the middle of a life-and-death situation and our "press event"—or whatever they were told it was—must have seemed inconsequential and irrelevant. In hindsight, I can see why Jim reacted the way he did after I refused Stan's initial request to postpone. They weren't asking for much—just a postponement.

I paced in the hallway just outside my bedroom. *What do I do? Do I cancel? Postpone? Can I get the same speakers back later in the week? What about turnout?*

My thoughts were interrupted by Lilia's voice. "Who was that on the phone?"

"That was Jim and Stan."

Lilia, knowing Sinema had called fifteen minutes earlier said, "Let me guess. They want you to cancel today's event. Sounds like Sinema is not giving up."

"Not cancel, postpone. Stan asked me to postpone the event." As I said these words out loud, I knew I was rationalizing what I knew was the wrong decision.

"You might as well cancel it then. There is only one first day of the legislative session. If you change the date, you are not postponing, you are canceling. Have you spoken to other members of the committee?"

I had not. I kept pacing. Seeing the concern on my face, Lilia continued, "You know this is not that complicated. Has UFCW pledged any money to support the Pearce recall effort?"

"No."

"Has Jim or Stan or anyone else from UFCW been involved in the planning process?"

"No. The Pearce recall is too much of a risk for UFCW at this time. Although Jim can't stand Pearce's policies, he cannot put UFCW and its 20,000-plus members in the crosshairs of the senate president by being a public supporter of the recall. And given that all previous attempts to recall any elected official have failed, Jim and UFCW are not involved at this time."

"Is anyone from UFCW turning out for the event or speaking at the rally?"

"No."

"I think you get my point, right? I am just sharing with you what you have already told me. The people that make the decisions on a campaign are those who pay for it or do the work."

"Yes, you are right about that." Still seeing me unsure of what to do, Lilia made one last comment that convinced me we had to move forward with the event.

"And, besides, you don't want to be perceived as someone beholden to any one particular group or organization. You need to focus on the few individuals who have been part of this effort from the very beginning."

She was right. Despite the support I had received from UFCW in the past, this new project had nothing to do with it. I did not work for the union now nor did I need its support to get this campaign off the ground.

I decided to move forward as planned and did not call Jim and Stan back to inform them of my final decision. If we succeeded, no one would be happier than Jim; if we failed, UFCW would not have exposed itself to Pearce's vindictiveness.

Call number three.

It was Luis Heredia, executive director of the Arizona Democratic Party. Unlike the previous two callers, Luis made it clear from the moment I picked up the phone that his call would not change anything.

"Randy, how are you?" he asked. "I know you are going to say no, but I have been instructed by someone to give you a call and ask that you cancel today's press conference."

I chuckled. I could tell by Luis's tone that he really did not want to make this call. "Luis, you are the third person to call me this morning on this issue. And you are right: we are not going to cancel the event. Can't *anyone* say no to Sinema? Or does she always get her way?"

Luis refused to take the bait and stayed on his talking points, "I am not saying it was Sinema who instructed me to make this call. Like I said, I am just following orders."

I explained again why we could not postpone the event. Luis remained respectful and calm during the entire call. After we hung up, I was a bit stunned that a newly formed group like Citizens for a Better Arizona would grab the attention of the highest levels of Democratic Party leadership.

Whether we showed up or not, I knew the Tea Party would be there espousing their anti-immigrant and pro-Pearce views. We needed to counter that by putting Pearce on notice on day one—not day two or three. As Lilia had said, there was only one opening day. We were not going to miss it.

That was the end of the calls. In organizing, the general rule is to do your best to engage individuals by not going too far outside their comfort level or personal experiences. We already realized that the notion of recalling one of the most powerful politicians in the state was just way too much for many progressive leaders—too daring, too risky, too reckless, and, yes, maybe even crazy. Unable to dream or imagine a successful campaign, many of these leaders refused to engage at all. Others took it a step further and encouraged their friends and allies to not get involved.

I gathered my things and headed out the door. The Facebook event we had launched from Rome a few weeks earlier had finally arrived. The genie could not be put back in the bottle.

CHAPTER 7

Birthing a Movement

A small body of determined spirits fired by an unquenchable
faith in their mission can alter the course of history.
~ Mahatma Gandhi

After the three-call intervention failed to get me to change our plans on opening day, we only had a few more hours to finalize our preparations and get to the Capitol grounds. Our supporters continued to send updates on all who planned to attend. Each message lifted our spirits, affirming our decision to launch Citizens for a Better Arizona.

The headline on our press release read, "Citizens Gather to Hold Senate President Russell Pearce Accountable for Setting a New Tone of Civility and Respect." This gathering at the Capitol was about inviting citizens to express their concerns about Pearce's new leadership role. We needed a leader who could unite all Arizonans and focus on real issues, especially during a time of budgetary crisis, job losses, and home foreclosures. Instead, Pearce exploited the politics of fear, hate, and division to champion bills and policies that had been detrimental to Arizona. Given the tragic weekend shooting of Gabby Giffords, citizens needed to take action and hold their leaders to a higher level of accountability.

We invited the press to our outside event and to observe the delivery of our "21-Day Notice" to Pearce's office asking him to focus on the budget, job creation, education, and health care. Our delegation also invited him to our January 22 town hall meeting in Mesa with members from his district. We intentionally set out to be reasonable in our message, actions, and tone. Whether Pearce joined us or not, our outreach to potential supporters and volunteers had begun.

The idea for the "21-Day Notice" came from the image I had of Martin Luther's attack against the Roman Catholic Church in the 1500s when he nailed his *95 Theses* to the door of Wittenberg's Castle Church and ignited the Protestant Reformation. A basic statement of principles, our "21-Day Notice" laid out what we wanted and when we would be back. And as part of the action, we taped (no nails!) the "21-Day Notice" to the glass windows near the entrance to the senate office building. Its text read, in part:

> ***Whereas*** Senate President Russell Pearce is the most powerful man in Arizona with a veto-proof majority in the Senate and a Governor, who he claims he got elected, willing to support his agenda;
>
> ***Whereas*** Senate President Russell Pearce only received 17,552 votes and now as President of the Senate works on behalf of over 6 million Arizonans…
>
> ***Whereas*** Senator Russell Pearce has a history of taking positions contrary to the voters of Arizona and his own district, including … an initiative that would have taken over $400 million out of early childhood development programs;
>
> ***Whereas*** Senator Russell Pearce has used divisive issues that have created an atmosphere of fear and mistrust, led to numerous challenges in court, millions of dollars of legal fees, and over $600 million of lost revenue to the state of Arizona from canceled conventions and other business and government contracts;
>
> ***Therefore be it resolved*** that we, Citizens for a Better Arizona, request that Senate President Russell Pearce … focus on issues

and concerns that will unite all Arizonans—issues like education, healthcare, and job creation.

Be it further resolved that we, Citizens for A Better Arizona … serve upon Senate President Russell Pearce this ***21-Day Notice*** to provide Senate President Russell Pearce an opportunity to pursue an agenda that serves the interests of all Arizonans...

Finally, be it resolved that we, Citizens for A Better Arizona, will reconvene here at the Capitol on ***January 31, 2011*** to evaluate Senate President Russell Pearce's performance and take appropriate action at that time.

The words "immigration" and "SB 1070" were intentionally left out. For many of us, though, SB 1070 and Pearce's racist views provided the fuel that motivated us to pursue the recall. Now, we wanted our public message to be about jobs, education, and health care—not immigration. To win, we needed to play to a much wider audience. Our 21-Day Notice included mainstream language and issues that spoke to millions of Arizonans. We also set out to interact with Pearce from a position of mutual respect by recognizing him as a power player and allowing him to respond. And finally, we made it clear we would be back at the end of twenty-one days. Although we did not mention that we would recall Pearce if he chose to ignore our notice, we did promise to "take appropriate action" once the twenty-one days had passed.

Our letter to Pearce was not an attack or declaration of war. In read in part, "On behalf of Citizens for a Better Arizona, I congratulate you on being appointed president of the senate by your fellow Republican senators. Given the current budget crisis we now face as a state, the decisions you make over the next six months will have an immediate and long-term impact on the lives of millions of Arizonans. We believe it is important for citizens to have an opportunity to interact with decision-makers like you so that we can build an Arizona that respects and represents our values as Americans."

The letter went on to say, "Citizens for a Better Arizona is a newly formed coalition of concerned citizens committed to improving the quality of life of all Arizonans—better schools, better health care, better jobs, better government, and a better, more civil tone of respect and decency when it comes to solving Arizona's problems."

We needed to move beyond the framework of party politics and activate our power as concerned citizens. This call to action did not come from nor was it inspired by any one political party.

At the start of the 2011 legislative session, Republicans appeared eager to cash in on Pearce's extremist agenda while Democrats seemed ready to play defense and wait him out—after all, the next election was only twenty-two months away. Given Pearce's record of extremism, I was strong in my position that waiting him out until the next election was not an option. We needed a strategic, dramatic, unexpected, and unprecedented intervention to free Arizona of Pearce's all-out assault on immigrants and their families. On that first day of the Arizona legislative session in 2011, no one—and I mean no one—could have predicted Pearce's removal from office within ten months. He was powerful, vindictive, and embedded at the center of decision-making in Arizona politics.

As people arrived at the rally, I had to remind myself how quickly this all came together. It had only been a few weeks since we'd created the Facebook event during our trip to Rome, and now, here we were on the opening day of the legislative session. Many participants brought their own signs with messages such as "Hate Not a Family Value." When the program started, more than one hundred people had gathered on the lawn next to the Senate building. We opened our program with a moment of silence in memory of Christina Green, a nine-year-old girl murdered at the shooting in Tucson. Her mother had called on all Arizonans to stop the violence and stop the hatred. Following the moment of silence, I then introduced State Senator Steve Gallardo to speak.

Gallardo had been the only senator to endorse and support the idea of recalling Pearce from the very beginning. I initially met with him back in November and although he did not think it was possible to successfully recall Pearce, he thought it was the right thing to do. For Gallardo, there had not been any real political wins for Latinos. "We got our ass kicked on SB 1070, ballot measures, Proposition 300's no tuition for undocumented students, Proposition 200's requirement of proof of citizenship register to vote, English only, the elimination of bilingual education and ethnic studies," he said. "We hadn't won in years."

Gallardo viewed the recall as an opportunity to strike back and go on the offensive instead of just sitting around and taking whatever Pearce threw at us.

When I told Gallardo of the idea to recall Pearce, he smiled with excitement and trepidation, "We were going after the one guy that hated us all—enemy number one—and one of the most powerful politicians in the state."

Steve reflected on how he felt at that time: "Was there a lot of hesitation? You bet. A lot of it was that we had been playing defense for so long, the Democrats didn't know how to go on the offense. I didn't think it would be successful. I didn't think we could get the signatures. At the end of the day, we were going after a very popular senator, an LDS senator (Church of Ladder-day Saints), in one of the reddest (Republican) districts in the state."

Despite any doubts Gallardo had about the recall, he was not about to miss out on the slim chance that we could prevail. He reserved a space on the Capitol lawn for us and was the first speaker and elected official to welcome Citizens for a Better Arizona.

Before launching Citizens for a Better Arizona, I had heard about Pearce's anti-women stances and claims of domestic violence by his wife,

LuAnne. So, I reached out to Ally Bones from the Arizona Coalition to End Sexual Abuse and Domestic Violence. She told me that as far back as 2002, Pearce worked to protect men accused of domestic violence from restraining orders, opposed stiffer penalties for men who assaulted pregnant women, and took strong stands against the safety of women in Arizona. Ally was our second speaker.

Then, Valeri Dosset from the Communication Workers of America Local 7019 addressed the crowd and listed every anti-worker, anti-labor, and anti-union bill sponsored by Pearce. We then heard more about the budget from Daniel Hernandez and Brian Barabe, both from the East Valley Patriots for American Values—a group founded to promote a more civil and family-centered conversation on immigration reform.

To broaden our message beyond Phoenix, Miguel Ortega, a small business owner from Tucson, spoke about how Pearce's brand of politics impacted small business owners throughout Arizona.

I saved the best speaker for last. All of our previous speakers, myself included, had been engaged in these types of political battles before—but not our next speaker. When I introduced Chad Snow, he hobbled up to the mic on crutches. His first words: "Forty-year-olds should not be playing soccer."

Chad spent the next three minutes hitting all the talking points: "I am a lifelong resident of Arizona, I am a lifelong Republican and like Russell Pearce, I am a member of the LDS Church, and I am here to say mainly that Russell Pearce does not represent the values of any of those groups. He does not represent the values of the majority of Arizonans, the majority of Republicans, or the members of the LDS Church."

Chad now had everyone's attention. With his calm demeanor and oratory smoothness, Chad outlined Pearce's record. He challenged the press and others present to examine Pearce's background. "I took a look at Russell Pearce's own website, a website where he touts the legislation that he has pursued over the last several years. The vast majority of his laws have to do with two things—immigration and deregulating gun control. There's not one bill about education, about health care, about improving our economy or creating jobs. I encourage you all to go to his website, review his legislative agenda, and ask yourself, 'Do these issues reflect my greatest concerns in the state of Arizona?' I think you will come to the same conclusion that I did and all of these people behind me did—that they do not."

In a matter of minutes, Chad's comments helped establish Citizens for a Better Arizona's credibility as a legitimate bipartisan watchdog group committed to holding Pearce accountable. We were not just disgruntled Democrats, but Republicans and independents who shared a common concern about the damage Pearce could do.

When our speakers finished, we led the group into the lobby of the Senate building to create some tension and place ourselves at the center of Pearce's seat of power. After we assembled in the lobby, Saul Solis, a member of East Valley Patriots for American Values, and former State Senator Maria De La Luz Garcia, set out to deliver the letter to Pearce's office. After meeting some initial resistance, Saul and Maria reached Pearce's office and delivered the letter to Pearce's secretary. When Saul and Maria returned, we all cheered.

I moved to the center of the group and unrolled our enlarged "21-Day Notice" declaration. I read loudly each "Whereas" that exposed the consequences of Pearce's record. At the end, I repeated that if he refused to pursue an agenda that benefitted all Arizonans, we would be back within twenty-one days to "take appropriate action."

The press seemed amused by our bold declaration. Once I finished, the questions started flying:

"What do you mean 'take appropriate action?'"

"What can you do to hold Senate President Pearce accountable?"

"Surely you are not threatening to recall Senate President Pearce, are you? You have no money. You have no organization. Is this just a publicity stunt?"

I attempted to clarify our intent: "We are not here today to recall Senate President Pearce or anyone else. We are here as concerned citizens to call on Senate President Pearce to put an end to his extreme brand of Tea Party politics of hate, fear, and division. If Pearce chooses to continue his attacks on workers, teachers, public schools, poor people in need of health care, and the US Constitution, then we will be forced to act." I left it at that.

Technically, we had to wait five days after the beginning of the legislative session to file a recall petition. We also needed to set up the proper legal entity—a formal recall committee—before money could be raised and signatures collected.

But we had shown up on day one of the 2011 legislative session, with about a hundred people, a threat, and an idea. As the crowd dispersed, I wondered where we would've been if I had listened to other establishment voices to cancel our opening day action. The next day, as we predicted, the *Arizona Republic* mentioned both Citizens for a Better Arizona and the Tea Party in the same article highlighting our actions at the Capitol.

We met the first test of our movement—getting people to show up for a bold idea. The next challenge involved keeping them engaged. Citizens for a Better Arizona, our supporters, our "21-Day Notice," and Chad's remarks generated enough friction to spark a movement.

Now we had to turn the spark into a flame and the flame into a fire—a fire for justice, a fire for redemption, and a fire for dignity.

CHAPTER 8

Who is Russell Pearce?

All politics is local.
~ Tip O'Neill, former Speaker
of the US House of Representatives

After launching Citizens for a Better Arizona and delivering our ultimatum to Pearce completed—change your ways or we will be back in twenty-one days—we had until January 31 to get everything lined up. We all knew Pearce was not about to change his leadership style or legislative priorities. In fact, we expected him to double down on his meanness, divisiveness, and attacks on the most vulnerable. After many years of being to the far right of his Republican colleagues, Pearce was now seated at the center of power, with the ability to set the legislative agenda. Extreme bills on immigration, education, or health care that might never have seen the light of day, now would be green-lighted and sent to the floor for passage where Pearce could strong-arm yes votes from his Republican friends.

With no money, no organization, and no real information about voters in LD 18, we needed to move on several fronts simultaneously. Shortly after our action at the Capitol, I called Ken and shared with him our need for data about how voters felt about Pearce being senate president. We decided to hold our first precinct walk during the Martin Luther King Jr. holiday weekend. We hoped to assemble five or six canvassing teams and talk to as many as three hundred voters.

I told Ken, "We need to know how these voters *feel* about Russell Pearce being president of the senate. That's it. We'll knock on the door and drop a Dr. Phil type question on them, 'How do you feel about Russell Pearce being president of the senate?'"

We agreed the Pearce question should come first and Ken suggested we could sign up anyone who responded negatively to Pearce for vote-by-mail. "We might as well start identifying our base of voters to take out Pearce now," he said.

On Saturday morning, we pulled into the Safeway parking lot at Main and Dobbins in Mesa and met up with Ken. Only about ten volunteers showed up. After meeting some of them and picking up my packet, it felt more like a run to the laundromat than the kickoff to a historic campaign. I just kept telling myself to be patient and thankful that I was not out there by myself.

It was one thing for volunteers and supporters to show up at the Capitol on the first day of the legislative session and quite something else to show up early on a Saturday morning in a parking lot to "fight the power." Most activists were still lamenting the November election and saw little need to begin canvassing just one week into the new legislative session. For those of us working on the recall, though, the clock was ticking; our "21 Day Notice" expired in sixteen days.

After a brief orientation and some role-playing, we headed to our assigned precincts to knock on doors and talk to voters about Pearce. Many of us were a bit nervous. For the past year, Pearce's extremist comments, positions, and bills such as SB 1070, kept Arizona in the national, state, and local news for all the wrong reasons. Passage of the bill was met with resistance at all levels. But every action—from civil disobedience at the Capitol to calls for a national boycott of Arizona to national marches with tens of thousands of participants opposing SB 1070—gave Pearce a platform too.

Despite a year of such protests, Pearce had emerged stronger and more relevant than ever. SB 1070 enjoyed support from Republicans *and* more than a third of Democrats. Because of that success, we assumed that Pearce was not only well-known in Mesa but also well-liked.

As we drove to our first house, I turned to Lilia and said, "A lot of the volunteers have never done this type of work before. I think they are going to be discouraged when people don't answer the door or, even worse, when they get a door slammed in their face. I am afraid to admit it, but a lot of people like Pearce."

Lilia smiled. "That's what you think. We really don't know. Remember, we live in Scottsdale."

I smiled back. She was right. We had never spent time in Mesa talking to voters. Given the immense amount of media coverage SB 1070 received and Pearce's long career in politics without ever losing a race, we assumed Pearce had achieved celebrity status with his base of Mesa voters. In addition to senate president, he was also the self-proclaimed Arizona Tea Party president and a hometown favorite. Or so we thought.

After about three hours of talking to voters, we headed back to Safeway to turn in our results and debrief our volunteers. We were stunned by the results, which seemed too good to be true. As each team reported its results and shared stories from the field, we realized we made a huge mistake on our tracking form. We forgot to include a spot for "never heard of him" as a possible response. As we tallied up the results, it became increasingly clear that when asked about the new senate president, almost two out of three voters responded with a question of their own: "Who is Russell Pearce?"

Ken looked ready to burst with excitement. Was it possible almost two out of three voters had no idea who Pearce was? Amid some of the most divisive, hateful, and combative times in Arizona's history, and one of the architects of these racist policies was a relatively unknown politician in *his own* district?

Ken and I breathed, ate, slept, and digested politics daily. However, politics for most voters in District 18 remained unattractive, inaccessible, unimportant, and unworthy of their time or attention. Based on the responses we received, it appeared that most voters did not watch CNN or the local news. Instead, they were working long hours and overwhelmed with the demands of parenthood or managing their own lives. Holding politicians accountable was not part of their weekly routine.

Given this new information, we could now define Pearce on our terms. We could essentially avoid discussing the polarizing issue of SB 1070 and create a narrative that Pearce's views were just too extreme for Arizona when it came to health care, public education, and the US Constitution. We could focus our efforts on persuading voters to support the recall against someone who caused citizens to die because of funding cuts to poor patients waiting for organ transplants.

As Lilia and I drove home that afternoon, we realized that we'd made the right decision in Rome to shift our attention from Arpaio to Pearce. He was vulnerable in ways that we did not realize, and now we had the element of surprise working for us.

Still, much work remained. We had to figure out a way to: pay for the recall effort; identify someone in LD 18 to chair the recall committee; find a LD 18 resident to sign and file the official recall petition; and most important to me, identify someone who would be willing to run against Pearce if we were successful.

Our precinct walk revealed that Pearce no longer possessed a veneer of invincibility. Not only was the oft-heard response "Who is Russell Pearce?" unexpected and comical but it unveiled the untapped universe of the tens of thousands of voters that would be more likely than not to sign the recall petition if asked.

If the voters in LD 18 did not know who Russell Pearce was, then we were duty bound to let them know—and the recall petition would be the means by which we would initiate those conversations.

CHAPTER 9

The $10,000 Bet

Life is either a daring adventure or nothing at all.
~ Helen Keller

To make sure we had enough money to launch the recall, we set an internal goal of $10,000 in pledged commitments. Given my financial situation (unemployed), I needed to be paid full-time for my work with Citizens for a Better Arizona. Apart from our volunteer operation, we had to hire a signature-gathering company to jump-start the campaign. There were a number of companies in Arizona that hired people to go out and collect signatures at piece rate. Depending on the campaign, each person collecting signatures could earn anywhere from $1 to $4 per valid signature.

With only 120 days to get it done, we needed to lock down donors now. We could not risk launching the campaign without the funds to keep us going for at least a month or two. Now that we had this bold, audacious idea, we had to get people to invest.

The first $5,000 came quickly. Chad Snow, who already agreed to chair the recall committee, was in for a $1,000 as was his law partner Alex Carpio. Lilia, a second-year law student at the time, could think of no better investment of her limited funds than to go after Pearce. Ken, in addition to his time and functioning as our undercover co-conspirator, also gladly invested his money, as did I.

Bob Lord, a tax attorney, former congressional candidate, and progressive blogger, heard about our plans and reached out to me. He said that given the controversial nature of this particular fight, he might not be able to give directly but he would help us identify those who would. After reviewing my campaign plan, Bob said, "I still think this is crazy, and your chances are remote, but I want to help. I am impressed with your plan, and I don't want to be the reason why it didn't work."

He offered to set up discussions with two people: Bobette Gordon and Doug Kahn. "Both of them should be good for $1,000," he said. "I'll call them and let them know to expect your call."

I followed up with both Bobette and Doug, and true to Bob's word, each of them pledged $1,000. Bobette and her husband Robert Cialdini, had a history of donating to various organizations and universities. Bobette served as the vice president for Influence at Work, a company started by her husband to "improve organizational and personal performance by understanding and using the psychology of influence." She was widely respected in the business community. Our discussion was short, direct—and productive. "Who do I make the check out to, and where do I send it?" she asked.

Doug had run unsuccessfully for Congress a few times in the 1990s in the Los Angeles area. By the time he arrived in Arizona, he had spent a considerable amount of money trying to get Blue Dog Democrats[1] out of Congress while supporting true progressive Democrats. A bit quirky and eccentric, Doug had a heart for progressive causes, especially anything that could help Dreamers. He had funded trips for Dreamers to Washington, DC, and other Dreamer activities and events. Doug detested the fact that these young people had become the target of so much hate

---

[1] Elected members of the Democratic Party who identify as centrists.

by Tea Party Republicans and leaders such as Arpaio and Pearce. When I asked Doug for $1,000 to recall Pearce he said yes immediately and wanted to hear more about our strategy. He chuckled when I explained the part about how we planned to run a moderate Republican against Pearce in the special recall election.

"Here I am spending upwards of $100,000 to get rid of moderate Blue Dog Democrats in Congress and now I am giving to a group that if successful, will replace one extreme Republican with a regular Republican," he said. "Did I get that right?"

"Yes," I told him, "but a Republican who would support Dreamers and immigration reform."

Doug, a seasoned political donor, knew that "anyone but Pearce" was a worthy strategy.

I continued discussions with labor leaders, prominent Latino lawyers and other community leaders who had the resources to invest $1,000 of their own money. However, unlike donations to a 501(c)(4) organizations, where donors' names remain confidential, every dollar donated to the recall effort would be made public while Pearce was still senate president.

The responses I received from these power players shared a common theme:

"Are you out of your mind?"

"Good luck with that."

"What happens when you fail? Then you would have poked the bear without killing him."

"What do you think he'll do to us during the 120 days you are collecting signatures?"

"Can't do it. My members are split on SB 1070."

"Even if you get the signatures, no moderate Republican will ever run against Pearce."

"There are many ways to make change happen; this is not one I can support."

I left many of these meetings angry and frustrated because I knew these leaders had spent thousands of dollars in the past on failed candidates and lost causes. Their reluctance reminded me just how far this idea of recalling Pearce was outside of their comfort zone. Within the labor movement in Arizona, no union wanted to take the lead on this particular campaign to get rid of Pearce, except one—the Communication Workers of America Local 7019 (CWA 7019).

The union represented line technicians, call center workers, and other workers in the communications industry. The political views of the members ranged from hostility to support for Arpaio. And most importantly, immigration and SB 1070 were not essential issues that motivated the majority of CWA's union members to get out of bed each day, go to work, and voluntarily pay their union dues every month. However, for CWA 7019 President Paul Castaneda, the likes of Arpaio and Pearce ignited his passion and inspired him to do whatever he could to take them out.

I first met Paul in 2010 during my run for US Senate at a solidarity meeting to support striking UFCW Local 99 members. Paul grew up in the mining town of Superior, Arizona. His father was a member of the International Brotherhood of Electrical Workers Union, and his grandfather and uncle had been members of the mineworkers union. So, it wasn't a surprise when Paul started working for the phone company, in Arizona's anti-union "Right to Work" environment, that he joined CWA and became an active union member.

By 2001, Paul became an officer in the union and was later elected president to help rebuild its political program. Paul supported my run for US Senate because he wanted someone from labor to be out-front speaking about labor's issues. As president of CWA 7019 and chairman of its state council, Paul knew Pearce's leadership posed a serious risk to not only immigrants and their families but to unions, workers, and all things progressive. Unlike other labor leaders, Paul strongly believed that Pearce was the kind of leader who we could not simply wait out. Pearce's leadership style demanded intervention, if not by other elected leaders, then by regular citizens.

Paul was open to just about any idea that involved holding Pearce accountable. After I explained our strategy, Paul was all in, especially for finding a moderate Republican to go head-to-head against Pearce. Paul knew the idea was a little crazy, but he also knew there were a lot of unregistered and low-performing Democrats in LD 18. A moderate Republican would be a gift compared to having Pearce as senate president. But to donate $1,000, Paul would need the state council to approve it. This was not a typical political contribution; CWA had never contributed to any recall effort, and its membership included Republicans, Democrats, and independents. Paul invited me to present the idea to the state council in Tucson.

After my presentation, I drove back to Phoenix, thinking a decision might take a while. Before I reached the northern edge of Pima County, I received a call from Paul. With his calm demeanor, Paul said, "One thousand dollars approved. We are in—all in."

"How the hell did you do that?" I asked.

"After you walked out of the room, we had a lot of discussion around Pearce's stance on anti-labor issues. Throughout his career, Pearce had sponsored or co-sponsored twenty-five anti-labor bills. If there was any chance to replace Pearce with a moderate Republican, then they had to take the risk. Plus, $1,000 wasn't a huge ask given just how huge the potential impact could be."

Paul acknowledged the donation would be "on the record" and went on to say, "At the very minimum we can embarrass him by making him the first senate president recalled in history and force him to run again during an off-year election."

"Anything else?" I asked.

"Oh yeah. Some voted yes just to give you something else to do following your failed race for US Senate." We both laughed.

Paul also loaned us office space at CWA. "We have an extra conference room that we rarely use. I figured it would be a bit much for us to expect you to work out of the back of your car." We laughed again and hung up.

I felt a deep sense of appreciation for the courage it took for an elected labor leader like Paul to take such a risk while others were ducking for cover. As word spread through the labor community Paul's decision was met with little enthusiasm. Most were not open to hearing the overall strategy and quickly responded with "What are you doing?" or "Why piss him (Pearce) off?"

Fear ruled the day as more labor leaders warned Paul that the Republicans would throw more anti-labor bills at them. Paul pushed back, arguing that playing nice with Pearce wasn't going to stop him from running anti-labor bills. Paul had seen labor withstand all sorts of attacks over the years and labor always lived to fight another day. Whether our effort was met with success or not, labor would soldier on. Paul just could not imagine sitting this fight out with so much at stake and with such a small buy-in (only $1,000).

* * *

When I returned to Arizona in August 2007, the Laborers International Union of North America hired me as their political director for a campaign to organize Latino immigrants working in residential construction. My routine included weekly meetings of Somos America, a coalition of organizations focused on protecting the rights and interests of the Latino community. Somos America functioned as an information-gathering clearinghouse for all groups working on Latino issues. Somos America was also at the forefront of the mega marches in 2006 that saw some 200,000 people march against anti-immigrant bills in Congress and demand comprehensive immigration reform.

Robert Reveles, a co-founder of Somos America, grew up in Miami, Arizona, a small mining town about eighty miles southeast of Phoenix.

A sign at the town's entrance reads, "Welcome to Miami, Copper Center of the World." When he was a child, Miami's segregated environment shaped his passion for social justice. He was born in the US but had to attend "Mexican school" in Miami. When his family attended Our Lady of the Blessed Sacrament Catholic Church, they were ushered to the "Mexican side" of the church. The public swimming pool and local theater all had special rules for when Mexicans could use the facility and where they could sit.

Eager to see the world and get out of Miami, Roberto enlisted in the military and spent time overseas. His desire to work with people from all walks of life was influenced by his military assignment in Southern Italy when he worked at NATO air headquarters. Roberto was impressed to see so many different nationalities coalescing around a common enemy—the Soviet Union. This experience convinced him to pursue a career in diplomacy, which eventually took him to Congress. There, he spent twenty-four years as a senior advisor to members of Congress, communicator, negotiator and advocate. He later served as a vice president for the oldest and largest gold mining company in the nation at that time. After twelve years with the mining company, Roberto "retired."

I say "retired" because since I met Roberto back in 2007, he was one of the busiest people I knew—chairing meetings, serving on various boards of directors, and volunteering for many causes. I found him to be grounded, articulate, intelligent, measured in both his speech and action, and, most importantly, a pillar of integrity. In 2007–08, Roberto, with the support of such leaders as Linda Brown, Hector Yturralde, and Mike and Janet Valder, helped me secure a $10,000 grant to help launch Maricopa Citizens for Safety and Accountability, during the height of Arpaio's popularity. Roberto did not shy away from righteous causes, and we were about to launch one of the craziest righteous causes in Arizona.

When I talked to Roberto about our recall plans, I knew he believed deeply in civic engagement—getting involved instead of complaining from the sidelines. He cared about the undocumented immigrant community and dedicated a significant amount of his resources, his time, expertise, and money to help in any way he could. As we met, Roberto reminded me of the fear SB 1070 unleashed on our community—especially the undocumented.

"The fear people felt as a direct result of SB 1070 had horrible consequences. This fear meant sick people not wanting to go to the doctor's office. It meant people choosing not to attend church services."

In one horrific case, an undocumented mother was afraid to take her teenage daughter to the doctor. She died from her illness.

"This fear caused people to stay home instead of going out to celebrate a special occasion or to wait nervously when a parent or relative went to the store hoping they would not be stopped, detained, and arrested once they left their home."

As Roberto continued to share stories, it became clear to me that he viewed SB 1070 from a moral framework of good and evil; it was definitely an evil law. Its purpose, he said, "was nothing more than making life miserable for a certain class of people so they would ultimately self-deport."

Unlike other progressives who winced at our bold strategy, Roberto smiled and his eyes lit up. "I think this is a very gutsy move. I feel that something has to be done to begin to put the brakes on Pearce and other anti-immigrant copycat legislative proposals that are now being introduced in other states. We need to do something now. How can I help?"

He was good for $1,000 the very next week, just as our legal recall committee was up and running.

Now $1,000 shy of our $10,000 goal, I made a quick call to my friend Dan O'Neal, the co-chair of the Arizona's chapter of Progressive Democrats of America (PDA) and asked if the group could help raise $1,000. Dan had been at the forefront of progressive causes for most of his adult life. A retired teacher with a relentless drive, Dan embodies the spirit of "never give up"—no matter the challenge or likelihood of success. Dan and his co-chair, Virginia Hauflaire, both attended our kickoff on the opening day of the legislature. Dan loved the recall idea. "It's a concentrated area, LD 18, and we can focus our resources and volunteers on one fight. Similar to the Saul Alinsky approach to organizing, this would allow us to target one person and stay on it for 120 days—and if successful have a statewide impact."

The call took less than five minutes. Dan pledged to pass the hat at the next PDA meeting and he assured me the group was good for $1,000.

This $10,000 commitment provided the investment we needed to launch our paid petition circulation within a week of forming our official recall committee. I would cover any other short-term expenses. I could never have predicted that our initial investment would come from such a diverse group.

We still had a few "to-do" items on our pre-recall checklist. The most important involved identifying and recruiting Mesa residents for key leadership roles and responsibilities.

As the countdown to the January 31 deadline continued, we tapped into every contact and lead we had to find the Mesa leaders we needed to launch the recall. Power, as it was explained to me during my early days as a community organizer, comes in two forms—organized money and organized people.

Now that we had some organized money, we needed to organize a few more people in Mesa to join.

CHAPTER 10

Three Confirmations

If you lose faith, you lose all.
~ Eleanor Roosevelt

As our January 31 deadline approached, several glaring holes remained in our strategy. We needed a Mesa resident willing to sign the paperwork to initiate the recall process—and someone in Mesa to serve as our chairperson, to be the local face of the recall. Chad would fill that role on a broader scale for press events at the Capitol, but he did not live in Mesa. We needed someone who would make it harder for pro-Pearce Tea Party supporters to label our efforts as outsiders and liberal agitators.

On a more personal note, I needed to know if someone would be willing to run. Publicly, I downplayed the concerns people expressed about us not having a candidate. Privately, I was deeply concerned about the strong possibility that all our efforts would be for naught. My stomach turned every time someone said, "Randy, even if you are successful and get the signatures, who would dare challenge Pearce? You are just wasting your time. You have no candidate."

My comeback was always, "You're right, we don't have a candidate—*but* no serious candidate to challenge Pearce would dare reveal themselves any time before a special recall election is called."

The candidate question was irritating, insulting, and mean-spirited.

Irritating because everyone who asked knew full well that Pearce and the Republican establishment would destroy any potential candidate who surfaced during the petition phase of the recall process. This would have a chilling effect on anyone privately considering such a run.

Insulting because given the lack of success of previous recall efforts, the odds were stacked against us to even acquire enough signatures. Why would anyone declare their candidacy for an election that had not even been called, scheduled, or not likely to happen? And yet that was the expectation or threshold for many people when deciding whether to support us.

Mean-spirited because most of these progressive people already knew we did not have a candidate and all the reasons why. Yet, they still asked so we could provide them the excuse they needed *not* to get involved.

For these reasons, most people were hesitant to volunteer or give money to the recall. And in truth, I shared some of their skepticism. I needed some confirmation, some indication that if we devoted ourselves for the next 120 days to recall Pearce that the right candidate would have the courage to run. Without that possibility, our efforts would only antagonize and embolden Pearce who would run unopposed in the special recall election. That "victory" of simply recalling Pearce without removing him from office would leave us feeling frustrated, angry, and defeated.

With only a week to go, I needed a credible candidate, someone who at least was Republican, Mormon, and willing to run if we got the signatures. I asked Ken if he knew anyone in Mesa who would be willing to work with us on this. Without hesitation, he said, "Dennis Kavanaugh."

In a city dominated by Republicans and members of the LDS Church, Dennis was the only Democrat—a gay, Irish Catholic Democrat—on the Mesa City Council.

Dennis moved to Mesa from St. Louis in 1975 to attend law school at Arizona State University. From grade school through college, he attended

Jesuit Catholic schools that cultivated his interest in and appreciation for social justice. The teachings of the Jesuits with their motto, "For human values in an urban society," sparked his flame to serve. Before 1975, he had never been west of Missouri and had never seen deserts, mountains—or so many Republicans. But when he arrived in Mesa, he found a welcoming town of about 75,000 (now a city of over 500,000). After participating in a Mesa leadership program, Dennis was elected to the Mesa City Council in 1996. When I walked into his office, he was in his fourteenth year on the city council and someone who knew the Mesa community very well, including many Republicans who supported him over the years. He was my best chance of finding the right people in Mesa to help.

I assumed Dennis, like any Democrat, would be excited to remove Pearce from office. He acknowledged that the idea struck him as crazy, but he also knew something needed to be done. "In 2008, Mesa elected a city council that was progressive on many fronts," he explained. "The council embraced the need for affordable housing, mass transit, investing in the arts and social services, and were not afraid to try new ideas. We did it in a way that encouraged consensus building. Everyone agreed, 'Let's leave partisan politics in the parking lot.' The previous four years we had a very conservative mayor. Things were now different. On most major policy issues, we now moved forward with unanimous votes. The council was also unanimous with the concerns pertaining to all that was happening with Arpaio and his worksite raids."

As Pearce and Arpaio ramped up their anti-immigrant efforts, Dennis was offended that Mesa seemed to be the epicenter of negative, anti-immigrant politics.

"That wasn't the city I came to live in. I didn't want Mesa to be known for Russell Pearce. We were better than that. I did a lot of traveling in and outside of the state. When people asked me where I was from, I would say Mesa, Arizona, and they would say, 'Oh, then, you must be with Russell Pearce.' I would always be quick to say, 'No, I am not,' but I felt the self-worth of our community was at stake."

As things heated up with SB 1070, the headlines about Pearce harmed economic development in Mesa. The city council dealt with the economic downturn as more companies rethought their interest in doing business there. In Mesa and other parts of metro Phoenix, people—primarily Latino immigrants—were disappearing during the economic downturn. SB 1070 became the gas to an economic fire already burning brightly that accelerated huge vacancies in the housing sector, depopulated neighborhoods, and slowed foot traffic to stores, shops, and restaurants throughout urban Arizona. Latino immigrants did not just work—they paid taxes and were consumers too.

During the run-up to SB 1070, Dennis, whose city council district overlapped Pearce's Senate district, began hearing from more constituents. They wanted to know what had happened to Mesa's image as a welcoming community. Like many elected officials upset about Pearce's politics, Dennis felt bound to the words of the Serenity Prayer, "God grant me the serenity to accept the things I cannot change, the courage to change the things I can, and the wisdom to know the difference." And given the makeup of Pearce's district, having Pearce as the state senator from Mesa was one of those things Dennis could not change and therefore had to accept.

I shared with Dennis that we needed to find someone in Mesa willing to serve as our local spokesperson and identify a potential candidate willing to challenge Pearce.

After ruminating for a bit, he had a suggestion. "There's a person who I think would be perfect to be the face of the recall in Mesa. She is older and wiser than us and she is also a Republican. Although she ran for office back in the 1990s, I think she is pretty much done with politics. Her name is Mary Lou Boettcher." I scribbled down her name and a couple of others, but Mary Lou sounded perfect.

My second ask was a bit more challenging. "Can you think of any Republican Mormon who would be willing to run? This information will not be used publicly, but it is for my own sanity. I need to know now, before we file our papers to recall Pearce, that someone would be willing to run. I need to hear a sign from the universe that, yes, this is possible and that, yes, someone would run."

This time Dennis did not hesitate. "There is one person who I know does not care for Pearce's politics. The person is a woman, a Republican, a Mormon, and from a prominent Mesa family." I leaned in, waiting for the name. "Her name is Beth Coons. She's a Farnsworth, Ross Farnsworth's daughter, and someone who really cares about children and public education. Here's her number. Give her a call and tell her I gave you her number."

Not knowing much about Mesa, or the Farnsworth family name and reputation, I now had a Mary Lou to visit and a Beth Coons to call—with four days to go before our January 31 deadline.

My first confirmation came in the form of an elderly woman with the passion and drive of a young organizer. I dialed Mary Lou's number.

Mary Lou answered the phone in a very sweet and high-pitched voice. I did not know her age or what she looked like.

After I explained my mission, she didn't hesitate.

"Say no more. Did I hear you correctly? You want to get rid of Russell Pearce, right?"

"Yes."

"I can't stand him. He is such a mean person. I don't know why people in Mesa keep reelecting him. He always has something against teachers and is always spearheading cuts to public education."

She agreed to meet with me, so I jumped in my car and headed to Mesa. Mary Lou lived in a very nice middle-class neighborhood on a cul-de-sac in East Mesa, just a few blocks away from Russell Pearce. When she opened the door, I almost dropped to my knees to thank God for the gift bestowed on our "crazy" campaign. There she was in front of me—an older White woman, seventy-eight-years-young, with short, curly snow-white hair, big round glasses, wearing a bright red sweater. I watched her walk slowly, partly hunched over, with a cane. We could not have asked for a better visual representation in a spokesperson for our campaign in Mesa.

As Mary Lou and I talked, I continued to celebrate the treasure we had just discovered. She had a nonthreatening, grandmotherly look about her and she sounded amazing. She was witty, intelligent, knowledgeable, strong, and clear with her thoughts. I asked how she'd come to live in Mesa.

Mary Lou was born and grew up in a small Kansas town during the Great Depression, then earned a teaching degree at Phillips University in Enid, Oklahoma. Her family moved to Topeka, where she worked as a teacher and met her husband Phil, who attended Washburn University. They moved to Mesa in 1962 for the desert climate, upon being told that it would help their son's asthma.

Politically, she described her family as Eisenhower Republicans. She was a lifelong member of the Arizona Education Association (AEA) and a charter member of the Mesa Republican Women's group. "I even ran for president of my local AEA chapter, the Mesa Teachers Association, and won," she said. "My slogan was, 'Bet your boots on Boettcher!'"

The more we talked, the more convinced I became that she was the perfect spokesperson for our recall campaign. When she spoke, I could see the sparkle in her eyes and feel the fire still burning inside to create a better Mesa.

I didn't sugarcoat my ask: "Mary Lou, our campaign to recall Pearce needs someone like you to represent us—a local resident like you who can help anchor our effort right here in Mesa. Pearce, his allies, and even the press are going to want to spin this as a story about outside agitators coming in to impose their radical left-wing agenda. You are going to be called all sorts of names and they are going to accuse us of undermining the 'rule of law' every day as we gather signatures."

I paused and let the information sink in. Mary Lou remained attentive but silent.

"However, they are going to have a hard time telling that story with you as one of our main leaders. They may still say those things, but they will look and sound ridiculous when you step up to the podium to speak as a representative of Citizens for a Better Arizona."

After her husband's death three years earlier, Mary Lou became less involved. "I miss him dearly, and I have been praying for something or someone to come along to help me reconnect to my purpose. I believe this cause has arrived at the right time."

In addition to becoming our spokesperson, she even offered to collect signatures at her church and in front of the library.

Feeling that our meeting had come to a close, I stood and helped Mary Lou out of her chair. I gave her a hug and thanked her for having the courage to get involved at the very onset of this historic campaign. As I turned towards the door to leave, I heard Mary Lou's voice again.

"Wait a minute, Randy, don't you need money to help get this campaign going?"

"Yes, and lots of it once this thing heats up."

"Well, then, hold on. I can't let you walk out the door without a donation. Let me get my checkbook. I want to give you some money."

I explained that technically I couldn't receive donations because the committee to recall Pearce would not be formed until Monday. I suggested she postdate the check.

"I want to be the first citizen from Mesa to donate to Citizens for a Better Arizona and the recall of Russell Pearce," she said while writing a check for $30. "I wish I could give more, but I hope this helps. I will also figure out a way to be there on Monday at the Capitol. See you then."

One confirmation down, two to go.

Given the resistance we encountered within Democratic circles, I could only imagine how Republicans might react to someone like me asking, "I know you don't know me but how would you like to be our candidate to run against Russell Pearce in a special election that has yet to be called? I know he is one of the most powerful Republicans in the state and is currently the senate president, but if we collect enough signatures to recall Pearce, would you run? And, by the way, this has never been done before."

How could I pitch my case to Beth Coons?

She was the daughter of Ross Farnsworth. At that time, I didn't know a Farnsworth from a Woolworth. Some Farnsworth families were much more conservative like Pearce; however, Ross was a well-known and highly respected businessman and leader in the Mormon Church. He developed many projects in the East Valley, including senior living communities Dreamland Villa, Sunland Village, Sunland Village East, and Sunland Springs Village. He also served on the Mesa City Council and gave a tremendous amount of his time and resources to help the YMCA, United Way, and other groups.

Beth was one of twelve children. Like her father, Beth cared deeply about serving her community. She was elected to the Mesa School Board and eventually served as president. Her passion was children—making sure they had basic needs such as food, healthcare, and shelter. Beth, or someone like her, would be Russell Pearce's worst nightmare—educated, Republican, a Mormon, and from a prominent Mesa family. Beth and her network of Republicans represented a large segment of the party that didn't share Tea Party views.

After staring at my phone for about five minutes, I dialed her number. To my surprise, she answered. I introduced myself and shared with her that Dennis Kavanaugh gave me her name and number. I then said, "There is something I want to run by you."

I paused.

She said, "OK."

"Dennis shared with me that you are not a big fan of Russell Pearce and that you are an advocate for children's issues."

"Let's just say Russell and I do not see things the same. How can I help you?"

I made the full pitch. "We are about to launch a recall on Monday so we can trigger a special recall election to remove Pearce from office. If we are successful in getting the signatures, no one thinks anyone would dare run against Pearce in a recall election. The only way we can beat Pearce in a special election is by keeping all Democrats out of the election and throwing our support behind one Republican.

"I have just one question for you, and I promise not to disclose your answer to anyone during this process. And before I ask you the question, I want to be clear that I am not here to ask you to support our recall campaign or get involved in the recall petition signing process in any way.

"However, what I need to know, as the principal organizer of this campaign, is that if we are successful in collecting the signatures and the governor calls a special election, would you seriously consider being the candidate to take on Pearce in the special recall election?"

I expected to be bombarded with questions.

To my surprise, it took Beth one second to answer. "Yes," she said. "And if not me, I would do my best to help identify someone else to run."

That was it. That was all I needed to hear to wash away any lingering doubts I had about pursuing the recall. Knowing it would be inappropriate for me to scream "I love you, Beth!" at the top of my lungs for giving me and the campaign such a gift, I remained calm, formal and composed. "Thank you, Ms. Coons, for taking my call. You will not hear from me again—unless, of course, Pearce is recalled. Have a great day!"

As much as I wanted to celebrate, I could not post this news on Facebook or do an email blast to all those who doubted the possibility that there was a Republican Mormon willing to challenge Pearce. Beth's quick response gave me the hope I needed to press forward. It fanned the flames of righteous indignation I had toward Pearce and his agenda. No matter what others said, should we complete the first phase of the recall process, there would be a candidate willing to run.

Two confirmations down, one to go.

Lastly, we needed to find a Mesa resident willing to sign the paperwork for the recall petition. Ken suggested I meet with Todd Selleck and his wife, Diane. Todd, Diane, and their two daughters participated in our first neighborhood canvass over the MLK holiday weekend.

"He is a Democrat and one of our precinct committee people in Pearce's district," Ken said. "He is someone we can rely on and will not back out. He will also cooperate with us, show up to key press events, and stay on message."

Todd lived in Mesa—in the same house where he was born and grew up. Not active in politics for most of his life, he was a registered Republican until 1994 when a man named Eddie Basha, a Democrat, ran for governor. Todd changed his party affiliation, voted for Basha, and has been a Democrat ever since. Todd's first entry into politics was in 2002, when a young organizer from Associated Communities Organized for Reform Now (ACORN) asked Todd to support a tax measure to raise money for Mesa's public libraries.

As a young father, Todd believed in the importance of public education and public libraries so he began attending meetings of ACORN, which eventually connected him to the Maricopa County Democratic Party.

Todd worked as a mechanic for a local country club and he saw Latino immigrants maintaining the golf courses every day. Many of the people Pearce deemed "illegal" and "invaders" were some of the hardest-working people Todd knew. When SB 1070 became law, Todd did not want to stay quiet. "Not too many mechanics are interested in politics. But I had two daughters—Jamie was eleven and Stephanie was twelve—in 2011. I had to do something. So, when Ken asked me if I would sign the official paperwork to initiate the recall Pearce campaign, I did not hesitate to say yes. Did I realize then how big of a deal it was going to be? I had no idea."

In a matter of days, a retired teacher/librarian, a Farnsworth, and a mechanic—all with very different economic, political and religious backgrounds—decided to do their part to bring Pearce's days as senate president to an end by November 2011.

As I drove home, I felt a deep sense of gratitude and appreciation that these three citizens were willing to do their part to indeed make Arizona better.

CHAPTER 11

On the way to the Dance

An empty cart rattles loudly.
~ An old proverb

With our January 31 deadline fast approaching, all the pieces for a successful launch fell into place:

A $10,000 commitment from individuals—check.

Someone to file the recall petition—check.

A Republican chairman for Citizens for a Better Arizona—check.

A Republican resident of Senate District 18 to be our key spokesperson—check.

Not so fast. Four days before the recall launch, I got a call from Stephen Lemons from the *Phoenix New Times*. He already knew about our plans to launch the Pearce recall that Monday. "Are you aware of what's happening?" he asked. "I think you guys are about to be upstaged later this morning."

"What are you talking about?"

"Another group is holding a press conference to formally launch their campaign to recall Russell Pearce."

"Another group? What group? No one has contacted us about it."

"Apparently, Dee Dee Blase from Somos Republicans is spearheading a different effort to recall Pearce. You should come check it out and see for yourself."

"Thanks, Lemons, for the heads up. I will be there."

I had met Dee Dee only once at an action in support of Dreamers. She was more of a social media online talking head than an experienced and seasoned organizer. She knew about our plans to recall Pearce because we had been posting messages on social media and inviting supporters to join us on January 31 at the Capitol to hold Pearce accountable. People may not have believed we could recall Pearce, but the word was out that we were going to launch a recall against Pearce on January 31. Our January 31 event was not intended to be a surprise attack. However, Dee Dee's move was. Knowing how difficult it had been to pull together so many campaign components during the past sixty days, this looked more like a gimmick than a serious effort to take down Pearce.

As I jumped in the car to head for the Capitol, the question of "Why?" pulsated through my head. Why would she or anyone else do this? Why now? Clearly, this was an effort to derail our plans to launch on January 31, to force us to join her recall effort or, for some reason, make it more difficult for our campaign to be successful.

Under the rules governing recalls in Arizona, anyone can launch a recall petition, and there is no limit to how many groups can file a recall petition against the same elected official. However, voters may sign only one recall petition. Each petition stands on its own and signatures from one cannot be combined with signatures from another. So, in this case, voters could sign only one of the competing petitions. If a voter signed both petitions, both would be invalid. The last thing we wanted was a competing petition.

I arrived at the Capitol expecting to see a large crowd of supporters for this historic announcement. What I saw was a pathetic attempt by this group to get in front of our efforts to be part of the story. They had no money. They had few supporters on hand for their big announcement. They had no strategic message. In fact, their petition focused on immigration and Pearce's desire to change the US Constitution to get rid of birthright citizenship—not exactly the message we intended to use four days later. Dee Dee even hijacked our name, Citizens for a Better Arizona, to form her group, Arizonans for Better Government.

None of this mattered to the media that attended and announced their message statewide. The headlines made me cringe, "Hispanic Group Files Papers to Recall Pearce" (*East Valley Tribune*) and "Hispanic group seeks recall of senate president" (*Douglas Dispatch*).

These headlines benefited Pearce. The last thing we wanted was a narrative that emphasized a "Hispanic only" effort to take on Pearce. We wanted the recall narrative to be more about Republicans reclaiming their identity, ideas, and values. However, Dee Dee had no problem misleading the public about Arizonans for Better Government. She claimed they had a broad coalition of Democrats, Republicans, and church leaders.

At the press conference, I did not see representatives of this broad coalition Dee Dee referenced. Where were the Democrats she claimed to be part of her coalition? Or members of the Mormon Church and their leaders? She had nothing, but now she was in the mix, and I started to get calls from the press and other supporters asking me if we are still moving forward as planned or joining this effort. By merely holding their press conference and filing their recall paperwork four days before our launch, they successfully inserted themselves into the narrative.

I immediately told our supporters that this was no more than a publicity stunt and we were in no way going to allow this attempt to delay all that we had been preparing for since November. The next day we put out a statement:

"Over the past couple of months people have been meeting in Mesa and other parts of Arizona to develop a strategy to recall Senator Russell Pearce. Out of those discussions came the idea of creating Citizens for a Better Arizona to bring together people from all walks of life with the same committed goal of removing State Senate President Russell Pearce from office.

"Strategies have been planned and implemented with our 'Hold Russell Pearce Accountable' campaign, including our January 10 event at the Capitol, our January 15 District 18 door-to-door canvass and our January 22 town hall meeting in District 18. These efforts also include fundraising, community outreach to other supporters throughout Maricopa County, and as of this morning the official formation of our newly formed political recall committee—Citizens for a Better Arizona.

"We are a well-established group that has what it takes to raise the necessary funds both across the state and across the nation and we're rapidly closing on $10,000 already raised to help us achieve our goals! And while anyone can draft a petition to start a recall, it is good organizational skills and dogged determination that will actually get the job done. We urge everyone who has a true commitment to removing Russell Pearce from office to be part of our diverse and non-partisan coalition. Together we can succeed!

"Finally, as planned, we are moving forward on Monday, January 31, 2011, at 12:00 noon to file our recall petition. Now is not the time to hold potlucks to plan strategy. Now is the time to implement the plan. We hope you will join us to show your support!"

As things turned out, we made the right call. The weekend following their announcement, Arizonans for Better Government posted Facebook photos of a handful of volunteers making signs at someone's home and volunteers standing on the side of the street attempting to gather signatures. This only confirmed our initial belief that they were making this up from one day to the next; they were putting together their campaign *after* their announcement.

A couple of months later, Dee Dee again tried to insert herself into our campaign by posting on social media that they had a $15,000 donor. Knowing that our ultimate goal was to get the signatures, I took the bait and reached out to Dee Dee directly. Until then, I had not spoken to her. But if she *did* have a $15,000 donor, I was willing to discuss ways we could collaborate. To me, collaboration meant using the $15,000 for our paid signature operation and chasing the 2,000 or more individual voters Dee Dee said already signed her group's recall petitions, assuming they existed.

Unlike their campaign, we entered into a database every voter who signed our petitions. It would be easy for us to cross-check their petitions and identify voters that we could then add to our recall petition. Once we identified these voters, we could send a volunteer to their homes and ask them to sign *our* recall petition.

I called Dee Dee and asked her if the $15,000 donor was real and how many signatures their group had collected. She insisted the donor existed and they had collected more than 2,000 signatures.

We ended up meeting in person twice. At no point did she provide the name of her $15,000 donor or copies of any recall petitions. But after our second meeting, she handed me a note expressing her desire to be our communications director. Seriously? No donor, no recall petitions—and you want to be our communications director? I laughed when I read her note. We never met again.

The presence of injustice does not mean that people will simply come forward to support a righteous cause. One thing you learn in organizing—you can say, claim, or declare just about anything—but you cannot hide from the outcome. Did a hundred people show up or not? Did your main donor come through or not? Most important, do you have the skills, capacity, and expertise to recall a senate president or not? Arizonans for Better Government had none of the above.

Despite this unwelcome diversion, we refused to get sidetracked or discouraged. We spent the next four days working on turnout for our January 31 launch of the Pearce recall and devising a strategy that would make this look, feel, and run like a statewide rejection of Pearce and all that he represented.

CHAPTER 12

Ready. Set. Recall.

Every public officer in the state of Arizona, holding an elective office, either by election or appointment, is subject to recall from such office by the qualified electors of the electoral district from which candidates are elected to such office.

~ Article 8, Arizona Constitution

Our "21-Day Notice" expired on Monday, January 31, 2011. Pearce had done nothing to indicate his willingness to govern in a more inclusive and conciliatory manner. On the opening day of the legislative session, we asked Pearce to focus on the most important issues for Arizonans—the budget crisis, jobs, public education and health care. Instead, Pearce ignored our warning to temper his agenda. He sponsored bills that provided guns for professors, limited tribal sovereignty, reduced funding for clean elections, outsourced airport contractors, privatized state parks, and required changes to the US Constitution.

In fact, Pearce was back on his soapbox about the need to end birthright citizenship. Of even greater concern to some families was his insistence on cutting Medicaid, rejecting billions of health care dollars from the federal government and eliminating funds to assist patients waiting for organ transplants. Two such patients awaiting organs died as a result of these cuts; they could no longer afford the six-figure price tag for the lifesaving operation.

Pearce's ascension to senate president meant that he now controlled the legislative agenda for some six million Arizonans. This was no longer a local fight in Mesa. Our launch would be an action, not a press conference.

To make it more of a shared experience and give our supporters a deeper sense of ownership, all of them would participate in submitting the official Statement of Support for Recall Petition. By law, one person (in our case, Todd Selleck) had to fill out the form and submit it to the secretary of state's office. We created more than one hundred similar petitions. Each of our volunteers filled one out, signed it, and turned it in right after Todd submitted the official one. We did this at the Capitol, but our volunteers across the state—in Tucson, Yuma, Nogales, and Flagstaff—did the same.

As we arrived at the secretary of state's office that morning, our new website was live and ready for online donations. One of Ken Chapman's reliable website designers, Lyle Dillie, worked tirelessly over five days to build a special online platform with a domain name—recallpearce. com—that was much more direct and clarifying than what we initially suggested. Anyone interested in helping as a volunteer or contributor could now do so online.

A few reporters had been observing our efforts since we unveiled our "21-Day Notice." They were eager to see what we would do once it expired, especially since there was already another recall petition circulating. Our press release declared our intention boldly and clearly, "21-Day Notice Expires Today—Citizens Across the State File Petition to Recall Senate President Russell Pearce." We were not a handful of unorganized, undisciplined, and "immigration only" novices about to launch a Hail Mary pass to take down one of the most powerful and divisive political figures in Arizona. We showed up with the right message, the right people, and the right strategy. At a minimum, we would force a recall election by collecting the 7,756 signatures we needed to win.

The message on the recall petition had a 200-word limit. A description would be placed at the top of every Recall Pearce petition; we intended it to be as inclusive as possible for all those who read it. The day before our filing, I drafted a statement and shared it with a few of our close supporters. We agreed to steer clear of immigration issues or other controversies that might prompt someone to tune us out and not sign.

Our final statement read: "We, Citizens for a Better Arizona and residents of District 18, submit this petition to recall State Senator Russell Pearce for his failure to focus on issues and concerns that affect all Arizonans. Mesa and Arizona need a leader who will pass laws to create jobs, protect public education and ensure access to health care for our children and those most in need. We deserve a representative that reflects our values, beliefs and vision for Mesa and all of Arizona. By signing this petition, we publicly withdraw our support for Russell Pearce and what he represents."

We made our case in less than a hundred words and kept our focus on jobs, public education, and health care for children. Depending on who we met at the door, we could still reference SB 1070, Pearce's desire to change the Constitution, and his other extremist views. For now, this statement would serve our purpose.

At the Capitol, we passed out the individual petitions for supporters to sign and turn in as part of the action. Everyone lined up on the seventh floor, right outside the service window for the secretary of state's office. More than a hundred participants stood in line.

Supporters included Carolyn Cooper, a self-described "army brat" and diehard Democrat who had spent more than fifty years living in Arizona; Dan O'Neal and Virginia Hauflaire from the Arizona chapter of Progressive Democrats of America; and Brian Barabe,

Carolyn O'Connor, Saul Solis, and Dan Martinez—all retired, lifelong Democrats and mostly former educators. We also had a significant group of Democratic activists, including Jeffrey Brown, who knew we could not let Pearce's power continue unchecked. Although we had a handful of Republicans in attendance, our success in getting signatures depended on recruiting Democrats and independents who could not stomach the thought of Russell Pearce serving as *their* senate president. The individuals that showed up on January 31 provided the jumpstart we needed to begin and sustain the recall during its challenging early days.

In January 2011, Republicans controlled the top offices and all branches of government; the Pearce recall was the only strategy that allowed us to go on the offense. Other organizations were already playing defense—attempting to block Pearce's extreme bills by engaging business leaders, church leaders, and other prominent leaders to derail Pearce's extremist agenda. Citizens for a Better Arizona was tapping into a reservoir of anger, discontent, and outrage of many lifelong Democrats. These activists, mostly retired, were involved in earlier struggles to fund public education and health care for the poor. No words of inspiration were necessary to fuel their dedication and commitment from day one through day 120 of the recall. They were fired up and ready to go the moment we said, "Recall Pearce."

With the media in full view, we began our action with Todd Selleck, his wife Diane, and two daughters walking up to the window and pulling out the official recall petition form. Before he turned it in, Todd turned to our supporters in line behind him and read it out loud. And when he finished with "By signing this petition we publicly withdraw our support for Russell Pearce and what he represents," the crowd erupted in cheers as Todd firmly placed the petition on the window counter.

Then our supporters, one by one, dropped off their signed, personal petitions. The language was the same, with this adjustment: "By signing this petition we are publicly demonstrating support for the recall effort of Russell Pearce filed on Monday, January 31, 2011, by Citizens for a Better Arizona in Maricopa County."

Meanwhile, the reporters started in on us:

"Why are you doing this when there is already a Recall Pearce petition circulating?"

"Why not combine efforts?"

"Is this just a publicity stunt?"

"How much money do you have?"

We reminded them about what we saw on social media over the weekend from the "other campaign"—people sitting in a room brainstorming and standing on a street corner with signs. We knew our campaign was the only real chance we had to recall Pearce. Although they were welcome to carry our petitions, we would not under any circumstances carry theirs. Unlike the other campaign, we said, we had $10,000 pledged, and our paid signature-gathering operation would be up and running within twenty-four hours.

It had been almost two and a half months since I had the idea of recalling Pearce. Now we had the recall petitions in our hands and the clock now ticking with 119 days to go to collect 7,756 signatures. Later that afternoon, Carolyn Cooper and Jeffrey Brown went to the Mesa Public Library to begin the work of gathering signatures. Carolyn would soon become one of our best and most loyal volunteers and canvassers.

Carolyn found out about our CBA kickoff event at the Capitol back on January 10 from Jeffrey Brown. She said, "When I found out more about Pearce, I was horrified. Jeff said he would make some signs, but he didn't have any time to do it. I made a sign that said 'Brewer and Pearce: Stop the Hate.' When I showed up to the Capitol on first day of legislature, I was over the moon. I had been begging—dying—for some Democrat to say in the public space what it truly means to be a Democrat. I was shocked to see how far Democrats had drifted to become more centrists—always claiming that we can't say this or that if we want to get elected."

The volunteers who gave their time were invaluable, but aside from our initial $1,000 investors, we had difficulty getting others to buy-in and donate money. Our initial paid signature-gathering operation went sideways within a week. Our volunteers at the Mesa Public Library told me someone who looked as if they were strung out on drugs was attempting to collect signatures. Sure enough, the person was strung out on drugs and part of the paid signature-gathering company I'd hired. That day, I canceled the contract and focused our efforts on fundraising and volunteer recruitment. However, volunteers alone would not get us enough signatures. We had to find a new vendor.

By the end of February our team was finally coming together and things had stabilized. With a core group of 25—30 volunteers already in place, we hired Geoff Esposito to coordinate volunteer walks, Randy Keating to set up and manage our database for verifying and entering all signatures, and we hired a new company to take over our paid signature-gathering operation.

It might be more accurate to say the new company, Sign Here Petitions, found us. My only experience with the paid signature-gathering business occurred during my run for US Senate. The work is seasonal, and some of the business practices can be a bit shady in terms of the tactics deployed, the treatment of the workers, and the handling of large sums of money. I received a call from Bonita Burks, owner of Sign Here Petitions, asking to meet. Companies such as hers received notices whenever a new campaign that needed signatures was filed with the secretary of state's office.

When Bonita arrived for the meeting, I was pleasantly surprised to see a Black woman who was the owner and principal officer of a petition-gathering company in Phoenix, of all places. Given the lack of diversity among those who own and operate political businesses, I was extremely pleased to give Bonita the opportunity to earn our business. Sign Here Petitions would be a partner in our drive to collect 7,756 *valid* signatures (I emphasize the word 'valid' because it would take upwards of 14,000 signatures to reach that goal). Bonita promised to stay away from the library and any events volunteers from Citizens for a Better Arizona attended, to verify every signature before turning them in, and meet once a week to turn in the completed petitions. We agreed to pay $2.50 per signature with incentives that could raise it to $3. With the contract in place, we soon surpassed 200—300 valid signatures per week.

Pearce had shown himself to be bulletproof when it came to marches, boycotts, prayer vigils, protests, civil disobedience, and other actions intended to bring him down or slow his rise. He would never envision being toppled by a small group of concerned citizens armed with clipboards, papers, and pens. In many ways, the recall petition served as our "Declaration of Independence"—without all the violence and bloodshed. Thousands of conversations, not armed rebellion, served as our means to restoring a sense of civility and decency and ending the anti-immigrant legislative attacks against Latinos and their families.

Our volunteers and paid signature-gatherers had 120 days. Every signature collected brought us one step closer to our goal. And every rejection at the door served as an ugly reminder of what happens when ordinary people are disengaged, uninformed, and, even worse—disinterested. Most of our volunteers thought we would never be able to recall Pearce, but they needed something tangible, something real, something they could measure that showed they were doing *something*. That occurred each time a voter in Mesa signed the petition.

I now could turn my attention to fundraising, social media, and weekly actions to help generate earned media coverage. This would help grow our numbers of volunteers and online donations. To accelerate fundraising, I also wanted another opportunity to pitch the campaign to key leaders within the Arizona Democratic Party—despite their initial opposition. Since the first day of the legislative session, we had made much progress, but we still needed help, especially when it came to raising money.

CHAPTER 13

"He's My Boss"

Here's to the crazy ones, the misfits, the rebels, the troublemakers, the round pegs in the square holes... The ones who see things differently—they are not fond of rules. You can quote them, disagree with them, glorify or vilify them, but the only thing you can't do is ignore them because they change things... They push the human race forward, and while some may see them as the crazy ones, we see genius, because the ones who are crazy enough to think that they can change the world, are the ones who do.

~ Steve Jobs

Even after we filed our official recall petition, some of the state's top Democratic leaders remained reluctant to join our campaign; some even tried discouraging others from getting involved. In February and March, we continued our outreach to elected leaders and other progressive community leaders who we thought would be more than excited to help recall Senate President Pearce.

True to her word in Rome, Lilia raised money, recruited volunteers and collected signatures. She carried recall petitions wherever she went and engaged anyone who was willing to listen. In 2009, Lilia had joined Emerge Arizona, which mentored women aspiring to run for elected office. Once Lilia completed that program, several colleagues

111

and Emerge Arizona leaders encouraged her to enroll in a leadership program organized by the Center for Progressive Leadership, CPL (today known as Leading for Change). Of all the groups she was part of, CPL appeared to be the most promising place to recruit volunteers for the recall campaign. The CPL curriculum required participants to develop and work on a project so they could apply class lessons on communications, fundraising, and organizing. Many of the instructors were elected leaders: State Senator Kyrsten Sinema (now a US Senator), State Representative Chad Campbell, and State Representative Katie Hobbs (now Arizona Secretary of State).

In 2011, CPL had a reputation as the best program for training and developing progressive leaders in Arizona. At first, Lilia hesitated to enroll because the costs exceeded $1,000 and she was still in law school. Because she wanted to hone her leadership skills and many people she trusted encouraged her to apply, she enthusiastically enrolled.

To Lilia's amazement, when she showed up to CPL with copies of our recall petition, her colleagues did not respond with much interest to get involved. She approached the director, Beth Meyer, whose social justice trajectory spanned decades. "A recall is crazy," she said. "It won't happen." Lilia pressed on and encouraged others to get involved thinking there still could be overwhelming support from other participants. Her colleagues Jackie Adams and Rhonda Bannard took a chance and agreed to carry recall petitions, but the rest of the class smiled politely and declined. Many quietly agreed the idea of recalling Pearce was "crazy."

At this point, Lilia reflected on the reactions from her classmates and attempted to reconcile CPL's mission and values with those of the recall campaign. For her, there was a strong connection between what CPL claimed to represent and what the recall set out to accomplish. Unlike the Arizona Democratic Party that was committed to recruiting, training, running, and getting Democrats elected, CPL's mission was much broader. This was what originally inspired Lilia to enroll.

Refusing to give up, she reached out to State Senator Kyrsten Sinema. Back in 2010, Lilia lived in Sinema's district, donated money, and volunteered for Sinema's campaign for state senate. Lilia knocked on doors and spoke to voters about why they should support a leader such as Sinema, whose passion for serving she admired. And when asked to introduce Sinema at an Emerge Arizona event, Lilia happily did so.

After one of the classes, Lilia asked Sinema for her perspective on how to best manage her leadership role with the Pearce recall.

"Oh, that's so dangerous," she warned. "You need to stop that right now. You can't get involved in anything like that. And, besides he's my boss and he would kill all of my bills. I can't get involved in anything like this."

This exchange revealed how key leaders in the Democratic Party viewed the recall and, more importantly, how they viewed a divisive and racist figure such as Pearce. Despite his anti-anything-progressive record, some Democrats still wanted to go along to get along in pursuit of their own agendas.

After more than twelve years in the labor movement, I can tell you the term "boss" is something we rarely had trouble defining. The boss had the power to hire and fire, someone who could literally and unilaterally deprive you of your economic means of earning a living. Pearce was not Sinema's boss, and she knew that. Could you imagine in today's national political climate, US Senator Sinema or any Democratic senator saying to someone leading a movement to get rid of the Republican Senate Majority Leader, "No, I can't get involved with that; he (or she) is my boss and would kill all of my bills." Of course not, and yet that was Sinema's go-to line to justify her position against doing anything to help the Pearce recall. And, to my astonishment, it not only worked, it also got her to where she is now.

Sinema's response illustrated both the extent to which Pearce's new position normalized his extreme beliefs and attitudes and the reason why we, Citizens for a Better Arizona, had to pursue a recall strategy.

Instead of sounding the alarm when Pearce was elected senate president, Democratic leaders assumed a business-as-usual posture. Shortly after Lilia was rebuffed by Sinema, I met with Andrea Cherni, chairman of the Arizona Democratic Party. Cherni ran unsuccessfully for state treasurer in 2010, but he had raised an impressive amount of money. When we met at the Democratic Party's office, I felt confident he would do something to help our effort.

After I made my pitch about all the reasons why we needed to recall Pearce, he calmly replied, "When it comes to raising money, elected officials like Pearce are more useful to us in office than out of office." Cherni shared the position of his Democratic colleagues that we would fail, and when we failed, Pearce would cause even more problems for Democrats and their legislative agenda. Before I left, I asked him to help us raise $5,000. He replied, "We'll see."

In politics, "we'll see" means "No."

Shortly after our launch, I asked one of our volunteers, Bob Unferth, to reach out to our elected Democrats and ask them simply to sign a pledge of support for the recall. Bob and his wife Nancy moved to Arizona more than thirty-five years ago from Chicago. After the temperature dropped to minus 27 degrees one winter, they felt the time had come to seek out a warmer place to live. I called Bob our honorary "Latino" because of his life experiences: his family had vacationed in Cuernavaca, Mexico, for more than thirteen years; he'd studied Spanish for more than forty years; and he enjoyed volunteering for causes that helped the Latino community. As a result of the time they spent in Mexico, both their daughters became fluent in Spanish.

Since 2008, Bob had been working with Mi Familia Vota, a national organization dedicated to educating and mobilizing Latino families to register and vote. "I had so much fun with them. We would stand in front of Ranch Market and register voters. They taught me how to say, '*Registrarse para votar?* (Are you registered to vote?)' and people, after looking at me, would respond, '*No hablo ingles* (I don't speak English).' I guess my Spanish sounded like broken English to them."

When Bob attended a meeting about organizing efforts in Latino neighborhoods and the horrible impact of deportations on families, he witnessed the consequences of extreme anti-immigrant policies and laws. "There was this nine-year-old little girl sitting there, and I could see the fear in her eyes. She was afraid of what would happen to her parents. I felt that Latinos were our friends. How could we allow this to happen?"

Bob found Pearce to be hostile, offensive, and short on intellectual prowess. Even though Bob initially agreed that these "crazy people" trying to recall Pearce would likely fail, he also noticed how Pearce kept helping their efforts by making one extreme statement after another. After we set up our signature-gathering table in front of the Mesa library, Bob showed up on the third day to help, and he kept coming back week after week. Similar to what some church members do, Bob "tithed" $100 every week, always on Mondays with a check tucked into a small envelope. "I could not give more than $100 at a time because of my wife. She was always after me, 'Why are you spending all this money?' Well, Lilia told me early money was most helpful, so I gave often and I gave early."

When we needed someone to ask elected Democrats to sign the pledge to support the recall, Bob happily agreed. After gathering signatures at the library, he had a good feel for what was happening on the ground. "Some people thought I was the devil incarnate. But most people were neutral to supportive. I knew we were never going to get the 7,000 plus signatures we needed, and we would never get someone to run against Pearce. But despite that, I kept coming back because it was worthwhile, and I liked the people I met."

As Bob began his outreach to Democratic legislators, a pattern developed. If he mentioned "the recall," most of his calls went unreturned or he received the boilerplate response, "I will pass on the message to the representative." However, Bob was not your typical volunteer. He had donated to various candidates, and he was an active member in his legislative district. Many of these politicians knew Bob personally, and they had no problem asking Bob for money when they ran for office.

When Bob approached his district's leader, State Senator Eric Meyer, someone he respected and admired, Meyer refused to sign the pledge of support, echoing the same go-along-to-get-along mantra.

Bob soldiered on and called State Representative Katie Hobbs. They talked briefly on the phone. Hobbs ending the conversation with, "I am with you but I can't sign the pledge of support." Although well short of a public declaration of support, Hobbs at least wished us luck and privately expressed solidarity with our efforts.

Bob continued to reach out to people he referred to as mostly "White privileged electeds," which left him saddened and disappointed each time they said no. "It was as if our Democrats put their trust in Republicans instead of progressives," he said.

Despite the disappointing response from electeds, other party leaders gave support.

At Ken's suggestion, I reached out to Ann Wallack, chairperson of the Maricopa County Democratic Party, to ask for financial support. Ann was opposed to SB 1070 from the moment it was introduced and wanted nothing more than for Pearce to be removed from office. Our meeting went well, and before I left, Ann reached into her purse, pulled out a check, and slid it slowly across the table, facedown. I mention this only because it felt a bit weird, as if we were involved in something shady and secret. I smiled, thanked Ann and picked up the check—a donation for $100. Given all the pushback we were receiving, I took this as a sign that things were about to change. However, we were still searching for our very first elected official to host a fundraiser for Citizens for a Better Arizona so others would follow.

During the first two months of the campaign, our fundraising efforts consisted primarily of small online donations and checks we received from supporters all over the state. Pearce's grip on elected officials from both parties went unchallenged for fifty-four days. Until March 26, no elected official—local, county, state or federal—offered to host a fundraiser. No elected official wanted to be *that* out-front in inviting their supporters to write checks to remove Pearce from office. However, one city council member from Glendale, a former nurse, social worker, and crusader for justice, Norma Alvarez, finally ended the 54-day drought. Yes, the first elected official bold and courageous enough to put her name on a public flyer with her home address inviting people to join our movement was a Latina from the Glendale City Council.

Norma perceived the situation as drastic, "With Pearce, the racism was just too much. He did not even attempt to cover it up. And our schools needed money, not more cuts."

I asked Norma if she was concerned Pearce might try to retaliate for her support of the recall. She grinned widely and said, "Let him come after me. What can he do to me? *Nada* (nothing)."

Exactly!

We posted Norma's fundraiser on Facebook and sent notices to our supporters. Following Norma's fundraiser, other elected officials began to step up. Soon thereafter State Representatives Ruben Gallego and David Lujan hosted a fundraiser in Phoenix, followed by State Senator Linda Lopez in Tucson. Each event allowed grassroots activists to become more engaged, while signaling to other power players in the party that this idea may not be that crazy after all.

CHAPTER 14

SB 1070 Supersized

Recognize yourself in the he and she who are not like you and me.
~ Carlos Fuentes

As leaders within the Democratic establishment and progressive circles continued to dismiss our recall movement, Russell Pearce's anti-immigrant train of hate, scapegoating, and divisiveness kept chugging along. By mid-March, several anti-immigrant bills were up for final passage. Pearce's omnibus immigration package made SB 1070 look like a Ford Pinto compared to his new Cadillac lineup of bills targeting immigrants and their families. With a 21–9 Republican majority in the Senate, Pearce wasted no time cashing in on his new position and what had now become a national platform.

These new bills, if passed, would:

- Deny entry to public schools for children in K–12 education if they could not produce a US-issued birth certificate or naturalization document
- Bar undocumented immigrants from driving, and the penalty, if caught, was one month in jail and loss of car
- Bar undocumented immigrants—including their children who were US citizens—from accessing public benefits

- Require all public employees—including public school and public health care employees—to report violations of national immigration laws; failure to do so would be a Class 1 misdemeanor, punishable by six-to-twelve months in jail
- Bar undocumented immigrants from enrolling in state universities and community colleges
- Sentence anyone convicted of identity theft to 180 days in jail
- Empower the state attorney general to sanction any business that did not use E-Verify to check the legal status of any potential employee
- Require hospitals to verify a patient's legal status before providing non-emergency care
- Restrict vehicle registrations to legal residents and citizens
- Issue state birth certificates to only those babies with at least one parent who was either a US citizen or green card holder
- Evict all residents, even US citizens, of a public housing unit if any undocumented person was found living there

The "reasonably suspicious" standard outlined in SB 1070 that legalized racial profiling of Latinos in Arizona didn't satisfy Pearce and his allies. From a legal perspective, they wanted Arizona to be one of the most unwelcoming places to live for any undocumented person and their families. And from a public relations perspective, they wanted to continue to use their public platform to instill fear of and foster intolerance towards immigrants.

Unlike the 2010 legislative session in which moderate Republicans and Democrats were overwhelmed and unprepared for the groundswell of public support for SB 1070, this year would be different. With a 21–9 disadvantage in the Senate, pro-immigrant rights groups focused their outreach on the one key constituent group that could persuade enough Republicans to vote against Pearce's agenda—Arizona's business community. No matter how much pro-immigrant groups such as Promise Arizona, Somos America, Puente or Border Action Network lobbied Republican senators, they were not going to be pressured into voting against their leader.

But three days before the March 17 vote, a broad, deep, and diverse group of business leaders signed a letter that strongly suggested legislators redirect their energies and let Congress take the lead on immigration. The letter was addressed to Senate President Pearce, but the message was meant for the conservative-to-moderate Republican senators who had not been swept up in the Tea Party movement.

They were more pro-business Republicans than anti-immigrant or anti-Latino zealots. The business leaders, reluctant to relive the fallout from SB 1070, made it clear they had no appetite to sit back quietly and watch Pearce pursue his crusade unchallenged. The letter read in part:

> "If the Legislature believes it is worthwhile to debate the question of citizenship, we believe that debate is best held in the US Congress … Arizona's lawmakers and citizens are right to be concerned about illegal immigration. But we must acknowledge that when Arizona goes it alone on this issue, unintended consequences inevitably occur. Last year boycotts were called against our state's business community, adversely impacting our already struggling economy and costing us jobs. Arizona based businesses saw contracts canceled or were turned away from bidding. Sales outside of the state declined. Even a business which merely had 'Arizona' in its name felt the effects of the boycotts, compelling them to launch an educational campaign about their company's roots in Brooklyn. It is an undeniable fact that each of our companies and our employees were impacted by the boycotts and the coincident negative image."

The letter's signatories included: PetSmart Chairman Philip Frances, US Airways Group (now American Airlines) President/CEO Douglas Parker, Banner Health President/CEO Peter Fine, Sundt Construction Chairman/CEO Doug Pruitt, Hensley Beverage Company President/CEO Robert Delgado, and other prominent business leaders.

In other words, the businesses' bottom line had been hurt and its leaders intended to make sure nothing like SB 1070 happened again. They wanted to lead the nation in innovation, productivity, and job creation—not anti-immigrant bills designed to make life miserable for thousands of immigrants who were needed to build, maintain, and grow those businesses.

The business leaders did not attack Pearce and his allies; instead, Arizona politicians were invited to be part of the effort to address these issues at the federal level. The letter drove home their message and strategy, "Therefore we urge the Legislature to redirect its energy by joining us in pressing the federal government for meaningful immigration reform. Together we can get results."

These presidents and CEOs would no longer keep silent as Pearce and his followers tried to use Arizona's legislature as a petri dish for more stringent and offensive anti-immigrant bills. The failure of these leaders to get involved in such a public way a year earlier not only hurt Arizona's image and thousands of immigrant families, but within a year of SB 1070's passage, some sixteen states introduced copycat punitive bills.

This letter arrived just in time to provide the kind of cover moderate, pro-business Republicans needed to vote against their senate president. Senators Allen, Barto, Crandell, Driggs, Grey, McComish, Nelson, Pierce, Reagan, and Yarborough followed the lead of the sixty business executives and voted down the omnibus immigration package of bills. Although they helped defeat Pearce's anti-immigrant agenda, these legislators were hardly a bastion of pro-immigrant liberators. Many of these very same senators voted for SB 1070. Given its political fallout, the negative economic impact, and Arizona's new image as racist state, these leaders now knew better than to allow Pearce to continue down this road again unchallenged.

"These immigration bills are a distraction," Senator John McComish (Republican) said. "They could be a detriment to the growth of our economy, and they are something people don't want us to be focused on. It's time for us to take a timeout on immigration."

Pearce, unfazed by the rebuke from business, refused to surrender. He declared, "I stand on the side of citizens, not a bunch of businessmen that write me a letter."

I had watched the vote from the gallery. As I left, I bumped into Petra Falcon, executive director of Promise Arizona, in the hallway. Promise Arizona was a relatively new community-based organization that worked on immigration reform, voter registration, and leadership development—with a focus on Latino youth. Petra is a lifelong Arizonan whose family goes back four generations. I met Petra back in 1995, when we were organizers with the Industrial Areas Foundation (IAF). As organizers, we attended monthly trainings to further our growth and development. Petra had an extensive background in church-based and grassroots organizing. We knew each other through our political work, but our social circles did not overlap.

I approached her to discuss the recall, and I knew it would not be an easy conversation. Up until now, Promise Arizona had done nothing to help us collect signatures in Mesa.

"Petra," I asked, "What's it going to take to get you guys involved with the recall?"

"I don't know, Randy," she said with a slight smirk. "Do you have a candidate?"

I smiled. She knew the answer the moment the question left her lips.

"Of course not. You know, Petra, that any candidate interested in taking on Pearce right now would be stupid to lift his or her head. Not only would the Republican establishment eat them alive, but Pearce and his allies would deal with such a person in such a way as to discourage anyone else from ever stepping forward."

"Well, when you have a candidate, come talk to me."

I made one last plea. "Petra, you could use the signature-gathering phase of the recall to identify and test out new leaders to help build your organization. If Pearce remains in power, today's victory will be temporary. He is not done, and you know he will not give up."

"Like I said, Randy, come back and talk to me once you have a candidate."

I held my tongue because I did not want to slam the door shut on Promise Arizona getting involved at a later date. What I wanted to say was, "By the time we have a candidate, we will not need Promise Arizona to win." We needed help now—not months from now when the special election would be set to go and the right candidate set to run.

Those like Petra, who had the mindset of "Come talk to me when you have a candidate," failed to conceptualize what that meant. By the time the "right candidate" emerged, a few things would have already happened—we would have submitted enough signatures to recall Pearce, Governor Brewer would have called a special election, and the right person (Republican, Mormon, pro-immigration, etc.) would have already declared their candidacy. In essence, by the time I met the "I have a candidate" requirement, all the hard work would have already been done.

What people were not talking about on the day Pearce's immigration bills failed was why he forced the Senate to vote on this bill when he did not have the votes to win. You know that old saying about playing checkers versus playing chess? Well, Pearce was playing chess. Pearce knew he did not have the votes for *this* legislative session, but he was setting everything up for the 2012 Republican primary. A Republican majority did not satisfy Pearce; he wanted a Tea Party majority and for that he needed five more senate seats.

By pushing this vote, Pearce now had ten non-Tea Party Republican senators on record voting against him—votes he could use against them in a Republican primary where turnout was low and the voters more conservative. With eleven hard-right senators already in Pearce's corner, he was laying out a strategy to take on and challenge at least five of his colleagues who he considered to be RINOs—Republican in Name Only—who voted with Democrats to defeat these types of immigration bills. Come 2012, Pearce would use his clout as senate president to raise money, recruit, run, and fund like-minded Tea Party candidates. With a more loyal and dependable voting bloc in place in January 2013, he would have the votes to pass his immigration bills. And with those senators in place, no letter from a bunch of CEOs would be enough to stop Pearce's anti-immigrant agenda.

As I walked to my car, Pearce's words from his November 2010 interview on *Sunday Square Off* echoed in my ears, "In the end, it is the game you play. You never slam the door shut." This was Pearce's response when asked if he might run for governor—just after he assumed his new role as senate president. Pearce's decision to force a vote on the immigration bills without the support of his entire Republican Caucus likely strengthened his position among hardcore right-wing extremists—those who turn out in large numbers in Republican primaries. Pearce had already shown himself to be patient. It took him ten years to work his way up from state representative to senate president; now, he was just one election cycle away from having the power and influence to move his entire anti-immigrant agenda. If left unchecked, Pearce would continue the work of building a Tea Party majority in the Senate, and a run for governor in 2014 would not be out of the question.

I had just witnessed a foreshadowing of Arizona's dark political future. As Pearce's adversaries cheered in the Senate gallery when the anti-immigrant bills were defeated, Pearce simply returned to his seat of power and plotted his next moves. Come 2013, with a new Tea Party majority in the Senate, it would be Pearce, not us, cheering the passage of these same bills. Time had been his ally … until now.

By the time Pearce forced this vote, we had set in motion the *only* possible legal and constitutional way to remove him from power, derail his agenda, and terminate any aspirations he held for higher office. The fight to stop Pearce could not be won on the floor of the Arizona legislature—an institution he had come to dominate and control. And by moving the fight from the legislature to the streets of Mesa, our canvassers and our operation remained for the most part under the radar.

The only way to undercut Pearce's ability to use time as his ally was to place a time limit on Pearce's political career. Dr. Martin Luther King Jr. described time as a neutral concept that could be used "destructively" or "constructively." Citizens for a Better Arizona had to use time constructively and build a new power base of voters in Mesa to swiftly and radically unseat Pearce from office.

And we planned to build that new base of power one signature at a time.

CHAPTER 15

The Power of Conversation

*Not everything that is faced can be changed, but
nothing can be changed until it is faced.*
~ James Baldwin

Who would have thought that a lawful and protected act such as asking a registered voter "Would you like to sign the petition to recall Senate President Russell Pearce?" could provoke adults to behave in such irrational and childlike ways.

But it did.

During 120 days of door-knocking and signature-gathering, we saw a little bit of everything. Some voters were eager to sign the petition, while others reacted with hostility. Our canvassers also learned something about their own values and their preconceived notions about the voters who lived in Legislative District 18 (LD 18). Perhaps most disheartening were the too-frequent conversations our canvassers had with voters who did not know of Russell Pearce, or worse, did not even care to learn about him. Those who said, "I don't want to have anything to do with that," or "I am not interested," without even listening to what we had to say frustrated me the most.

A vibrant and functional democracy requires engagement and participation.

Each time we knocked on a door to initiate a new conversation, we invited these residents into a political process that elevated their importance as voters. We could not move forward without their consent. The recall movement was an attempt to remove Pearce from office, and it was a throwback to shoe-leather democracy in which face-to-face conversations, not slick commercials or radio ads, determined the outcome.

For the door-to-door canvassing, we put together lists of Democrats and others who declined to state their party preference. To limit the number of negative experiences at the doors, we removed all declared Republicans.

Throughout the signature-gathering, I emphasized that this was not a "persuasion" campaign but an "opportunity" campaign. We needed volunteers to reach as many doors as possible so the thousands of anti-Pearce voters who already existed could sign without having to leave their homes. As an organizer, I knew part of our approach was merely a numbers game—being able to knock on so many doors to collect enough signatures. This was a mission to connect, especially with Democratic voters who had been ignored for far too long because Pearce's district had always been represented by a Republican.

Still, many Democrats supported SB 1070, and we also found out many independents were conservative Republicans. So, our volunteers had to be kind and determined, respectful and strong, and—above all—resilient. No matter how often they heard "No," they had to approach the next door with a smile and positive attitude.

Bob Unferth, our tither in chief, became one of the most effective canvassers in Latino neighborhoods. White, male, English-speaking, and seventy-one years old—Bob's outgoing demeanor and warm personality had a way of winning over Latino voters. "There's always a certain anxiety with White people driving into poor ethnic neighborhoods," Bob said, "but during the Pearce recall, this all switched. Going into poor Latino neighborhoods turned out to be fun."

People invited Bob in for coffee or on hot days for a cold drink and a chance to get out of the sun. Sometimes it would lead to an offer of food. "It was hard to get out," he said. "This became a little problematic for me because I needed to knock on more doors."

Bob's experiences in most working-class Latino neighborhoods were warm and welcoming, which contrasted sharply with the treatment given in some of the fancier, higher-income White neighborhoods in Mesa. One particular home visit stood out to Bob: "My wife, Nancy, and her walking partner, a Latino high school student, knocked on a door, and the man, after laying eyes on both of them, issued a direct threat: 'If you bring that guy back here again, I am going to shoot him.'" The simple act of "door-knocking while being brown" caused this particular voter to react in such a threatening and de-humanizing manner.

That home was taken off the walk list.

We hardly had an army of volunteers; we functioned more like a small and well-rehearsed choir of about twenty-five "singers" who always showed up to practice and who consistently hit their notes of recall, recall, recall and Pearce, Pearce, Pearce.

One of those core choir members was Brenda Rascon, a Mesa resident in LD 18. A child of undocumented parents from Mexico, Brenda spent many weekends in lawyers' offices or community-based organizations with her parents while they tried to get their papers in order.

Brenda said her hardworking parents were scrupulously law-abiding and had never received as much as a parking ticket. As a child, she couldn't fathom why anyone would want to take her mom from her.

Brenda and her family relocated to Arizona in the 1990s to escape gang-related violence in their Los Angeles neighborhood. The Rascons settled in Mesa in a predominantly Mormon neighborhood. Brenda studied hard, graduated from Arizona State University, and then entered a doctorate program in biology. Her only political involvement was volunteering for the Obama campaign in 2008. That changed in 2010.

"I remember driving to ASU one morning," she said, "and hearing Governor Brewer on the radio saying, 'Mexicans are drug smugglers and under the control of drug cartels.'"

She was shocked. The governor of the state where she lived, worked, and studied was calling her parents drug-smuggling criminals. She could not believe it.

This incendiary talk came as SB 1070 made its way through the legislature, and Brewer and Pearce stoked fears about the "illegals" they claimed were supposedly smuggling drugs and taking our jobs. Brenda could no longer ignore what was happening in her own backyard.

"Oh my God," she said, "Pearce lives about a mile from me. He is saying these horrible things. My dad is a citizen and a voter. Pearce is talking about people in his own district. Pearce needs to represent us all."

So, Brenda showed up at the state Capitol on the day Brewer signed SB 1070. She and her friend April Bojorquez made their way through the large crowds of protesters until someone caught their attention—State Senator Kyrsten Sinema. They approached her, and Brenda said, "I know you're an opponent of Pearce's and I know you tried to oppose this legislation. But how does something like this happen?"

This triggered an expletive-laden response. "I have been trying. I have been doing my fucking best to stop this!" Sinema said while turning the tables. "Why don't *you* do something about this? I have been trying to fucking stop him!"

Brenda ignored the crude reply and tried again. "I realize you are angry about what happened. I just never thought I'd see a day like this where I feel betrayed by my government. Is there something I can do? I am a graduate student. Is there a way for me to help?"

"You need to become a precinct committee woman. You need to organize your precinct and do something." Sinema told Brenda to reach out to Wayne Mansky and Michael Conway, leaders of the LD 18 Democratic Precinct Committee.

So, Brenda started going to the precinct meetings. She felt welcomed but soon realized these meetings were not the vehicle for the type of change she envisioned.

When Citizens for a Better Arizona launched the recall, Brenda, like a true academic, did her research and then showed up at the Mesa library to volunteer. She never left. "When I learned that there was a provision in the Arizona Constitution for the recall and you explained how we were going to do it, I was convinced we had a chance."

It did not take long for Brenda to be tested at the doors.

"I knocked on one door where a White woman answered. She told me she was a teacher. She was unlike anyone I had ever talked to before. She said, 'Yeah, I like Russell Pearce. He is going to take all that Mexican trash out of here.'"

I wondered to myself, "Has this woman not looked at me? Is she not aware of who she is speaking to?"

Brenda continued. "I'm sorry. How does this affect your ability to teach? Don't you have a diverse student body?"

"I just think all the illegals need to get out. I don't care if you come here legally. We just need to keep out the illegals and Pearce is the man to do just that."

Shocked that a woman who taught math at a local high school would have such views, Brenda then said, "You do realize that this law will not just affect people who are undocumented, but it will also affect people who are citizens of this country. How do you feel about that? How do you feel about education? Healthcare for the poor?"

"I hate those illegals and want them out. Leave me alone," she said, slamming the door.

For every voter who slammed the door, another door opened. Later that day, Brenda had a White woman practically jump through her screen door to sign the petition. "All I had to do was mention Pearce's name, and she said, 'Oh my God. Yes!'"

As this woman signed the petition on her porch, another woman came out of the house. She was beaming with a megawatt smile. She said her son had just called from Europe and asked her to do something about Russell Pearce because "everyone makes fun of him." She could not wait to tell him that they had signed the recall petition.

On another occasion, when a White woman answered the door and was asked to sign the recall petition, she blurted out, "Russell Pearce was the best man in our wedding." The volunteer was just about to turn to leave when the voter grabbed the clipboard and signed the petition. After signing, she said, "My husband will be back later this afternoon. Please come by then, and I will make sure he signs as well. We do not support what he is doing."

Many of our liberal volunteers found their stereotyped images of a Pearce supporter challenged every day. At one home, a White guy was working on his car in the front yard, his motorcycle leaning against the garage. The volunteer thought, "This guy is a right-wing gun owner and Pearce supporter."

Despite her discomfort, she still made her pitch, "We are here to talk about Senate President Russell Pearce. Do you know who he is?"

The man looked up, paused for a moment, and said calmly, "Yes, I know who Russell Pearce is."

"Do you know his views on health care and education?"

"Yes, I do. And the stuff he says about immigrants. What an asshole. You know people are just trying to get by and make a living. I think if someone is willing to cross the border illegally and risk everything for their family, then I want them in this country. These are hardworking people."

People such as this man who were coming to the defense of immigrants reminded our volunteers to let go of their prejudices. We had to stop ourselves from profiling voters—making judgments based on how they looked and where they lived.

When Amanda Zill, a registered nurse and one of our star volunteers, approached a home expecting to speak to a seventy-eight-year-old woman, she noticed a big motorcycle in the driveway, a US flag flying in front of the house, and a scruffy-looking White guy in the garage. Seeing his tattoos, full beard, and white tank-top T-shirt, Amanda thought he *must* be a Pearce supporter.

She hesitated, made her pitch and then waited for the callous rejection. "Instead," she recalled, "the man calmly and politely responded, 'Yes, I will sign that.'" He asked Amanda to wait, went into his home, and returned with his son, who seemed to have a serious health condition, and said, "My son is all I have. He is dependent on me for his care. I cannot afford to be without his health care."

During another visit, Amanda was invited into a Mormon home. Their opinions about Pearce caught Amanda by surprise. "We know Russell very well. We don't recognize him now. He has gone off the deep end."

Amanda lit up and shared her story of why this movement was so important to her. When she left the home, she realized that absent the recall effort, Republican and Mormon voters like this couple would have no other viable candidate to vote for but Pearce—despite their disapproval of what he was doing. The recall provided voters from all backgrounds the rare opportunity to challenge Pearce's reign as senate president.

On a few occasions, our volunteers came across Black citizens who had never voted or been involved in politics. One seventy-five-year-old woman said she did not vote because, "Politicians are going to do whatever they want, anyway. What's one more vote? It doesn't matter. Me going to the polls to vote doesn't make a difference."

Just then, her grandson joined the conversation. After some more discussion with our canvasser, both grandmother and grandson registered to vote and signed the petition.

When it came to door-knocking we had another secret weapon: With her white hair in a ponytail, an apron tied around her waist, and a moist towel wrapped around her neck to beat the heat, Carolyn Cooper always showed up with a sense of purpose and conviction that was second to none. While eating at restaurants, she spoke so loudly and proudly of the campaign, someone would stop and ask to sign the petition. When Carolyn knocked on doors, people took to her immediately, especially in Latino neighborhoods. "Once they understood I was part of the campaign to get rid of Pearce, they would hug me and ask me to come inside."

On one of the 100-plus-degree days she'd spent knocking on doors, Carolyn accidentally hit a parked car. She knocked on the door of the closest house. "I'm so sorry," she said, breathing heavily and sweat dripping down her face, "Is that your little car right there? I just hit it." Instead of being outraged, the man was more concerned about Carolyn's health. "He then invited me into his home and offered me water. After we worked out the details about the car accident, I had to ask." Because the man was not on the walk list, Carolyn assumed he was a Republican and a Pearce supporter. She made a pitch for the recall, anyway. "Without missing a beat, he took the petition, signed it, and asked me if I needed anything else."

By that time, Carolyn's husband Howard arrived to pick her up. As she got in the car, she turned to him with a smile on her face, "I hit his car—and he signed the petition. Maybe I should do that more often." They both laughed.

Our volunteers stayed focused and on message—no matter the challenge or personal setback. When one of them, Virginia Hauflaire, tripped and sprained her ankle as she approached the door of a voter, the woman brought out some ice and a small towel. Despite the distraction, Virginia got her and her husband to sign. Another volunteer, Fred Barlam, saw a voter shift from being annoyed by his presence to being excited when she learned Fred was part of the recall. She signed and took Fred to five other neighbors who signed too.

I approached signature-gathering as a scavenger hunt. On some weekends, I started with a list of voters only to abandon it midway through my shift. After each person signed, I always asked, "Do you have any family, friends, or close relatives who would sign?" If the answer was yes, I would ask them to call them right then and let them know I needed their signature. Personal referrals like this were the best and quickest way to fill a petition sheet. On a few occasions, people who had signed and expressed certainty that their sister, brother, aunt, or friend would also sign, were surprised and disappointed to find out that when asked they gave a resounding, "NO!"

The most memorable example of this occurred during an encounter with a Latino voter named Fernando, who was also a member of the LDS Church. After signing the petition, Fernando pulled a list of names off his refrigerator door of other church members in his ward who he said would "definitely" sign the petition. Fernando spoke most highly of his stake president[1] and gave us his name and address. He also instructed us to let the stake president know that he had sent us.

Within minutes, we arrived at the stake president's home. But when we presented the petition, he said, "I hate what Russell Pearce is doing. But I am sorry you have been led to believe I will sign the petition. I will not sign the petition, and I do not wish to be involved with the recall in any way." Given the controversy surrounding the recall, many Mormons did not sign, even though they disapproved of Pearce's politics.

One weekend, I was at the Mesa library manning the sign-up table. When a White man passed by, I asked, "Can we count on you to sign the petition to recall Pearce?" He ignored me. I asked him again in a

---

[1] A stake president oversees LDS Church programs in a defined geographic area composed of smaller individual congregations called wards. He is responsible to support members of his stake in their efforts to follow Jesus Christ.

slightly louder voice as he continued to walk to his car. At that point, he flipped me off and shouted, "Fuck you!"

Our volunteers never knew what was brewing just beneath the surface of each person they met. To some, we were doing the "Lord's work," for others, the "devil's deeds."

Some of the most intimate conversations about the recall occurred in the homes of Latino voters, especially the elderly. Several times, Lilia Alvarez found herself at the kitchen table of many Latino families. She will forever remember seventy-four-year-old Antonio, who had to be awakened from a nap to sign, and his daughter, who registered to vote so she could sign the petition. The impact of face-to-face conversations cannot be overstated.

Another elderly couple, the Gonzalezes, welcomed Lilia into their home, offered her something to drink, and insisted that she sit in the best chair in the house, the one reserved for company. As they signed, they took Lilia on a stroll down memory lane and shared stories about the photos on their walls.

In another Latino home, the granddaughter walked into the family room soon after her Nana signed the petition. The granddaughter had just turned eighteen. Although she did not know the difference between a Democrat and a Republican, she did know who Russell Pearce was. While helping her complete a voter registration form, Lilia asked her what party affiliation to check. The young woman said, "I don't know. I have no idea."

Lilia provided additional guidance: "Well, Russell Pearce is Republican. Your Nana is a Democrat. I'm a Democrat. You choose." She chose Democrat.

For so many voters, especially older Latinos, our canvassers served as the bridge to helping citizens become first-time voters. When Lilia and her canvassing partner knocked on the door of seventy-three-year-old Andres Arreola, only to find out within seconds that Mr. Arreola had been deceased for three years, they did not expect much else to happen. But Mrs. Arreola added, "Andres always voted. He always was involved."

Caught up in the moment, Lilia responded, "Oh my gosh, I hope that he's blessing this campaign. I know he would have signed this petition."

Mrs. Arreola then asked Lilia, "So how does one vote? I just became a citizen because I waited until I was old enough to take the test in Spanish. So that's why I'm asking you because I am a citizen and I want to vote."

Lilia walked her through the process, translating for her when necessary. She informed Mrs. Arreola that she could both register and sign the petition in matter of minutes. As she signed, Mrs. Arreola said some Latinos did not understand the importance of voting against Russell Pearce. They were *torpe*—Spanish for "hard-headed."

Not every Latino we spoke with supported the recall. One such man said he agreed with Pearce. When our canvassers asked why, he said, "I am tired of people using welfare. I do not like politics either way. I am just tired of people using up the public funds by taking advantage of the system." He admitted that neither he nor his wife voted and that he had given up on politics. He was a naturalized citizen and felt people must come to this country the right way, just like he did. Before our volunteers left, he said. "I consider myself to be very hardworking but there are people that come over and are very lazy. So, for that reason, I support Russell Pearce."

We also stationed some of our volunteers in front of the post office where weird things always seemed to happen. One guy on a bike stopped to sign the recall petition, then rode off yelling, "Now we've got to get Osama out!"

Our folks, not sure who he was referring to, shouted back, "Osama who?"

Without missing a beat, he replied, "The guy in the White House."

Another time, the branch manager came out and ordered us off the property. He made it clear that he did not approve of the recall. We made it clear we did not care about his political views and demanded to speak to his supervisor. He then called Mesa police, who told us to move to the sidewalk. The political content of our petitions, not the petition-gathering itself, was what triggered so many people to use whatever power they had to shut us down.

When it came to maintaining peace in opinion-divided households, the wives usually dictated the outcome. One of our volunteers walked up to a home that had a parked car in the driveway with an Obama sticker on the bumper. The name on the list was a female Democrat, which indicated that she would most likely sign the petition. She did, then asked whether her husband, a registered Republican, could sign. Upon hearing that members of either party could sign the petition, she called him to the door and said, "You better sign or else you're not going to get any dinner." He signed.

Some Pearce supporters tried to block us from speaking to their anti-Pearce family members. One pretended to be the person on the list and declined to sign. As our volunteer left, three people ran out of the house and asked what the visit was about. When they learned it was about the Pearce recall, all three signed, including the woman whose name was actually on the list.

The more conversations we had, the more we realized that families were deeply divided about Pearce's record. We instructed our volunteers to make every effort to speak to every voter on the list in each household and not to make any assumptions based on one negative response from someone who lived at the same address.

An extraordinary story came from Molly Duran, a volunteer who lived in Phoenix. She drove out to Mesa a few times a week to make calls, walk precincts, and help out. A single mother of two, Molly exercised at a locally owned gym on Saturday mornings. During one of her workouts, she got a sobering reality check when she overheard a conversation among five people in her spin class. She relayed her memory of that conversation:

One man said to the group, "Hey, did you hear about all those people gathered in Mesa yesterday to collect signatures to recall Russell Pearce?"

A woman said, "Yeah. I heard there would be about a hundred people there."

Then another man said, "Wow, imagine all those liberals in one location."

The first guy who spoke added, "Yeah, where's Timothy McVeigh when we need him?"

Molly stood there, shocked by the reference to Timothy McVeigh, a domestic terrorist who killed 168 people by blowing up a federal building in Oklahoma City. Instead of confronting them, Molly pulled out her "Recall Pearce" button and wore it for the duration of the class. Other than some disgruntled looks, no one said a word.

As we neared the final week of the 120-day signature-gathering phase, the work had taken on a life of its own. Some people in Mesa undertook covert actions to gain more signatures. A few days before the final turn in, Lilia and Sara, our new office manager, went to lunch at a Mexican restaurant in Mesa. As Sara paid the check, she confirmed that the man behind the counter was the owner. Sara asked, "Do you know who Russell Pearce is?"

The owner's facial expression became one of deep concern. "What do you mean?" he asked.

"I mean, are you aware of his laws like SB 1070, what he's doing, and his policies?" The man stayed silent and shook his head in disapproval. Sara added, "We work for Citizens for a Better Arizona, and we think he's abusing his power."

Hearing that, the owner broke into a smile. "Actually," he said, "I keep up with the laws he writes. When we elected him, we elected him to take care of his district. That is his main priority—Mesa. We have not experienced any benefit from him being our representative."

He then reached below the counter and handed a piece of paper to Sara and Lilia. He had been quietly collecting signatures for the past week and informed Sara that this was his second petition sheet. Other business owners were doing the same, he said.

Sara reminded him that the deadline was only days away and instructed him to come by the office the following day. Before they left, Sara and Lilia invited the owner to join us at the Capitol on May 31 for the official submission of the recall petitions. He smiled and said, "*Como no* (of course)! And I will bring my family."

Given all the controversy surrounding the recall, I can say neither side used violence as a means to further its cause during the 120 days of collecting signatures. The closest I came to a violent encounter occurred at the Mesa library when Pearce's nephew, Talmage Pearce, showed up with a small group of supporters. Dressed in Pearce T-shirts, Talmage and his friends edged closer to our workspace.

One of our volunteers from Tucson, Sal Baldanegro, refused to move as Talmage pressed forward. Within minutes, Mesa police arrived and separated both groups—arresting no one from either group. No real damage done. Talmage, however, used this incident to discredit our efforts and persuade others to reject the recall. He sent out an email that read in part, "Randy and one of his progressive thugs began to physically assault me by pushing into me and stepping on my feet and not letting me go. As I asked them politely to get off of my foot and let me go, they began telling me to leave or they will call the cops and tell them that I was physically assaulting THEM! This is the kind of people who are behind this recall election."

Yes, we were "the kind of people" who volunteer to stand in front of a library on a Saturday morning to calmly and peacefully collect signatures. We had not gone to Talmage's event. He came to ours, looking to instigate some sort of confrontation. Thankfully our volunteers remained focused and disciplined, depriving Talmage of the fight he came to initiate. Without a well-thought-out strategy to counter the recall, Pearce, his nephew Talmage, and other supporters did virtually nothing to stand in our way.

Signatures continued to pour in. March numbers surpassed February, and in April we nearly doubled what we collected in March. Once we passed 8,000 signatures, we knew that the only thing that could stop us would be a shortage of funds.

As Pearce continued to ignore our recall, someone in Dallas, Texas, took notice. Our concerns about having enough money to finish what we started in January would be resolved with one unexpected and timely email.

CHAPTER 16

The Texas Surprise

*If you are neutral in situations of injustice, you
have chosen the side of the oppressor.*
~ Archbishop Desmond Tutu

By April, we still struggled to raise enough money to keep the operation afloat. Snail mail trickled in everyday—$10 from a retiree in Payson, $25 from a teacher in Surprise—but no major donor in Arizona stepped up. Our largest individual donation was $1,000.

I started each day by combing through emails to monitor the level of activity of our online fundraising efforts. On this particular morning in April, I came across an email from our PayPal account that indicated that someone had unsuccessfully attempted to donate $25,000! I looked closer to make sure I read the number correctly. I did. At that point, a donation of this size would've guaranteed our ability to get enough signatures to recall Pearce. I scanned the email for more detail. I needed a phone number, a name, an email—anything so I could follow up. I found the donor's email and sent off a quick message. Within minutes I received a response, "This is Domingo Garcia. You can reach me at (214) ...."

Domingo Garcia. Why was that name so familiar? Within seconds my memory kicked in and I remembered: Dallas City Council, 1995.

In spring 1995, after I took the California bar exam, I packed up all my belongings and headed to Texas, to start my career as an organizer with Dallas Area Interfaith (DAI). DAI was part of the Industrial Areas Foundation (IAF), a national organizing network established in 1940 by Saul Alinsky. When I was a graduate student at Harvard's Kennedy School of Government, I met one of the top leaders from IAF, Ernie Cortés. Cortés had been selected as a fellow at Harvard's Institute of Politics and I attended his seminar on organizing and building power. This turned out to be one of those life-altering moments for me. Before meeting Cortés, I never thought of organizing as a profession. Although I had been involved in numerous actions, protests and marches as an undergraduate and graduate student, I had received no formal training about power, politics, and moving people into action.

After a few meetings, Cortés offered me a junior organizer position in Dallas. I remember him telling me, "You will be more of a liability to us at first. We will have to undo a lot of what you have learned in college. What we teach and train is counter-culture to what main stream universities offer students. But we are willing to invest in you if you are willing to learn. My biggest concern about you Randy is—are you teachable?"

When I arrived in Dallas in the spring of 1995, Domingo Garcia was mayor *pro tempore* of the city council and a lawyer with a small but growing law practice. Leaders from DAI met with Domingo frequently to push their citywide agenda consisting of after-school programs, job training, and a living wage.

Some sixteen years later our paths had crossed again—via a PayPal email! Since my time in Dallas, Domingo had settled a number of multimillion-dollar lawsuits and his law practice had expanded to other cities around the state. The success of Domingo's law firm had turned him into a major donor for Democratic candidates and progressive causes. I called him immediately.

"Mr. Garcia, this is Randy Parraz and I am president of Citizens for a Better Arizona. I am following up on your donation of $25,000. You did try and donate $25,000 to our effort to recall Senate President Russell Pearce, right?"

"Yes, that was me. How is it coming along? Are we going to get enough signatures?"

"We are now." We laughed.

He had seen a Citizens for a Better Arizona email seeking help and told me, "I was excited to see someone taking the fight directly to Pearce. With all the racism and bigotry going on in Arizona I wanted to help."

It hit me then that Domingo had also donated to my run for US Senate in 2010. As the only Latino candidate for US Senate in the country at that time—and given Governor Brewer's signing of SB 1070—Domingo decided to invest in my campaign. When we started the Pearce recall, I had included all the emails from my US Senate race in our email blasts to raise money.

"So, do we have a chance?" he asked. "Or is this just some Don Quixote adventure?"

I explained our progress and he seemed satisfied. "I am glad to see that you all have quite an operation up and running. I know from my experience without the necessary resources up front, efforts like these don't have a chance."

I had another favor to ask Domingo: "Instead of running your credit card again, would you be willing to mail two smaller checks, each less than $10,000?"

"What do you mean?" he asked.

"The last thing we want is to give the press an angle that works against our overarching narrative. A single donation of $25,000 from an individual from Texas is newsworthy. However, two donations of $9,900—one from you and the other from your wife, Elba—gives us the money we need without hitting the $10,000 threshold for any one individual donor." We wanted the money, but we did not want increased scrutiny from the press or from Pearce's allies.

This must have sounded odd to him, but reporters had asked me repeatedly about our donors:

"Has anyone given you $20,000?"

"What about $10,000?"

"What outsider or out-of-state entity is funding this effort?"

I did not want to lie. But I also did not want to say "yes" to the $10,000 donor question. By breaking down the donations this way, we would stay under the $10,000 threshold and still have enough money to finish gathering signatures. Besides, I could always go back to Domingo and Elba for more support during the special recall election. When the overnight package arrived the next day, I opened it. Inside were two checks for $9,900 and a note from Domingo with three words: "Hasta La Victoria!"—onward to victory!

Anyone who has met Domingo knows he looks distinctively Mexican with his dark skin, mustache, and dark hair. His father was an undocumented worker from Coahilia, Mexico, and his mother a Native American Apache. At seventeen years of age, Domingo's father swam across the Rio Grande River in pursuit of the American Dream. After walking for five days in the desert, he got a job at a ranch earning $40 a month. Domingo experienced discrimination at a very young age. As a child of non-English speaking parents, he often had to translate for them. When he was eight years old, he and his father stopped at a gas station in West Texas to buy some food: "Right when we were about to enter the store," Domingo said, "I noticed a sign that read, 'No Mexicans, No Niggers, No Dogs Allowed.'" Domingo had to translate these hate-filled words to his father so he would understand why they couldn't walk in the front door. Stories like these were etched in Domingo's mind as he grew up.

I did not want to provide the pro-Pearce forces an opportunity to use Domingo's image, money, and out-of-state residency to rally support for Pearce. A good Republican political consultant could do a lot with Domingo's photo, a $25,000 check, and the image of Texas. To the extent that I could, I wanted to keep outside supporters below the radar and make this a statewide fight for a better Arizona.

Domingo understood politics and the optics I was seeking to avoid. "Sure, not a problem," he said. "Send me the address and I will overnight the checks tomorrow."

I had not known how closely Domingo was following Arizona's swing to the far right and the passage of SB 1070. The combination of Sheriff Arpaio's worksite raids and roadblocks, and Dreamers chaining themselves to the Capitol building in protest of SB 1070, moved Domingo to action. After SB 1070 passed, Domingo and his supporters organized three "freedom buses" from Dallas to Phoenix. The riders included Black leaders who had participated in the freedom rides in the South—including Rev. Peter Johnson who marched with Dr. King—and activists from the League of United Latin American Citizens in Texas.

Their first protest was outside Arpaio's office. For several hours, this coalition of Black and Latino activists marched, chanted, and rallied. As the protest wound down, someone shouted, "Let's go to the governor's mansion," though no such mansion existed. Governor Jan Brewer lived about twenty minutes from downtown Phoenix in Glendale. The organizers obtained Brewer's address, loaded up the buses, and converged on her home.

When the buses arrived, they were surprised to see one police car parked in front with only one officer inside—and he was asleep. Seeing no other barriers, Domingo and a few other leaders walked up to Brewer's front door and rang the doorbell. They told the person at the door they came from Texas to speak to Brewer about SB 1070. After a few minutes, they were told Brewer was not available.

So, the delegation decided to hold a prayer vigil on the sidewalk in front of Brewer's home. "We prayed for her and asked that she find a way to deal with these issues more compassionately," Domingo said. "Unknown to us at the time, the former governor of Alaska, Sarah Palin, was also inside the house. They were going to a fundraiser later in the evening."

It didn't take long for the cavalry—the city of Glendale's finest—to arrive. Within thirty minutes of the buses' arrival, more than a hundred officers were on site and took positions around the home. The police asked the group to leave, stating it was an unlawful assembly.

The group refused. Domingo informed the officer that they were "assembling" on the public sidewalk. Because they were not on private property, they were not leaving.

Now the officers needed to figure out a way to get Brewer and Palin out of the house and into their vehicle. The officers regrouped and formed a wedge in the driveway from the garage to the street so Brewer and Palin could leave.

If the officers thought that was the end of the situation, they didn't know Domingo. While waiting outside, the group found the location of the event Brewer and Palin were to attend. After they left, everyone got back on the buses and headed to the Marriott Hotel in Scottsdale. They set up a similar picket line at the hotel until they were asked to leave.

Domingo's support for our efforts reflected his deeply held belief that bigotry should come with a price. And the price for Pearce would be a recall. Domingo still was not sure how successful the recall in Arizona would be, but he had seen it work in Texas. In Dallas, he and others launched a recall of a city council member who had made some bigoted comments. It was not successful, but the recall campaign damaged this elected official so severely, that when he ran for reelection, he lost.

Like Citizens for a Better Arizona, Domingo felt there needed to be an immediate response—and immediate consequences—when politicians pursued a racist agenda. We were learning to become more vigilant, more creative, and bolder when politicians appealed to people's worst fears and insecurities. Although Domingo is a firm believer that all politics are local, the situation in Arizona had become a national crisis. "We had to stop it in Arizona, or else it would come to Texas," he said. "Arpaio and Pearce were the poster children of this new politics of using race and immigration as wedge issues to win elections. I knew it would take a national effort. We could not just sit on the sidelines and watch from Texas."

Domingo continued to show up, literally and financially, from the time of our first phone call until the night of the special recall election. He flew in when we turned in our recall petitions and for the historic election night celebration. When things heated up and the death threats became more frequent, Domingo offered to mail me a gun for protection. And when we needed to produce an ad and purchase time on local cable TV, Domingo kicked in another $75,000 to make it happen. He then connected us to Laura Barberena, a brilliant and talented political strategist in San Antonio, to make it happen.

We kept Domingo's and Elba's donations secret for as long as we legally could. Our paid signature-gathering operation continued through May 31, without any interruptions. And like clockwork, Bonita and her team at Sign Here Petitions turned in signatures every Monday in batches of 300, 400, and sometimes 500 or more.

For the first time, this investment allowed us to believe—with absolute certainty—that come May 31, Pearce would be Arizona's first senate president recalled!

CHAPTER 17

Let's Party

Instead of hate, celebrate.

~ Prince, the Artist

April 2011 turned out to be the month of many gifts. In addition to the donation by Domingo and Elba Garcia, more stories surfaced exposing Pearce's "entanglement" with a scandal related to the Fiesta Bowl. He received tens of thousands of dollars in unreported gifts from Fiesta Bowl officials in the form of football tickets, hotel accommodations, extravagant meals, and limousine rides. Most of us were not shocked by such behavior by Pearce, but to his Tea Party "patriots," the scandal mocked his "Rule of Law" mantra.

Meanwhile, Citizens for a Better Arizona had already amassed more than 8,000 signatures and registered 600 new voters. The news that he accepted kickbacks and bribes happened at the perfect time. Chad Snow, our chairman, immediately issued the following statement on behalf of Citizens for a Better Arizona: "These illegal gifts represent a culture of corruption in our Capitol, and Russell Pearce is at the heart of it. When a politician places their hand on that bible and takes that oath to support our laws, that means all of them. Russell Pearce has decided the rules don't apply to him. His district, and all of Arizona, deserves better."

Pearce was consumed by this scandal and continued to ignore us.

By late May, our campaign surpassed 15,000 signatures. We were now closing in on 20,000. I kept these numbers private and mentioned the goal of 15,000 publicly to keep our volunteers motivated. In that final week, reporters kept asking:

"How many signatures do you have?"

"Can we see them?"

"Where are they being kept?"

I told them we would not disclose the final number until May 31, but I knew we had enough. To protect the signatures from being damaged or stolen, we stored them in a vault in Chad's law office, formerly a bank. We would "deposit" new petitions a few times each week in the vault which had a security system with video cameras. If we came up short, it was not going to be because someone had stolen the petitions.

During the final week, we hired Sara Ryan to work closely with Lilia as our office manager to tighten up our operations and oversee our volunteers. Sara, then a junior at Arizona State University, showed up a few months earlier at another Arpaio action at the Maricopa Board of Supervisors. Accompanied by her father, attorney Tom Ryan, she offered to help out. Sara's addition to the team would pay dividends the first week—especially on the May 31 turn-in day.

A skilled organizer can visualize an action—in every detail—well before it happens. The better an organizer becomes at visualization, the more likely it is that the intended outcome will unfold as planned. When the time came to turn in the recall petitions, I did not want to hold a press conference with a bunch of petitions positioned behind a podium or stacked on a table. We needed an action to dramatize what we accomplished. It needed to visually reinforce our message and feature some of our main leaders from Mesa. To make sure all our volunteers felt appreciated and valued, we decided to hold a rally and march from the senate office building to the secretary of state's office.

A few days before the big event, we still did not have a location for our Pearce recall celebration. I'd hoped to use the Wright House, a well-known and respected business in Mesa where families—Republican and Democrat, Mormons and those of other faiths—gathered for weddings and all sorts of celebrations. Owner Mike Wright supported our campaign and donated to the recall. However, hosting such a celebration would not be well-received by many families and potential customers who had supported Pearce (and the Wright House) for years. When I called Mike about this, he said he needed to make a few calls first. Within minutes Mike called me back with a two-word response, "Let's party!"

On May 31, Citizens for a Better Arizona returned to the scene of its first action—the Arizona Senate Office Building—Pearce's seat of power. Lilia, Sara, and I drove to Chad's office to pick up the recall petitions and to take some photos. When we arrived, volunteers were still in Chad's conference room combing through the last batch of signatures. Chad entered, confident and calm, but curious.

"Where are we at with the signatures?" he asked. "Did we hit our goal of 15,000?"

"No," I said. "Higher."

"Sixteen thousand?"

"No. Higher."

"Seventeen thousand?!"

"No ..." and before I could reel off the number, Chad interrupted.

"Twenty thousand? Are you telling me we collected over 20,000 signatures?"

"Well, let's just say we came close. With the signatures that came in over the weekend we are now over 18,000 strong!"

"Wish I could be in the room when Pearce receives the news," Chad said. "Kind of hard to dismiss 18,000 signatures as a bunch of outside agitators!"

We headed to the Capitol as people gathered outside the Senate building. By the time we kicked off our mini-rally, more than a hundred volunteers and supporters were in the lobby ready to celebrate.

With the Capitol police in full force and the sergeant at arms on the scene, Chad came forward and welcomed everyone. Our gathering in the lobby served as the starting point for our march to the secretary of state's office. The lobby served as the backdrop for unveiling our "Special Limited Edition Recall Resolution." We asked our volunteers to dress up for the occasion—to wear collared shirts, ties, slacks, dresses, jackets, and other business attire. We did not show up to protest; we were there to do the people's business of recalling one of the most extreme politicians in the history of Arizona.

With cameras rolling and people amped up about what was about to unfold, I moved to the center of the group to recite our recall resolution. I had just finished the final draft earlier that morning and my heart was racing with excitement. I now could reveal what we had accomplished in the past 120 days and remind the citizens of Arizona why we had taken such drastic and unprecedented action. I firmly declared:

> "***Whereas*** Senate President Russell Pearce has chosen to pursue a political agenda that ***DOES NOT*** reflect the values of the majority of Arizonans;
>
> "***Whereas*** Senate President Russell Pearce's behavior over the past five months clearly demonstrates that he is ***TOO EXTREME*** for Arizona;
>
> "***Whereas*** Senator Russell Pearce has demonstrated a ***RECKLESS DISREGARD*** for public education by calling for hundreds of millions of dollars in cuts to K-12 and state universities;
>
> "***Whereas*** Senator Pearce supported the ***TERMINATION*** of health care for the poor and refused to support funding for Arizonans in need of organ transplants to survive;

"*Whereas* Senator Pearce has pursued an agenda that has severely **DAMAGED** our economy and **TARNISHED** our reputation both nationally and abroad;

"*Whereas* in the 100th year of Arizona's statehood and the 235th year of the United States of America as a country, no sitting senate president of any legislature has ever been successfully **RECALLED**—until now; AND...."

When I said, "until now," the crowd erupted. Yelling, hollering, clapping, whistling, cheering, and making all sorts of sounds to express their deep satisfaction and appreciation for what we had accomplished together. Seeing the Capitol police and sergeant at arms uneasy with the loudness of our group in the lobby, and not wanting to be pushed out of there too soon, I continued:

"*Whereas* citizens from Mesa, District 18, and the rest of Arizona have come together in a 120-day effort to exercise their right as citizens to recall Senator Pearce and create an Arizona more appreciative and tolerant of all those who live here;

"*Therefore be it resolved* that we, Citizens for a Better Arizona, respectfully and appropriately, officially name this day, May 31, 2011, **RECALL RUSSELL PEARCE DAY** and invite citizens from Mesa and Arizona to join this historic campaign to remove Senator Pearce from office."

The place erupted again with a loud outburst, and I knew we had to start our march before the Capitol police moved in. Before leaving the building, we taped the enlarged Special Recall Resolution to the window of the entrance to the Senate building for all to see. We then lined up, with Saul Solis, from East Valley Patriots for American Values, and Paul Castaneda, president of CWA 7019, leading the procession—each of them carrying a long pole, one with the US flag and the other with a flag of Arizona.

As we walked across the open space between the House and Senate buildings and around the corner to the front of the Executive Tower building, we did not chant or carry any protest signs or Citizens for a Better Arizona banners. We did not want our procession and message to be hijacked in any way or portrayed as a protest. We wanted this to be a somber moment—a moment to remind us all of the pain, hurt, and suffering of too many families because of Pearce's misuse of power. The decision to recall Pearce was not a gimmick, a ploy, or an act of desperation; it was a *necessity*.

We gathered at the main entrance to the Executive Tower building and waited for the recall petitions to arrive. Unlike statewide ballot initiatives that require hundreds of thousands of signatures and many boxes in which to carry them—we could fit all our recall petitions in one box. Although 18,000 signatures sounded like a lot, we had less than 1,500 pieces of paper.

To add suspense, drama, and children to our action, we staged a drive-by drop-off of the recall petitions at the entrance to the Executive Tower building. We decorated a minivan with large, bright yellow "Recall Pearce" signs on each side, loaded it with four crate-style file baskets, and distributed the recall petitions evenly among them. The van pulled up to a cheering crowd minutes after we'd all arrived at the front of the building.

We recruited children, mostly White children, to carry each crate into the lobby of the main building. I brought my two daughters, Chad brought his kids, Sara recruited some of her younger cousins, and many of our volunteers brought their sons, daughters, nieces, and nephews. So, when the van door slid open, and with all major media outlets present, a group of kids wearing Recall Pearce T-shirts ran up to the van door, grabbed the crates, and carried them into the lobby.

The lobby then filled with our supporters, and everyone gathered around a podium we'd set up earlier that morning. Before we turned in the petitions, we held a brief press conference for our special unveiling. Mary Lou Boettcher, Chad Snow, Todd and Dianne Selleck, Julie Jorgensen and Amanda Zill stood close to the podium. Everyone except Chad lived in Pearce's district and supported the narrative that predominantly White, older, Democrat and Republican, male and female, Mormon and non-Mormon voters in Mesa had recalled Pearce—not some Latino from Scottsdale.

After each of them spoke, I moved to the podium to present our only visual for the press event. We had compiled a chart that captured the enormity of what we had accomplished. Across the top of a two-by-three-foot foam poster board, it read, "One Door at a Time: 'People Power' in Mesa."

It was a bar graph showing the total number of votes—17,552—Pearce received when he was reelected to the state senate in 2010. Next to this figure, another bar graph showed more than 18,000 voters had signed the petition to recall Pearce.

"Today we want to make it clear to all those who doubted our ability to gather enough signatures to recall Senate President Pearce that they overestimated Pearce's power and support," I said. "Not only did we surpass the 7,756 signatures required to recall Pearce, but we collected more signatures to recall Pearce than the total number of votes Pearce received in his last election."

A collective sense of accomplishment filled the room as people cheered, applauded, high-fived, and hugged one another. This was no longer a dream, a long shot, or a crazy idea. We were now only an elevator ride away from submitting our recall petitions and adding one more title to Pearce's resume—Recalled Senate President Pearce.

For the official petition submission, we passed out portions of the papers to our supporters who had volunteered, donated, and turned out. We made sure each person had some petitions to turn in. One by one, each volunteer came to the service counter and submitted the recall petitions. Some did so quietly, while others posed for photos or shared what this event meant to them.

After the last person turned in the final recall petitions, Todd, who 120 days earlier filed the original petition to recall Pearce, picked up the entire stack of petitions with both hands and raised them over his head. His hands shook as he held them up, turning towards reporters as if he had just won a world heavyweight title.

Todd and the clerk then went to another room for a formal inventory of the recall petitions. When Todd returned about twenty minutes later, he had a signed receipt that showed the state's official tabulation of our signature count at 18,315. That number meant we'd collected approximately 152 signatures per day in 120 days.

That ended our official business on the seventh floor, though the press continued to interview our supporters. As I stepped into the elevator, I shared the immense pride, satisfaction, and yes, pure joy expressed by all those who joined us. Citizens—not political parties or elected officials—but a group of citizens finally intervened to call into question Pearce's extreme brand of politics. The time to party had finally arrived! And we did just that later in the evening at the Wright House.

By now, grassroots Democratic leaders such as Lauren Kuby, vice-chairwoman of LD 17 next door in Tempe, had embraced the recall, recruited volunteers, and helped us organize our recall party. The recall was no longer something to be ridiculed and ignored. It was a movement to join.

Our efforts put Pearce on the defense. He would have to justify himself, his ideas, and, most important, his agenda at a time when he had reached his highest level of power and influence. Pearce's decision to ignore and dismiss Citizens for a Better Arizona, our "21-Day Notice," and the recall campaign from the very beginning provided us the space and time for the campaign to take hold and build momentum. By the time Pearce finally reacted, we had already identified over 18,000 potential voters willing to recall him.

We knew our continued success depended on Pearce saying and doing things to reinforce how his politics were too extreme for Arizona.

He did not disappoint.

CHAPTER 18

Pearce Reacts ... Finally

You have no enemies, you say? Alas, my friend, the boast is poor. He who has mingled in the fray of duty that the brave endure must have made foes. If you have none, small is the work you have done. You've hit no traitor on the hip. You've dashed no cup from perjured lip. You've never turned the wrong to right. You've been a coward in the fight.

~ Charles Mackay

One of the biggest mistakes Russell Pearce and his supporters made while we collected more than 18,000 signatures was to ignore us. For 120 days, Pearce did virtually nothing to obstruct, undermine, or complicate our operation. By the time he decided to fight back, we'd had close to 20,000 conversations with voters in his district, built a committed team of volunteers, and raised enough money and momentum to make it difficult for even someone as powerful as Pearce to survive our recall movement.

However, only days after we turned in the petitions, Pearce escalated the fight to a whole new level of lies, deceit, and character assassination. He and his supporters accused us of carrying swastikas, called us "social thugs," and referred to us as "anarchists," "pro-law breakers," and "not pro-America." I guess being called a "social thug" is better than being an "anti-social thug." One of the leaders of Pearce's anti-recall campaign, Matt Tolman, called us an out-of-state and out-of-district special interest group. He also launched a new pro-Pearce website called "protectanamericanpatriot.com" to help fight back the recall.

Unwilling to analyze the extent to which our recall movement had gained traction in his backyard, Pearce pushed the false narrative that we did not follow the law, we paid for all our signatures, and those opposed to the recall would challenge the signatures in court. Pearce lied when he told his supporters both the law and constitution were on his side. Pearce's dismissal of the recall process as a legitimate option for citizens to pursue affirmed our most basic assertion that Pearce was just too extreme for Arizona.

We continued to highlight the silliness and foolishness of Pearce's lies and outrageous statements. But Pearce did not let up with his attacks against Citizens for a Better Arizona and me. On a local radio show Pearce again attempted to play the role of the victim—as if something illegal had occurred. "The guy (Randy Parraz) doing this does not live in my district," Pearce said. "This is an attempt to overturn a legitimate election. He is a union thug … a former official in the AFL-CIO. And a failed Democrat in the US Senate." Putting the "thug"characterization aside, what Pearce said about where I lived and my background were true. But none of this had anything to do with voters in his district exercising their right to recall Pearce. By calling me a union thug and accusing us of overturning a legitimate election, Pearce used the power of his position to diminish the wound we had inflicted during his inaugural year as senate president. The submission of over 18,000 signatures caused Pearce and his allies to panic and lash out at me, while Republicans such as Mary Lou Boettcher and Chad Snow remained the faces of our recall campaign.

As the county recorder continued to verify and count the signatures, Pearce remained confident that he would prevail, boasting that he had never lost an election. "I am 16–0 in my district. I believe like Ronald Reagan, government is the problem and not the solution for most issues." With each passing week, Pearce stepped up his rhetoric and described us as "radical extremists" and "far-left anarchists"—an upgrade from just "anarchists."

Pearce's allies in the Maricopa County Republican Party piled on and made up stories about who was behind the recall. Republican Chairman Tom Morrissey issued a statement, "The attempt to recall Senator Pearce is an obvious political stunt the Democrats are using to vilify a strong conservative advocate and distract voters from the real issues like border security."

Had the Republican Party bosses done their homework and analyzed the recall signatures, they would have figured out that Republican voters in District 18 made up more than 10 percent of the recall signatures. In other words, more than 1,000 Republican voters from almost every precinct—voters whom we did not target, door-knock, or phone bank—came to the library on their own and signed our recall petition. This was not a Democratic stunt—and the Arizona Democratic Party definitely was not spearheading this campaign. This was a grassroots, multi-partisan, citizens' revolt.

Political pundits, without talking to me or other leaders in the recall movement, reached the same conclusion about our chances of removing him from office. Aside from Steve Lemons at the *Phoenix New Times*, the consensus among reporters who covered the Capitol and politics in general believed that Pearce would win a special recall election. And he'd do so handily, emerging even stronger. Instead of seeing the successful recall movement in one of the safest Republican seats as a warning sign, Pearce supporters, of course, echoed that theme. State Rep. John Kavanaugh told the *New York Times* the recall effort was, "a gnat on the rump of an elephant."

As Pearce's attacks continued, Chad emerged as one of our best weapons to counter Pearce's lies, name-calling, and outrageous statements about the legitimacy of the recall effort. In an opinion piece in the Arizona Republic, Chad wrote: "Mark Twain once said 'If you can't beat a man's argument, don't panic. You can still call him vile names.' This seems to be the mantra taken on by State Senate President Russell Pearce in response to the recall effort against him. In one hundred years of statehood, over a thousand Arizonans have served in the state legislature. Never before has one of them been so extreme, so out of touch with the values of everyday Arizonans, that they have been recalled—until now. Senator Pearce has a fanatical obsession with one issue that he has pursued at the expense of everything else that is important to Arizonans. He has gone around the country painting Arizona as a lawless frontier—the "kidnapping capital of the world"—to drum up support for his pet legislation. One of the leaders charged with attracting new business to the state said that task has become almost impossible because of the climate of fear created by Senator Pearce, stating that 'we're trying to convince them that we're not Afghanistan.'"

Chad also cited education as one of the main reasons for the recall. "Mr. Pearce has presided over a senate that cut a quarter of a billion dollars from K–12 education—in a state already ranked 49th in per-pupil education spending. The CEO of Intel, the state's largest creator of high-wage jobs, recently said that if the decision to build a new $5 billion plant here were made today instead of several years ago, 'Arizona wouldn't even be in our top 10' because of the lack of priority given to education by the state legislature."

Chad finished the piece reminding people why tone and civility matter in politics. Pearce's response to the recall "has been to call the over seven hundred people who participated in the recall 'socialist thugs who carry swastikas,' 'extreme leftist anarchists,' 'the open borders cartel,' and 'mafia' members. This response is not befitting a senate president and is only further evidence that Mr. Pearce is simply not fit to lead our state. At the end of the day, the only name we will be calling him in return is '*Recalled* Senator Russell Pearce.'"

Chad's hard-hitting response to Pearce's attacks allowed us to elevate and reshape the discussion from name-calling to real issues that impacted ordinary citizens. To generate negative press stories, we continued to use his words against him on issues that resonated with all Arizonans. When Pearce referred to extending unemployment insurance as "paying people to sit at home," we held an action at the Capitol calling for a special session by the legislature to support workers who had been laid off during the economic crisis. We printed out an oversized unemployment check made out to Russell Pearce for $212, dated December 5, 2011—the date we expected him to be out of office and unemployed—and delivered it to his office. Yes, $212 was the weekly amount unemployed workers received in Arizona. We also reminded people that instead of working to make sure Arizonans would be eligible to extend their unemployment benefits, Pearce chose to champion causes such as allowing guns on college campuses and draconian immigration bills that failed to pass.

Meanwhile, I received daily updates by phone from Karen Osborne, the Maricopa County director of elections. Each day the numbers increased—1,500 valid signatures, then 3,500 valid signatures, then over 5,000 valid signatures. I loved seeing these voice mail messages pop up, knowing that we were closing in on our ultimate prize of 7,756 valid signatures. By June 15, only fifteen days after we submitted our signatures, I finally received word from Osborne that we surpassed 7,756 valid signatures. We called a press event to confront Pearce's false allegations.

"We are tired of dealing with fiction, having to listen to Pearce and his supporters talk about duplicate signatures, invalid signatures and signatures from voters outside of Pearce's district," I said. "Today, let's talk facts. As of June 15, 2011, this is what we know to be *true*:

- On May 31, Citizens for a Better Arizona submitted 18,315 signatures to the secretary of state's office.

- The secretary of state's office reviewed the signatures and concluded that 16,948 signatures met the basic legal criteria for further review and sent the signatures to the Maricopa County Recorder's office.
- As of today, the Maricopa County Recorder's office has reviewed 13,583 signatures.
- The total number of valid signatures is 8,239.
- Our signature validity rate is 61 percent. If this holds, we will surpass 10,000 valid signatures by the time all the signatures are reviewed.
- And by the way—all—yes, all, of these government-run offices handling and processing the recall petitions and verifying signatures are headed by *Republicans*."

If there was any illegal activity going on, or fraud of any sort, then it was being committed by Pearce's supporters. As I continued to go over the numbers, one of the reporters interrupted, "OK, let's assume you have enough valid signatures to force a special recall election. You still do not have a candidate."

I had to exercise some serious restraint again because such a question was way too premature; the governor still had not even called a special election. With my best attempt at humility, I countered, "Of course, we don't have a candidate; the special election has yet to be called. What I can say is this, I don't care who the candidate is—Mickey Mouse, Donald Duck, or whoever else—it doesn't really matter because that candidate will begin their campaign with over 10,000 votes. And we will launch the largest paid field operation LD 18 has ever seen to make sure every voter who signed the recall petition turns out to vote Pearce out of office."

We had just made history by successfully recalling not only the first senate president in the history of the United States but one of the most powerful politicians in the state of Arizona. The reporters acted as if this was an everyday occurrence. Instead of diving deeper into the real story of how Citizens for a Better Arizona forced someone they thought so powerful and invincible to now have to reclaim his seat in a special recall election, they immediately shifted the narrative to "we don't have a candidate."

On July 12, after receiving the official notice that CBA did submit enough signatures to recall Pearce, Governor Jan Brewer set the special election for November 8. The very same governor who signed SB 1070 and owed her recent election in large part to Pearce's passage of SB 1070, was now called upon to sign a different kind of declaration.

Instead of calling the governor's action anti-American or illegal, Pearce toned down his response and for the first time acknowledged the rule of law:

"I spoke with Governor Jan Brewer's office regarding my potential recall election. While I know her role is basically ministerial in this process, I conveyed my support of her calling the election on November 8, 2011. I intend to remain in office. Additionally, my legal team has not yet completed its analysis of the certification process undertaken by the County Recorder and the Secretary of State. Arizona law allows me until July 18 to make a legal challenge. In the weeks and months ahead, I will campaign actively to promote and defend my long record of promoting economic recovery, job creation, balanced budgets, law enforcement and secure borders ..."

In other words, see you in court.

Unable and unwilling to discredit the secretary of state, county recorder and governor's offices—all headed by Republicans who collectively oversaw the entire recall process—Pearce had to accept for the moment that he had been legally recalled. Still unable to restrain himself or tone down his rhetoric, he directed his anger and frustration at those who had no vote in the upcoming special election. He ended his statement with, "I have never lost an election and will fight these outside forces that support lax law enforcement, amnesty, and open borders."

In that single sentence, Pearce declared war on an adversary that did not exist. None of us who led the recall had ever called for amnesty or open borders. Pearce once again went to his well of anti-immigrant hate and fear to discredit us and drum up support from his base. And by doing so, he all but ruined his chances of building the coalition he needed to survive the recall.

During a radio interview on August 11, Pearce reverted to what had worked for him in the past. He again questioned the legality of the special election by claiming we had "collected fraudulent signatures" and reduced the recall to something brought about by "a union thug and outside money."

When the conversation turned to immigration, Pearce unloaded his parade of "hits" against immigrants. "We are the import capital of the nation when it comes to illegal aliens … over half of them come through Arizona." Followed by, "These are gang members, drug runners, human smugglers, child molesters … where three out of ten have a criminal record." Pearce even invoked John Adams by reminding viewers of Adams's declaration that "this republic only answers to the shedding of our blood." Whose blood needed shedding? Nobody had stolen anything from Pearce or committed a crime. Pearce remained senate president and all he needed to do to maintain it was run again in his home district, where he boasted of being 16–0.

Finally, Pearce blamed the recall on "out-of-state folks, George Soros money, and union money." Although we would have taken any amount of money from Soros and national unions, the vast majority of our donations came from people who lived and worked in Arizona. I never received a phone call or donation from Soros or his foundation, but that did not stop Pearce from using his platform and influence to create an alternative set of facts.

Our success with the recall up to this point was still not enough to convince high-profile Democrats such as State Senator Kyrsten

Sinema to collaborate with Citizens for a Better Arizona. After seeing an interview Sinema did on cable TV where she made some misrepresentations about the recall—the same recall she characterized as "crazy" and "dangerous" and something that should be stopped—I emailed her. I reminded Sinema that our decision to recall Pearce was not tied to SB 1070 initially as she suggested (our recall movement started after the Republicans elected Pearce senate president). She also said Chad Snow was a Republican Mormon from Mesa, instead of the city where he actually lived, Peoria.

I suggested a meeting so she would have the most up-to-date information about the campaign—especially some of the basics. My email closed with: "I would welcome an opportunity to sit down with you to discuss messaging and other details about the campaign that would help prepare you for other interviews you do. You are one of the best at what you do on camera so it would help our cause tremendously if we can amplify our message with each interview. Please let me know if you can meet this week. Thanks."

In declining my invitation to meet, Sinema made it personal. She wrote in part, "...please leave me alone and don't pretend like we are friends. We are clearly not—your attack against me to Lemons (the *New Times* reporter) makes that crystal clear." I only knew about Sinema's interview because Lemons called me to get my reaction. Admittedly, I was surprised to see her make any comments about the recall—something she had characterized as "so dangerous." I preferred that she not say anything and direct all reporters to Citizens for a Better Arizona.

Although Sinema's response was tone-deaf to the message I had just sent, she made clear here unwillingness work with Citizens for a Better Arizona. I complied with her request to leave her alone. The email exchange ended here.

Sinema may have been appalled by Pearce's horrible record, but our interests were not aligned. Citizens for a Better Arizona's recall agenda conflicted with Sinema's long-term goal of running for Congress and eventually the US Senate as a centrist candidate. Instead of meeting with "radical left-wing extremists" like me, she invested more time in working closely with right-wing extremists like Pearce. So much so that when Pearce was challenged about his divisive tone as senate president during a debate on *Horizon* (a news show on local PBS channel) he flatly denied it. He went on to say that Sinema, during a debate on a televised news show, interrupted the moderator to defend him. According to Pearce, Sinema said, "I love President Pearce. He is fair and he helps anybody get their bills heard."

That played into Pearce's strategy of using the words of prominent Democrats such as Sinema—who did not support the recall—to defend Pearce's actions as senate president. Fortunately, the list of prominent Democrats who said flattering things about Pearce's leadership style was short. At this point, there was nothing Sinema or any other Democrat could do to rehabilitate Pearce's record.

Even when a candidate emerged in late July, Pearce and his supporters lacked the sophistication to deploy a different strategy to address a new situation. Instead of reconnecting to his base, they continued to make the recall about me—the failed Senate candidate who lived in Scottsdale.

In mid-August, Jim McLaughlin, president of UFCW Local 99, called to let me know how that strategy was taking shape. With the recall completed and the special election set, Jim became one of our strongest allies.

"Dude are you running for office?" he asked.

"Am I running for office? Hell, no, I am not running for office. Why are you asking?"

"Have you had a chance to drive around Mesa this morning?"

"No, I am still at the CWA office in Phoenix. What's up?"

"Someone just invested a lot of money to give you some serious name ID in the East Valley. I am driving into work from Gilbert and there you are on the side of the road—huge red signs with your photo and name plastered all over them. Apparently, you oppose the rule of law and have the recall candidates in your pocket. I'll take a photo and send it to you." The signs, he said, were four-by-eight feet.

"So, this is their winning strategy?" I asked. "As long as they keep attacking me, then we are in good shape. Last time I checked my name was not on the ballot. Thanks, Jim. I'll head over there shortly to check it out."

Sure enough, when I drove to Mesa and exited the freeway, there it stood—a large, bright red sign with an enlarged photo of me. The photo was of me speaking at a Maricopa County Board of Supervisors meeting about Sheriff Arpaio's abuse of power. Pearce and his allies had concluded that by using me as the far left-wing boogeyman, voters would stay the course and keep him in office. In big, bold letters the sign read, "Randy Parraz and his Recall Candidates" followed by three main bullet points, "Oppose the Rule of Law," "Support Open Borders," and "Supported by Labor Unions Who Boycotted Arizona." Near the bottom it read, "Stand for the Rule of Law—Oppose the Recall."

If anyone needed more convincing, they added a smaller message at the very bottom: "Randy Parraz—a liberal extremist and community organizer who supported the boycott of Arizona—supports gay marriage and is opposed to East Valley values."

Pearce's supporters posted over a hundred of these signs throughout Mesa; some even turned up in neighboring cities. Our favorable reaction to Pearce's decision to waste money on signs attacking me was cut short by new developments on the ground.

We had internal problems of our own—problems, if left unattended, would guarantee a Pearce victory in November.

CHAPTER 19
Mutiny Avoided

The thorn from the bush one has planted, nourished, and pruned pricks more deeply and draws more blood.
~ Maya Angelou

The moment everyone warned us about had arrived—a successful recall campaign with no viable candidate in sight. I could hear their voices in my head: *Even if you get the signatures, you don't have a candidate. No serious candidate will step forward to challenge Pearce. It would be political suicide.* The signature verification process at the county recorder's office was a formality. We had already checked and verified the majority of our signatures before we turned them in. On May 31, we knew we had more than the 7,756 signatures needed to initiate a special recall election. But the critics observing from the outside were right. As Karen Osborne and her team checked and verified signatures, we, in fact, did not have a candidate—at least not yet. I had not spoken to Beth Coons since January, and even then, she never promised to be the candidate.

Our inability to announce a candidate within days of the governor announcing the special recall election encouraged reporters, especially obnoxious know-it-alls like Howie Fischer, to ridicule our efforts and conclude that we were just on some quixotic adventure. Fischer was a veteran journalist who had been reporting on state government and legal affairs in Arizona since 1982. In 1991, he founded Capitol Media Services and his reports appeared in daily and weekly newspapers throughout the state and aired on Arizona Public Radio.

From the beginning of our recall campaign, Fischer would show up at our press conferences at the Capitol. Instead of covering our recall effort, he would pursue a line of questioning to undermine our credibility. Fischer would ask loaded questions such as:

"What office are you running for?"

"Isn't this just a publicity stunt?"

"You don't have a candidate, so what do you hope to accomplish?"

"Isn't this just about SB 1070 and immigration?"

It got so bad that during one of the protests outside Pearce's office, I suggested that Fischer take the letter addressed to Pearce to his office since Fischer appeared to be working for Pearce. I grew impatient with Fischer and could no longer listen to his arrogant, obnoxious voice. Towards the end of the campaign, I ignored him completely and didn't care what he wrote.

Our path to defeat Pearce had a few unique challenges. The strategy had been to challenge Pearce with a more moderate Republican in a head-to-head race with no other candidates. However, others thought they knew better.

Within weeks of submitting our signatures, we discovered that members of our staff had been encouraging Andrew Sherwood to run against Pearce again—this time in the recall election. Pearce defeated Andrew by a wide margin in 2010, and Sherwood was now the Democratic chairman of LD 18.

The ringleader was Jim Parker, a true progressive and Democrat who was our best signature-gatherer. He alone, as part of our full-time paid campaign, collected close to 1,000 signatures by being relentless and persistent in the field. No one could match Jim's energy and success when it came to knocking on door. However, once we transitioned from signature-gathering to the special election, the notion of replacing one Republican with another did not sit well. Jim and our former volunteer coordinator, Geoff Esposito, were already contemplating joining Andrew's campaign to take on Pearce.

Once I became aware of this, I called Jim into the office and had Lilia and Sara present to make sure nothing too volatile occurred.

"I will just get to the point," I said. "I hear you and Geoff are in talks with Andrew about working with him to take on Pearce. Is that accurate?"

Jim had been promoted to our field director. He had keys to the office and was someone I trusted to implement our strategy. His face began to turn red and he could not contain his anger and frustration.

"Yes, that's right. I can't work to get a fucking Republican elected. I busted my ass collecting signatures and I'll be damned if I am going to be part of any campaign to elect another Republican."

I was a bit surprised by Jim's candor, but this made it easier for me to do what I had to do next. "Well, Jim, we appreciate all that you have done for the recall effort, but we explained the strategy to you early on. Like you, I would love to have a Democrat run and defeat Pearce. However, we know that if we run a Democrat in a head-to-head race with Pearce, Pearce will win."

Before he could respond, I continued. "Of even greater concern, the moment Andrew or any other Democrat declares their candidacy, any and all other Republicans thinking about challenging Pearce will respectfully decline. You know why? Because the votes they need to win will now go to the Democrat who can't. It's just that simple."

I don't think Jim heard a word I said. He held his ground, "I did not put in all those hours to get a Republican elected!" he blurted.

"Jim, I understand. Unfortunately, I will have to let you go. Please give me your keys to the office. You can pick up your check at the end of the day. I am sorry it had to come to this. Thanks again for all you have done."

Firing Jim did not resolve our main problem—Andrew's desire to challenge Pearce again.

When Andrew ran against Pearce in November 2010, after SB 1070 became law, he lost by over 20 percentage points. Pearce's victory had very little to do with how good of a campaign he ran. LD 18 was a safe, really safe, Republican seat. Any Republican, no matter how great a campaign Andrew mounted, would have won. Because Andrew was the Democratic chairman of LD 18, I met with him early in the petition phase to inform him of our strategy so he would not be surprised by our plans to run a moderate Republican against Pearce. I didn't expect Andrew to do more than run interference for us with some of his Democratic precinct committee people. Andrew embraced the strategy and wished us luck. We didn't have another real conversation until I called to address this situation.

"Andrew, I hear that you are considering throwing your name in as a candidate against Pearce in the recall election."

Sounding a bit surprised, Andrew asked, "Where did you hear that from?"

"I just had a conversation with Jim Parker. I had to let him go. He would rather work to get someone like you elected than some Republican. Is this true, Andrew?"

He paused. "Yes. I think I can take him out. I have looked at the numbers, and in a special recall election, I have a chance. Democrats will be super motivated to turn out."

"And so will Republicans the moment you or any other Democrat jumps in the race. We discussed this back in February. You agreed to stay out then."

"Yes, but things have changed."

"The only thing that has changed is that we, Citizens for a Better Arizona, have done the work to recall Pearce and force a special election. And now you want to risk any chance we have to defeat Pearce by declaring your candidacy? All of our work to recall Pearce will be wiped out because people like you can't resist inserting yourself into such a high-profile campaign."

"I disagree. Pearce is now vulnerable. I can take him out this time."

I could not hold back my anger and frustration. I blurted out, "If you run, I will destroy you!"

I hung up the phone and let my own words sink in. I had to laugh at myself. I had no real power over Andrew: He did not work for me and I definitely couldn't *destroy* him or anyone else. Further, anyone could file to be a candidate, be it Andrew or some other Democrat. Our whole effort was now at risk of being torpedoed by someone ill-equipped to take on Pearce. Andrew's candidacy, or that of any other Democratic candidate, would have been Pearce's dream matchup.

I stared at my computer screen unsure of what to do next. Turning out Democrats to vote for a Republican who rejected Pearce's extreme positions was one thing. However, getting Democrats to vote for a Republican when they still had the option to vote for a Democrat would be too difficult to overcome.

A few more minutes passed. I called my "fixer" Ken Chapman. He was the person most likely to hold some sway over Andrew. The last thing guys like Andrew wanted was to be ostracized by the Democratic establishment.

"Ken, you are not going to believe this."

"What is it now?"

"I just got off the phone with your boy Andrew and it did not go well. He says he wants to run against Pearce in the special election."

Ken sounded unsurprised. "I didn't think it would get to you this quickly."

"What do you mean?"

"Some Democratic precinct chairs want to run a Democrat and don't want someone like a Pearce-Lite. As Democrats, they cannot support a Republican. I told them this was an anti-Pearce campaign not a pro-Democrat candidate campaign. This is new for our party volunteers. I told them we have to respect the people who were doing the work and the people who are most impacted."

Any candidate matchup with Pearce in a special recall election would be a statewide and potentially a national story. The press coverage would be widespread and intense; anyone who ran against Pearce would benefit personally, even if they lost. I should have expected something like this would happen despite our best efforts to keep everyone informed and on the same page.

"Unfortunately, Andrew is stirring the pot and trying to make this more about him. I need you to call him. The last thing we need is Andrew or any other Democrat fucking this whole thing up by filing candidate papers. Do you think you can get through to him?"

Ken remained calm and agreed to set up a face-to-face meeting. I slumped back in my chair and waited—hoping Ken could put out this fire immediately.

While waiting, I called Paul Castaneda and asked him to tell Andrew how his local union would react to his candidacy. Paul could not believe that Andrew or any other Democrat would undercut all the work we had done to reach this point. We cut our call short so Paul could reach out to Andrew as well.

Andrew had an overabundance of self-importance. He liked to be called "Mr. Chair." This day, though, Andrew was about to be taken to task for undermining our entire recall strategy. Once Andrew arrived, Ken and Doug Mings, the legislative caucus director for the Arizona Democratic Party, sat Andrew down. The meeting started with a nice exchange of ideas but soured quickly.

Raising his voice, Ken told Andrew, "If you do this, we will make sure you pay the cost. I have been part of this effort from the very beginning and I agree with the strategy. It is the only way to defeat Pearce."

Ken knew of Andrew's desire to run again with the support of the Maricopa County Democratic Party. Doug reminded Andrew that redistricting in 2012 could create a better opportunity for him to win in a new, more Democratic-leaning legislative district. And most importantly, if the recall strategy failed, Andrew would not want to be remembered as the person who helped Pearce survive and win.

Paul kept up the pressure as well. He called Andrew and held nothing back. "This is important to us. This is not a partisan race. If you run, we will not support you during this race or any other race in the future. Stand down." When Paul said "we," he was referring to all unions affiliated with the Arizona AFL-CIO.

After a few hours, Ken called back. "Are we still alive?!" I shouted.

Ken just chuckled and I knew right then that we were back on track. "You are not going to have to worry about Andrew any longer. If a Democrat does choose to run it won't be Andrew. He now gets it."

Half-joking and half-serious Ken then inquired, "Please tell me you have the right candidate about to declare; this wait-and-see is killing me."

It was killing me too. With Ken running interference at the Democratic Party, the field had now been cleared for the right type of Republican to emerge.

Before I could reach out to Beth Coons, the one Republican who told me back in January she would either run or help me find the right candidate to run if we recalled Pearce, the right Republican in Mesa found me.

CHAPTER 20

Hermano Hernández

Because you believed I was capable of behaving decently, I did.
~ Paulo Coelho, author

By late June, a special recall election was all but certain. That was when I received *the call*. I add the emphasis because this call would open the door to a world of which I knew very little about—Republicans, Mormons, and well-established Mesa families that went back generations.

Republicans had always been the enemy, always on the other side of issues I cared deeply about. My father raised me as a Democrat and my earliest political memory goes back to Jimmy Carter's election in 1976 when I heard my father arguing with his compadre as to why Carter, and not Ford, was the right choice. Two years later I remember my father putting up a yard sign in front of our home for a man running for Congress, a Democrat named Robert Matsui, a Japanese American who was interned during World War II. However, my dislike and disdain for Republicans went even deeper than my father's influence.

Shortly after my father's tragic death, another suitor quickly came knocking on our door to "rescue" my mother from this horrible nightmare. He shall remain the man without a name. He made all sorts of promises to gain her trust, including economic support, as she struggled to raise three young boys. In time, this man's relentless pursuit resulted in marriage. Before this marriage, I had no idea what the term "domestic violence" meant, what it looked like or even sounded like. My father never hit my mother, never cursed at her, or called her any insulting and derogatory names. During my eleven years as his son, I could recall only two times when I heard them "fighting"—and that was some late-night yelling when they came home after some social event. For the most part, my father adored and respected my mother and took care of her.

It did not take long for my mother's new husband to show his true nature. For the next few years, I lived with a Dr. Jekyll/Mr. Hyde; he'd be charming on Monday and a raging alcoholic on the weekends. I'd never seen a grown man cry with so much pain, curse with such righteousness, and show so much violence towards people he lived with and claimed to love. Words like "bitch" and "whore" were yelled at my mom, and phrases like *cabron chavalos* (fucking kids) were directed at my brothers and me, too often to count. Once, I ran from the house in my socks to avoid being hit by a piece of furniture he was about to drop on my head during one of his demonic outbursts.

My mother found the courage to fight back the moment she no longer cared whether she lived or died. I came home from a high school party to find my mother in tears, her hand bruised from blocking the golf club he swung at her. Her neck was dark red from when he picked her up off her feet with his hands around her throat, threatening again to kill her if she told anyone. After they divorced, we learned the extent of her nightmare and how much she hid from us. This person threatened my mother's life the night before their wedding day. She had serious reservations then and when she expressed them to him that night, he threatened to kill her if she backed out. He was not about to be embarrassed and have to tell his family why the wedding was called off. After the incident with the golf club, my mother finally reached out to her brother who then helped her get an attorney to free my mother from this horrible marriage.

I share all this to say that the person I refuse to name was a loud and proud Republican. I understand that not all Republicans beat their wives, curse at family members, or are violent alcoholics, but that man definitely shaped my views about Republicans. Once I became aware that he was a Republican, I vowed never to be one and never to vote for one. And to this day, I have yet to break those vows.

So, when I received a call from an unknown number, I did not expect it to be *the call.*

"My name is Tyler Montague," he began. "I think I can be helpful with your campaign against Pearce."

"How so?"

"Well, I am a Republican. I live in Mesa. I am a member of the Church of Latter-day Saints, and I disagree with many of Pearce's positions, especially SB 1070."

The person we needed to help us navigate the inside world of Republican politics in Mesa among members of the Mormon Church had just arrived. Other than Beth Coons, I did not know any other Republican Mormon who lived in Mesa.

We needed a Republican Mormon to defeat Pearce, and I never expected someone like Tyler to reach out to me directly. He sounded friendly, calm, and easygoing. By the next day, I was heading over to Mesa to break bread with Tyler and see how we could work together.

We met at the Asian Café Express, where Tyler held many of his political meetings. He was a big guy, tall and wide, thick neck, with a round, friendly face and welcoming demeanor.

Tyler acknowledged that he and others were not fans of Pearce, but they initially weren't fans of the recall.

"Even though a lot of people I know don't like Pearce, they also don't like the idea of a recall. When I first heard about it early in the process I thought, 'This is not going to work. This is just sour grapes.' Well, my friends and I have been watching this whole recall thing and we have never seen anything like this. We never would have launched a recall to get him out of office. Heck, when your volunteers came knocking on my door, I did not even sign the recall petition."

"So, why get involved now?" I asked.

"Because we realize that Pearce can no longer be ignored. Pearce's anti-immigrant positions are truly authentic and if left unchallenged, Pearce will only get worse. Pearce deeply hates undocumented immigrants. While a deputy sheriff in the 1980s, an undocumented immigrant shot off his finger and the bullet entered his abdomen. Later, his son was also shot by an undocumented immigrant. How Pearce feels about Latino immigrants and what he says about them is not done for political theater; this is what he truly believes."

"Are you telling me there are a lot more Republicans willing to speak up now? Once Pearce successfully pushed SB 1070 through the legislature and then became president of the senate, we figured Republicans were resigned to sit back and wait to see how this would all play out."

"I can only share my experience. Look, I will admit that I have voted for Pearce in the past. However, back in March 2010, during the SB 1070 deliberations, I wrote Senator Pearce a letter and argued unsuccessfully that as the law was written, I was guilty of harboring illegal aliens or committing some felony. I then added, 'When one of our bishops helps one of these families with rent, they are breaking the law. You are criminalizing Christianity.'"

The response back, Tyler said, from Pearce's office was simple, direct and unhelpful: "That is not our intention."

A few days after Governor Brewer signed SB 1070, Tyler saw her speak at a precinct committee meeting. "She was so angry. Her whole vibe was so dark. This was not right. It was un-Christian. It was how they were dealing with people who were already here that really upset me. As I left the meeting, I said to myself, 'This isn't my Republican Party.'"

After that, Tyler was all in to do something. He and a friend planned to take over their LD 18 Republican precinct committee. In the 2010 November election, Tyler, for the first time, demonstrated his opposition to Pearce at the ballot box by voting for the independent candidate, Andrea Garcia, for state senate.

When I met with Tyler, I knew very little about him and the Montague family. I now know Tyler's life experience shaped him for this moment. He was born and raised in Mesa and his father Dea Montague was a lawyer and church leader. As a teenager, Tyler watched his father and other prominent Mormons such as Ross Farnsworth form a group called "Mormons for the Martin Luther King Jr. Holiday."

In 1987, Governor Ed Mecham, immediately upon taking office, signed an executive order to rescind the federal MLK holiday. Instead of falling in line with other Republicans, Tyler's father took a stand that left a huge impression on Tyler. He boldly declared, "That's just not who we are." Five years later, voters approved a statewide measure to recognize and reinstate the MLK holiday.

In high school, Tyler heard the racist comments that followed the changing demographics. "In the late 1980s, more and more Mexican immigrants started moving into our neighborhoods. I would hear comments like, 'What's up with all the Mexicans moving into the neighborhood?'"

Before those types of attitudes could become part of Tyler's character, he received word that he would serve his mission in Vina del Mar, Chile. Immersing himself in the Latino culture was eye-opening. "Through my service in Chile, I came to love Latino culture and developed a better understanding of Latinos in general," he said. "Any xenophobic attitudes that started to form in high school had been permanently dispelled once I completed my mission in Chile."

Tyler eventually married, had five daughters and settled in the neighborhood where he grew up. As a leader in the community and his church, Tyler served as the assistant district commissioner with the Boy Scouts and a youth minister with his church. In these groups, Tyler encountered adults and children who were undocumented immigrants from Mexico or some other Spanish-speaking country. For Tyler, SB 1070 hit too close to home.

"We had a bishop in our church who was undocumented. And part of our conversation was like, 'What are we going to do, let them round up our bishop?'"

For Tyler and others like him, SB 1070 forced them to become more active, and more political.

"So, are you telling me SB 1070 triggered some sort of revolt among Republicans in LD 18?" I asked. "I would not say revolt, more like a spiritual awakening. Because of our efforts, Pearce came very close after the November 2010 election to *not* even being selected as a precinct committee person in his own district."

"What do you mean? Pearce had just been elected president of the senate."

"Yes, but earlier in 2010, after SB 1070 passed, some of my friends and I got involved in our LD 18 Republican precinct committee and recruited anti-Pearce individuals to run and serve as LD 18 precinct committee people. We figured it was too late to run someone against Pearce in the Republican primary so we attempted to take over the LD 18 precinct committee."

"So, what happened?"

"Initially, we succeeded. At the first vote of the statutory organizational meeting in November, we ran a slate of people, and when the votes were counted, Pearce did not receive enough votes to make the final list of fifty-three precinct committee people. We had outorganized him in his own backyard."

"Let me guess what happened next: The Republican Party leadership got involved?"

"You got it. The very next day someone raised some issue about how the original call letter for the meeting did not meet the required 10-day notice and subsequently the vote that took place was ruled invalid. Early in December another vote was held for precinct committee people; this time overseen by the Maricopa County Republican Party leadership. We almost pulled it off again. After everyone voted, they read out the results in order of highest vote-getter to lowest vote-getter until they filled all committee slots.

"The person announcing the results had reached the 40s and still Pearce's name had not been called. Names 49, 50, 51, and 52 were called, and still no Pearce. But when they got to the last and final slot, number 53, our efforts fell short when the announcer read out the final name—Russell Pearce. They literally had to cheat to get Pearce elected as a precinct committeeperson—so much for the rule of law." We both laughed.

Pearce's face must have been bright red when it became apparent that even with an election run by his allies in the county Republican Party, he still almost lost. He received the fewest votes *from those who knew him best*. After Pearce did not make the list of fifty-three precinct committee people in the first vote, he sent out an email blaming others and making a call to the faithful to wake up. It said, "We had an effort by folks outside of our district handing out a flyer as to who to vote for and it appeared they were trying to unseat many of our longtime hardworking conservatives. I know many of the new folks who showed up for the very first time ever at our meeting are good folks who come from good families, but this effort was damaging to our unity and hurtful to our longtime hardworking PCs."

Pearce needed to sound the alarm so his Tea Party loyalists would show up for the next meeting.

Many people outside of Mesa were not aware of the growing anti-Pearce faction that had been brewing for quite some time, even in this very red and Tea Party-strong district. To Pearce's surprise, the extent of their reach, persistence, and influence nearly got him removed as a state committee person at a time when he had just become one of the most powerful Republicans in the state.

"What an embarrassment it would have been for Pearce to be president of the senate and voted off his own LD 18 Precinct Committee," I said.

"I share all this with you to let you know that now, and even before SB 1070, we have had a significant minority of Republicans in Mesa, I would say 30 to 35 percent who do not support Pearce's anti-immigrant policies. However, that's not enough to win a Republican primary. That's why I called you."

"You want to know if we have a candidate, right?"

"Well kind of. First, I wanted to find out if my team and I can work with you because all we hear from Pearce and his supporters is how crazy you are and that you are out to destroy America." We both smiled. "I also wanted to find out if you would be open to hearing us out on how we could be helpful. Now with a special election about to be declared by Brewer, how are you thinking about who to run?"

"First, I will tell you that we will do everything we can on our side to keep all Democrats out of the race. Second, we want this to be a one-to-one matchup between Pearce and what we hope to be a kinder, gentler Republican, and most importantly, someone who respects and appreciates the Latino immigrant community. These attacks, these anti-immigrant bills, have to stop."

"Glad to hear that we are on the same page. We are willing to identify, recruit, and support the right candidate *only* if we can get assurances from you that the field will be clear of all Democrats. We feel confident we can win the special election with our significant minority of Republican votes plus all the Democrats and independents who are opposed to Pearce."

"Who do you have in mind?"

"We have reached out to a couple of potential candidates: one of them is Robin Harris. Robin is opposed to what Pearce is doing, he is well respected, and he has an impeccable reputation within the LDS Church and the general Mesa community. Robin feels strongly that Pearce's views on immigration are an unfair and an inaccurate representation of the LDS Church and members like himself.

"Right now, Robin and his wife are still considering it and we should have an answer soon. But like I mentioned before, we need to know that there will not be any Democratic candidate. You need to know, that no matter who we run, the moment a Democrat gets on that ballot, our candidate will withdraw the same day. We cannot afford to divide the anti-Pearce vote."

"I get it Tyler; that has been our strategy from the beginning. You have my word that my team and I will do everything in our power to keep the field clear of Democratic candidates. You are the final partner we have been waiting for to get us to the promised land." We both laughed again.

"One more thing before you go."

"Sure, what is it?"

"Well, you know that our LDS community is a tightly knit group, and because of our weekly worship services, community outreach programs, and other volunteer activities, we always seem to find ourselves in mixed company. I mean, on any given day of the week, we could have a number of social events where the company is very mixed with both pro-Pearce and anti-Pearce supporters. So, to keep the peace as much as possible, my friends and I have developed a code name for you when we need to share information."

"What do you mean?"

"Well, sometimes when we talk about you and the recall, there are others within earshot who would be upset to hear that we would associate with someone like you. And now that we are going to be in communication, I need to let my friends know when I have heard from you or when you are coming by for a visit. So, we have come up with a secret code name for you: Hermano (brother) Hernández."

"Hermano Hernández? Come on, Tyler, is this really necessary?"

"Hermano Hernández, you have no idea the reactions we get when the name 'Randy Parraz' is mentioned in mixed company. For some individuals it is as if you are the devil, some anti-Christ figure that has come to steal our wives and children."

Tyler grinned widely and laughed. "All kidding aside, you know what I am talking about: Pearce and his supporters are blaming this recall on you, so we thought it would make things easier for us to just call you Hermano Hernández."

"Well, then, Hermano Hernández it is, and whether it's Robin Harris or someone else who eventually decides to run, I feel confident that you and your team will make the right decision. Now that we have each other's number, let's stay in touch and please let me know the minute you—I mean, *we*—have a candidate."

"¡Cómo no Hermano Hernández, nos vemos!" he said, which means, "Of course Brother Hernandez, see you later!"

As I drove away, I felt six months of pressure leave my body. For the first time since we launched our recall campaign, I no longer had to worry about finding a candidate to take on Pearce. Beth Coons, and others like her opposed to Pearce, would now be contacted by Tyler. Our recall movement had created room for others to maneuver—others who never would have taken such action but for our efforts. Without making one phone call, we now had a semi-secret committee of Republican Mormons in Mesa to identify, recruit, vet, and support the right candidate to take on Pearce in the special recall election.

And I had a new secret code name: Hermano Hernández.[1]

---

[1] Whenever I call Tyler, my number still comes up as Hermano Hernández.

CHAPTER 21

The Banana Patch

Ignorance of the law excuses no person—from practicing it.
~ Italian proverb

It took only forty-two days for the county election officials to process and verify all the signatures we submitted. This quick turnaround guaranteed what we always wanted—a November 2011 special recall election.

On July 12, Governor Brewer made it official by announcing the date for the special election. On Tuesday, November 8, 2011, voters in Mesa would be given the chance to remove Pearce from office.

Of the signatures we submitted, more than 10,000 were deemed valid—a cushion of some 2,600 signatures from the required minimum of 7,756. Within six short months, Russell Pearce—the untouchable, unbeatable, and invincible Russell Pearce—now had to run again in an off-year election.

Still convinced that some sort of fraud or other illegal acts had been committed, Pearce refused to concede that he had been fairly and legally recalled. Six days after Brewer announced the special election, Pearce turned to the courts.

Somehow, one of Pearce's neighbors, Franklin Ross, secured the counsel of a high-powered attorney, Lisa Hauser, from the law firm of

Gammage and Burnham, and filed a lawsuit with eight separate causes of action. The lawsuit claimed that the special election would cause "irreparable harm" to its petitioner, Franklin Ross, a registered voter in District 18. "Irreparable harm" is a legal term referencing harm that cannot be corrected through monetary compensation or the conditions cannot be put back the way they were. In layman's terms, the only way to avoid "irreparable harm" was to cancel the election.

A background check on Franklin Ross showed that he owed more than $1.8 million in defaulted mortgages in the past two years, and he owed Citibank more than $22,000 in overdue credit card payments. And yet, somehow, he still managed to secure the resources to hire Ms. Hauser. The legal challenge to derail the election was more likely funded by Pearce's lobbyist friends or other supporters committed to doing whatever it took to keep Pearce in office.

During the signature-gathering phase of the recall, we worked closely with the Arizona Secretary of State's office to make sure we followed all constitutional and statutory provisions. We wanted to save our limited resources to get out the vote in November; if forced to spend our money now defending a frivolous lawsuit, our efforts would be hurt significantly. I did not want to spend a dime proving what we knew to be true.

Despite my objections to the lawsuit, we still needed legal counsel. We got off to a rocky start. On a recommendation from Ken, I contacted the highly reputable law firm Perkins Coie. I mistakenly assumed they would represent Citizens for a Better Arizona *pro bono*, but when I received the first invoice for more than $2,500, I realized that was not the case. After some clarifying conversations, Perkins Coie disengaged from representing us, but to its credit, agreed that Citizens for a Better Arizona could pay an amount we believed to be fair.

That misfire with Perkins Coie wasted several weeks, and now I was about to jump on a plane to the East Coast for a weeklong vacation I had promised my daughters months earlier. As our plane took off, we had no legal strategy, no team, nor lawyer in place.

Our response to the lawsuit was due in three days.

When we landed, good news awaited. Sara Ryan, of our recall campaign staff, had told her father, Tom Ryan, president of the Arizona Trial Lawyers Association, that Perkins Coie had dropped us. When I checked my voicemail, Tom had left a message for me to call him the moment I landed.

I called Tom and he informed me that he had discussed our situation with his wife and office manager, Anita; they agreed he should take the case.

"I will represent Citizens for a Better Arizona all the way through," he said. "I mean, I would not be surprised if the other side takes this case all the way to the Arizona Supreme Court since they are not likely to win at the lower court level. From a legal point of view, we are in a very strong position."

Tom had more good news. "We are deeply impressed and inspired that you and Citizens for a Better Arizona have made it this far and we want to do our part. You are not going to have to worry about anymore legal invoices ... We will do this *pro bono*."

"Tom, you and Anita, are about to make a grown man cry," I said. "Thank you so much for taking this on. Looks like the Ryan clan is all in."

While I attempted to enjoy the next few days, the pressure on Tom ramped up. He received a call from Janice Goldstein, executive director of the Arizona Trial Lawyers Association.

What Tom originally thought to be a general check-in call became something much more pressing when Tom asked Janice how she was doing.

"Not good," she said.

"I'm sorry. What is it?" Tom asked.

"I am standing on the ledge of my balcony wondering whether I should jump off. A little birdie just told me that you are going to represent the recall movement against Russell Pearce. Is that true?" she asked.

"Well, yes. Yes, I am."

"You can't do this."

"What do you mean, I can't do this?"

"Tom, you are the president of the Arizona Trial Lawyers. If you fail, it is just going to make (Pearce) more powerful. We can't have our name associated with this."

"Well, I have already said yes and there are a number of deadlines fast approaching. I cannot and will not go back on my word."

Shortly thereafter, the Arizona Trial Lawyers Association decided that Tom needed to take a leave of absence as president if he represented Citizens for a Better Arizona. Tom was not one to go back on his word or put some title or position above a righteous cause for justice. He took the leave and stood with us throughout the legal fight.

Tom was raised in Arizona, one of eleven children of an Irish Catholic family. He attended Catholic schools, graduated from the University of Arizona and attended Arizona State University School of Law. While there, Tom was student bar president, led a march of one hundred students to the dean's office in support of minority students, and helped start the La Raza Law Students Association.

Tom worked at a few law firms before setting up his practice. He met his wife, Anita, along the way. He proposed and she accepted but with one condition: No politics. By that, though, she meant no running for elected office. At that time, Tom found that tough to accept, but in retrospect, Tom has come to appreciate Anita's foresight. "I am still involved in politics but on my own terms. I have gotten better at picking and choosing my battles."

Tom did not want to sit out our effort to defeat Pearce. This was a battle he needed to fight.

After two days of intense research and writing, and with only minutes to spare, Tom finished the brief. Anita and Sara rushed to court and filed it at 4:58p.m., two minutes shy of the deadline.

Given the time sensitivity of the case, Judge Hugh Hegyi quickly scheduled a hearing. With the general seating area filled, members of the media sat in the jury box. Right before the hearing started, Tom asked Lilia, Chad, and Sara to join him at the lawyers' table for a front-row view.

Empowering citizens to recall their elected officials was established at the Arizona Constitutional Convention in 1910. Accountability was so entrenched in the minds of Arizona's founders, that when President Taft mandated that Arizona exempt judges from the recall provision, they did so just to gain statehood. A year later, true to their original intent, they amended the constitution and deemed judges recall-eligible.

The Arizona courts had already taken the position that "the recall procedure is not intended to protect incumbents from being ousted by dissatisfied voters." The courts even went on to say that because the provision is to benefit the public rather than elected officials, "we construe the language liberally in favor of permitting recall elections."

Tom set out to dismiss all eight claims brought against Citizens for a Better Arizona. "Citizens are free to write down any reason whatsoever on their petition to recall an elected official," he said. "Even nonsensical statements like 'we choose to recall this person because he is an odious cretin with commodious pants' or 'for fribben in the banana patch in his tighty-whities' meet the statutory requirement for a recall petition."

Superior Court Judge Hegyi denied Pearce's petition, so Hauser appealed to the Arizona Supreme Court, hoping to benefit from its conservative leanings. Normally, such a case would be heard by the court of appeals, but given the urgency of the situation, it was fast-tracked to the Arizona Supreme Court, which agreed to hear it.

We asserted that Pearce's lawsuit gave no cause of action and should be dismissed for failing to state a claim for relief. Given the absence of fraud, confusion, or unfairness, the only reasonable outcome would be to affirm the lower court's decision.

On September 14, the Arizona Supreme Court did so. Pearce, Franklin Ross, and all his other supporters had to put down their legal briefs and lace up some shoe-leather: The special recall election was on!

Ironically, the supreme court's official opinion was not published until November 14—six days after the election. It basically laid out how every claim brought by Pearce's team had no legal foundation. It also stated, "CBA's petition for the recall of Senator Pearce substantially complies with the constitutional and statutory requirements."[1]

Initially skeptical about the strategy of recalling Pearce, Tom was swept up in the momentum of our court victory and about the possibility of us winning the November election. "At the beginning of it all, I didn't know if it was possible. Many political pundits and reporters like Howie Fischer said Pearce could never be recalled. However, I believe you don't just engage in fights where you know you will win. There are fights you take on because it is the right thing to do."

While Pearce wasted time and resources in court, we continued to raise money, build our base of volunteers, and ramp up our field operations. Because of Tom's efforts, we did not have to waste tens of thousands of dollars to defend our right to recall Pearce.

Just as we shut the door on Pearce's legal attempt to delay or cancel the special recall election, Pearce and his supporters now had to cook up some other gimmick, trick, or diversion to win.

And we still needed a candidate.

---

[1] On March 5, 2014, the Superior Court of Arizona Maricopa County designated *Franklin Bruce Ross v. Ken Bennett, et al* as a historically significant case because of the unique legal issue or controversy involved, the prominence of one or more of the parties to the action, or because of other high-profile or newsworthy reasons.

CHAPTER 22

Divine Intervention

In a gentle way, you can shake the world.
~ Mahatma Gandhi

As our legal battle came to an end, our new Republican friends in Mesa continued their search to find our "unicorn" candidate—someone who had all those unique characteristics we needed to win. But did such a "unicorn" candidate exist?

Towards the end of July, Tyler and his team had narrowed their search down to one person, who, if he said yes, would be the ideal candidate to challenge Pearce. As they were working out the final details, there was still much speculation in the media that no legitimate candidate would emerge to run.

A few days before the name of the candidate became public, Lilia and Sara ran into Howie Fischer, the Capitol news reporter, at a bagel shop. Sara recalled how much of a jerk Fischer had been when we turned in the recall petitions. Despite her disdain for Fischer, Sara tried to strike up a friendly conversation.

"Hi, Howie," she began, "I don't know if you remember me but I am Sara from the recall."

Fischer didn't say hello, and instead asked, "Who is this magical unicorn you think you are going to produce to be a candidate in this

191

recall? This special candidate who happens to be Mormon, a Republican, and willing to challenge Pearce." Fischer recently posted an article about the recall with an image of a blank face and a big question mark covering it. Fischer continued, "You guys are idiots if you think you have anyone that can be put in this position."

Sara knew that this was not the time to go toe to toe with one of the most influential Capitol beat reporters in Arizona. Sara, knowing considerable progress had been made on the candidate recruitment front, politely responded, "OK. Nice to see you, Howie. Just wanted to say hello." And she walked away.

Maybe our candidate wasn't a unicorn, but he had one unforgettable name: Jerry Lewis. Because of the famous comedian Jerry Lewis, just saying Jerry's name made people smile. Moving forward, Jerry's campaign would have many challenges, but name recognition would not be one of them.

Fischer was right in one sense; no politician would ever do what Jerry did. Fortunately for us Jerry was not a politician. Jerry's entrance into the race would be best described as a man called to serve a mission—a call he and his wife, Janet, reluctantly, painstakingly, and even grudgingly answered.

Fischer had not done his homework. He refused to get to know me, our team, or learn more about our strategy and field campaign. He was not interested in what voters were telling us or in the significant number of Republican voters in District 18 who did not support Pearce. In January, even I had been able to find someone willing to run—Beth Coons—who was Republican, Mormon, and a community leader from a prominent Mesa family.

Jerry grew up in the San Fernando Valley near Los Angeles. Many of his childhood friends were Hispanic. He played sports with them, hung out with them, and got to know their families. In high school, Jerry studied Spanish and spent part of the summer after his junior year in Taxco, Guerrero, as an exchange student in the Eisenhower Sister City Program. When Jerry reconnected with the Church of Latter-day Saints as a teenager, he again came in contact with lots of Hispanic kids and other Hispanic members of the LDS Church through softball and other sports. Jerry attended seminary in ninth grade, went to church every week, and routinely read the Book of Mormon.

Jerry's immersion in his faith led to a spiritual awakening about the purpose of life. Jerry believed that we were all God's children, regardless of where we lived, the color of our skin, our gender—or anything else, for that matter. At nineteen, Jerry accepted Jesus as his Savior. His faith deepened as he embraced the journey of discovering God's purpose for him.

Jerry completed a two-year Mormon mission in Hong Kong, where he became fluent in Cantonese. His time abroad helped him appreciate and respect other languages, cultures, and people. He finished college at Brigham Young University, where he met Janet Merkley, who became his wife. At Sunday school, Janet was asked to sing a solo, and Jerry listened intently. "I saw this wonderful, talented girl singing this solo," he said. "Man, I need to meet this girl."

Later in the day, Jerry met Janet in one of the breakout sessions and immediately asked her out. That evening, at a fireside meeting, the speaker talked about eternal and celestial marriage. "Perfect timing," Jerry thought, already imagining his future with Janet. A month later, he drove from Provo to Portland, Oregon, to meet Janet's family.

Because Jerry and Janet had taken a golf class together, Jerry promised to propose on a golf course when the time was right. The special moment occurred on the 9th tee of the Dinosaur Golf Course in about two to three feet of snow in Vernal, Arizona. Soon after, Jerry accepted an accounting job with Deloitte, the international consulting firm, and they moved to Phoenix before settling in Mesa. This was thirty years before the recall election, so Jerry may have been politically naïve—but he was definitely *not* an outsider.

Jerry and his family were deeply disturbed by the attacks of Pearce and Arpaio on the Latino immigrant community. The LDS Church had very strong feelings about using the correct principles to guide the immigration discussion. Pearce's claim that SB 1070's punitive approach was consistent with church teachings compelled the leadership of the LDS Church to clarify its position on immigration. A June 2011 statement from the LDS Church read in part:

> *"What to do with the estimated 12 million undocumented immigrants now residing in various states within the United States is the biggest challenge in the immigration debate. The bedrock moral issue for The Church of Jesus Christ of Latter-day Saints is how we treat each other as children of God.*
>
> *As those on all sides of the immigration debate in the United States have noted, this issue is one that must ultimately be resolved by the federal government.*
>
> *The Church of Jesus Christ of Latter-day Saints is concerned that any state legislation that only contains enforcement provisions is likely to fall short of the high moral standard of treating each other as children of God.*
>
> *The Church supports an approach where undocumented immigrants are allowed to square themselves with the law and continue to work without this necessarily leading to citizenship.*
>
> *The Church of Jesus Christ of Latter-day Saints supports a balanced and civil approach to a challenging problem, fully consistent with its traditions of compassion, its reverence for family, and its commitment to law."*

After the church released this statement, Pearce could no longer make any claim that SB 1070 was consistent with LDS Church's principles on immigration. The statement referred to undocumented immigrants as "children of God," and it said no group should be targeted. And finally, the church said, a tradition of compassion, not hate, should guide the framework or approach to immigration reform.

As stake president, Jerry sat in meetings and heard all the horrible things that Latino immigrant families were confronting in Mesa and the surrounding cities.[1] Arpaio's worksite raids resulted in deportations of the main breadwinners of these immigrant families. Jerry knew the names and faces of these families. He knew the children who were being torn from their parents. These children were American in every sense of the word, but because of this anti-immigrant environment, they were now forced to grow up without the love, protection, and support of their parents.

"We saw good people, even those mistaken as being undocumented, being herded up and treated as criminals," Jerry said. "The targeting and profiling that ensued was a travesty of justice and of the US Constitution."

Jerry recommitted to furthering his Spanish-speaking skills after he was assigned to a Spanish-speaking unit within his stake. Many of the families Jerry had come to admire, love, and respect were forced to go underground after SB 1070 passed; some families chose to leave the state.

Jerry thought somebody had to do something about this. "We needed a twenty-first century solution to this crisis," he recalled. "Washington had abdicated their responsibility. Senators McCain and Flake tried, but they were maligned for even trying to put forward a comprehensive immigration solution."

Shortly after SB 1070 passed, Jerry was asked to become a precinct committee person. Jerry agreed but he had no intent to become a candidate. However, his adherence to his faith led him to become knowledgeable about politics. Besides, before they married, Janet told

---

[1] A stake in the LDS Church congregation is a geographical area composed of 6 to 15 wards or branches. Each ward is headed by a bishop with 300 to 400 congregants. A branch is smaller, 15 to 200 members, and may be organized around a foreign language.

Jerry that she would follow him anywhere and support him in whatever he chose to do—so long as it was *not politics*. Jerry agreed and pursued a career in accounting. All this would change in 2011.

That February, Jerry participated in the Ragnar Relay—a two-day running relay with teams of seven to twelve men covering upwards of 200 miles. The same weekend, his duties as stake president were ending. En route to a meeting to discuss his replacement, Jerry received a phone call from Dea and Tyler Montague, prominent LDS Church leaders in Mesa. Congressman Jeff Flake had decided to run for US Senate, they said, which would create an opening for his congressional seat. They heard that Pearce might run for Flake's seat. If that happened, the Maricopa County Board of Supervisors would appoint a successor to Pearce's state senate seat. Three Republican names would be submitted for consideration. They wanted to know if Jerry would be willing to be considered for such a role.

Jerry told them he was "flattered" and agreed to run it by Janet.

He did and his wife was quick to respond. "No," she said. "Remember, we don't do politics."

"Well, let's consider it," Jerry responded. "I think there might be some opportunities here to correct some of the problems with immigration. I might be able to be a positive influence. Let's think about it for a week."

During Fast Sunday, a time when members go without food or drink for two meals or twenty-four hours and donate to the church, Jerry prayed and asked for clarity about his role in all of this. Something special happened to Jerry during this fast. He said, "As I prayed and pondered, I received a message which I believe was a personal revelation from God. I received this impression: 'Your wife has sustained you throughout your entire marriage—through college, church callings, bishop, stake president, teacher, and other changes in your career—she has been there by your side and has sustained you in everything you have wanted to do. Listen closely to what she tells you.'"

After dinner, and with the spiritual impression fresh in Jerry's mind, he approached his wife. "Janet, I need to listen to what you want. This is going to affect you and the rest of the family."

Again, Janet said, "No way."

Without hesitation, Jerry called Dea and Tyler and told them, "No thanks. Not interested. We don't want to do this."

Despite his "no politics pledge," Jerry could not shake off a desire to do something. Interestingly, though, Jerry refused to sign the Pearce recall petition. "If we put Pearce in office, we have to live with the consequences," he reasoned. Jerry's desire to help was not restricted to running for office. Surely, he could serve in some other capacity. Besides, a long time had passed since he held his last elected office—senior class president in high school.

By mid-June, it became apparent that a recall election would be held in November. In July, Dea and Tyler Montague, Kenny Smith, Chad Haywood and Dave Johnson approached Jerry again with another political opportunity—the chance to run against Pearce in the recall election. Jerry agreed to meet.

"Here's the deal, Jerry," Tyler explained. "We thought we had someone ready to go against Pearce. We just found out Robin Harris can't run. The recall is about to be officially signed off on. The signatures have been verified and the governor is about to call a special election. We need you to run."

"Thanks for thinking of me," Jerry said. "However, you all know Janet and I have already discussed this—it was a *no* back in March, and it is still a *no* now. But I will ask Janet again. It is really her call. But I am not going to do anything that jeopardizes our relationship or in any way affects our children's safety."

Jerry believed the family to be an eternal unit—as the family goes, so goes the nation and the world. It became increasingly difficult for him to ignore what was happening in Mesa. He felt Congress's refusal to enact immigration reform led to the creation of new state laws to fix all that was broken in our immigration system.

Further complicating Jerry's decision to run was that he knew Pearce. Jerry had signed candidate petitions for Pearce and even voted for him in 2008. Pearce's uncle, Keith Crandell, the founder of the East Valley Institute of Technology, was a dear friend of Jerry's. Keith not only supported Pearce, he also campaigned on his behalf. Even as far back as 2003, when Pearce was a state representative, Jerry had called on Pearce to help him with a constituent matter and Pearce helped resolve the matter to Jerry's satisfaction.

By 2010, though, Pearce had lost Jerry's vote. The tone had now changed. The immigration battle had touched Jerry's life in a very personal and meaningful way. And because so many of his Latino friends were now suffering because of Pearce's behavior, Jerry wondered what he could do to help. How could he stop this?

Jerry struggled to reconcile the "no politics" pledge he made to Janet when they got married, the impressions he received during his fast, and his deep desire to do something now to help his immigrant friends.

Jerry made one more attempt with Janet.

"I have been thinking a lot about this. It's only getting worse. There are other anti-immigrant bills on the table. There was more discussion about clamping down even further in Arizona since the federal government wasn't doing its job," he told her. "Janet, things have changed since our conversation in March. I am only asking you this because I have been asked to reconsider. I am going to do whatever you want. Nothing has changed in that regard and our relationship and the safety of our family is much more important than anything else."

"Thank you for that, Jerry. My answer is still no."

"I tell you what. Let's think about it. Let's allow it to percolate a little bit."

Janet agreed, still not sure what needed to percolate since their agreement to steer clear of politics was something they both had agreed to decades ago. The following Sunday, Jerry approached Janet again.

"There is something there. I am not sure what it is. I am feeling drawn to it. I don't want to do it, but I am feeling drawn to it."

Janet was still adamantly opposed and warned Jerry. "Think about our children. What's going to happen to them? We still have kids in elementary school and grandkids. Look at what they do to politicians. I don't want anything to happen to our children."

"Yeah, I know but I have been told by these guys that they will only come after me and leave the family alone. By the way, here's a list of names of families who are involved in politics you can call if you want."

"No. I do not need any list to call. We are not going to do this to our family."

The following week, Jerry and his youngest son Sam had a weeklong Boy Scouts trip. Before he left, he told Janet, "Here is what I propose. Sam and I will be out of the house for a week and a day. You will be here with our daughters and it will be pretty quiet for you. You will have a whole week to think about this. I am inviting you to reconsider." He shared the list the Montagues had given him of other families in politics who she could contact to learn more about their experiences.

"Jerry, I just don't want our family dragged through all this stuff, but I will pray on it. I know you are doing your best to make sense of what you are feeling called to do."

From the road Saturday morning, Jerry checked in with Janet. No change of heart. Same thing Sunday night. And, no, she had not called anyone on the list.

Monday. "Hey, any more thoughts?" Jerry asked.

"No. Nothing," Janet replied.

On Tuesday, Jerry had no cell phone reception.

By Wednesday, Janet still had not checked in with the wives of other politicians, but she now had something different to share.

Jerry asked again, "So what do you think?"

And this time Janet declared, "We *need* to do this."

Shocked by her response, Jerry asked for clarification, "What? Did I just hear you correctly? We *need* to do this?"

"I have struggled with this, but I received my own impressions and my own ideas as to why you need to do this. Our friends are getting persecuted like nobody's business. And families are being torn apart. Someone needs to step in and do something about it."

"OK. Great!"

Now Jerry had to reconsider whether *he* really wanted to do this. Jerry's next call was to his employer.

Ron Neil, CEO of Edkey Schools, attended the same church as Jerry. He had a reputation as a deep-thinking, kind, and considerate man. "Oh, by all means, if you want to run, we will support you one hundred percent."

Jerry then called the two owners of the charter school where he served as CEO. They were both very conservative members of the LDS Church. They agreed Jerry needed to do this; it was the right thing to do. Both men spoke Spanish and had served missions in Spanish-speaking countries.

Then Jerry called two spiritual confidants and invited them into the decision-making process. "Hey, I want to make sure I am not doing this for my personal gain and recognition. I want to make sure this is for the right reason. Please ask me the questions you think I need to answer before I move forward." Their feedback was all positive.

Jerry then called Tyler with a three-word greeting: "Let's do this!"

Within twenty-four hours, Jerry was inundated with calls from reporters asking whether he planned to file as a candidate. Until now, no one thought any credible Republican would dare challenge Pearce in the recall election. On his drive home from his trip with Sam, Jerry received numerous calls from wonderful friends from other LDS churches, prominent civic and business leaders, and former church members, applauding his decision to run and offering their support as individuals.

Jerry even got a call from the pollster Mike O'Neal who offered to help. Jerry had a long 15-hour drive back from Idaho, and he spent most of the time talking to reporters, family members, friends, and other allies. However, Jerry was still reluctant to go on the record as an official candidate. But Brahm Resnik from NBC Channel 12, Steve Kraft from FOX Channel 10, and Steve Lemons from the *New Times* kept pressing him. When Jerry pulled into his driveway, Lemons was waiting for him on his doorstep. Instead of pressing for an on-the-record confirmation, Lemons said he wanted to get to know Jerry and promised an "off-the-record" conversation. Jerry agreed and realized there was no turning back now.

Jerry's advisers did not want to announce Jerry's candidacy for another week and a half. But the buzz of his candidacy was generating more excitement and interest. But now the calls—from legislators, strategists, and good friends—were pleas for Jerry *not* to run. The sentiment was: *Jerry please don't do this. This is going to tear apart the community. This is going to tear apart the LDS Church. This is going to tear apart the Republican Party. And this is going to be really tough on you. They are going to come after you really hard.*

To which Jerry responded, "You know I have my personal witness; this is something I have to do. I can't go back on what I felt I am being directed to do. The cathartic and revelatory experience Janet and I have gone through over the past four to five months has only strengthened our resolve to run."

He also told them, "There is a bigger cause here that I can't fully explain, but a lot of it I can. And it has to do with how my friends are being treated. And it is wrong."

Still, the pressure mounted on Jerry to bow out. Once it became clear to those set on derailing Jerry's candidacy that they couldn't convince him otherwise, their words and actions turned hateful. Various Republican leaders informed Jerry that Governor Brewer was dead set against him running and would soon be calling to make the direct ask. The "Don't run, Jerry" campaign went on for at least a week. Despite the threats from those closely aligned with Governor Brewer, she never called.

But then things took an unexpectedly violent turn. The following Saturday, Jerry was scheduled to do a 20-mile run with two of his brothers-in-law. The run started in Apache Junction at 3:30 a.m. About three hours into the run, the group had reached the intersection of Stapley and Brown in Mesa.

"All of a sudden, something hit me in my groin and dropped me," Jerry said. He turned and saw a white, newer model Chevrolet truck pulling a black trailer. Jerry could see the driver laughing as they drove away.

He had been hit by a heavy padlock, but the blow was cushioned by his fanny pack. The impact was so strong that Jerry had bruises on both thighs near his groin. As they waited for the police officers to arrive, they wondered who would do such a thing. Had that padlock struck Jerry in the head, the injury to Jerry's head would have been severe if not fatal.

Fortunately, Jerry recovered to the point where he was able to finish the last three miles of his run. When he arrived at his home, Jerry called Tyler.

Jerry, with a bit of nervousness, started in, "Tyler, you are not going to believe what happened. My wife's worst nightmare has just been confirmed. This was a personal attack and I don't want to even think about what would have happened had that padlock hit me in my head."

Jerry added he needed to tell his wife about this immediately. He then said, "I don't want to tell the press. We need to keep this quiet."

Tyler disagreed. "Jerry, we have to tell the story. We cannot let this go without a response. This was not a random act of violence. You were targeted."

Tyler eventually convinced Jerry that the best way to protect Jerry would be to leak the story to the press so everyone could assess for themselves what motivated the attack. Once Tyler leaked the story, the press asked Jerry: Was this random, or was it organized?

"I have been running marathons for three years and nothing like this has ever happened. I don't know, but what a coincidence, you think? I still haven't even made my formal announcement yet and this happens."

Instead of forcing Jerry out of the race, this cowardly, violent act strengthened Jerry's faith in the decision to run.

During the next few days, Jerry's team finalized his formal announcement and held Jerry's first press event at the now-famous Wright House in Mesa to introduce his candidacy. Jerry told reporters that voters expressed a desire for a new start in Mesa politics and he would bring a new tone of civility to address some of Mesa's most pressing problems.

Pearce would now be forced to go toe to toe, not with a liberal Democrat, but with a conservative Republican and former leader of the LDS Church, with deep ties to the community and close to three decades of service in the Mesa area. He had a name—Jerry Lewis—voters would never forget. His George Clooney looks only made things worse for Pearce, who had a rough outward appearance. The large crowd of friends and colleagues who attended Jerry's announcement emboldened and inspired Jerry.

Don Stapley, a Republican from Mesa who had recently retired after serving eighteen years on the Maricopa County Board of Supervisors, also showed up and endorsed Jerry. Given the atmosphere of fear and intimidation being cultivated within the Republican Party to get everyone in line behind Pearce, Jerry felt former supervisor Stapley's endorsement was a real act of courage—especially since Jerry had never run for office and Pearce had never lost an election.

Now everyone knew the answer to Howie Fischer's snarky question: "Who is this magical unicorn candidate who happens to be Mormon and a Republican and willing to challenge Pearce?"

Hey, Howie, his name is Jerry Lewis.

CHAPTER 23

What a Sham!

Facts are threatening to those invested in fraud.
~ Dr. DaShonne Stokes, sociologist

Soon after Jerry Lewis's announcement, Pearce and his supporters recognized that Jerry posed a significant threat in a head-to-head matchup. Jerry not only represented conservative values, but he did so with kindness, humility, and compassion. Pearce needed help to survive the special election. Enter Constantine Querard, a conservative political consultant with a history of backing some of the wackiest and extreme right-wing politicians in Arizona. Querard volunteered to run Pearce's independent expenditure campaign, which meant Querard could advocate for Pearce without being tied to his official campaign; in fact, Querard would be forbidden from coordinating with the candidate and allowed to operate without the candidate's permission.

Querard got right to the point in an email to his Republican allies. "You still know lots of folks in LD18? I need to find a couple of people to be candidates for the Pearce recall. Know any patriots out that way who are team players?"

Querard wanted to enlist a few good "patriots" to *run to lose*, but do so in such a way as to take votes away from the real challenger, Jerry Lewis.

Some Republicans found the strategy to be dishonest, fraudulent, and illegal, but one person had no problem doing whatever it took to help Pearce win. That individual was Greg Western, a local Republican activist and head of the Red Mountain (Mesa area) Tea Party.

By mid-August, Western enlisted members of his LDS Church ward to find candidates who would be willing to run to lose to help Pearce win. But as the deadline approached for all candidates to turn in their signatures to qualify for the November special election, Jerry remained the lone challenger.

On the last day for candidates to turn in their nominating petitions, I sent our office manager, Sara Ryan, to stake out the secretary of state's office all day to see if any last-minute candidates surfaced.

About 4:30 p.m., Sara was just about to head back to the office when the unimaginable happened. The elevator doors opened and out walked Greg Western, with papers in his hand. He approached the service window and placed the nominating signatures on the counter for a candidate to run in the upcoming special election.

Her name was Olivia Cortes.

Sara took photos and videos of Western turning in the signatures. She also captured him on video explaining to reporters why he was supporting Cortes and not his good friend Pearce.

Western recruited Cortes from his church ward to be a candidate. He convinced Cortes, also a Pearce supporter, that by doing this she would be helping her friend Pearce get reelected. Don't let the last name fool you. Like Pearce, Cortes harbored anti-immigrant feelings. As someone who immigrated legally to the US from Mexico, Cortes supported Pearce's policies to crack down on and deport the "illegals." Believing Western's assurances that she would not have to do anything, Cortes agreed to have her name placed on the ballot. However, she had no idea what it meant to enter this particular race at this particular time. Cortes trusted Western and other Pearce loyalists to guide and protect her through this process. The moment her name became public, no one could protect her from the avalanche of public interest and media scrutiny that ensued.

We wasted no time helping her gain notoriety. That evening we posted on our Facebook page, "BREAKING NEWS: Head of Tea Party in East Valley, Greg Western, turns in signatures on behalf of Olivia Cortes ... unbelievable! Isn't Senator Pearce the President of the Tea Party movement in Arizona? Why would leaders of the Tea Party: recruit a candidate to run against their hero; help the candidate collect signatures; provide the resources to pay for signatures; and send in the chairman of the East Valley Tea Party to turn in signatures ... because Russell Pearce is finally vulnerable."

The desperation of Pearce and his supporters reached a new high with this move. Pearce denied any knowledge of, or involvement with, recruiting Cortes as a candidate. However, Pearce's close ties to Western made that impossible to believe. Regardless of what anyone thought, Pearce's team nonetheless had recruited a candidate to divide the anti-Pearce vote. Now it was our turn to respond.

Mike Wright was one of our biggest supporters, a lawyer, a Democrat, Mesa resident, and member of the LDS Church. As he heard more of the story behind Cortes's conversion from anonymous churchgoer to candidate, he wanted to join the fray. Mike belonged to the same stake as Jerry and saw Jerry's commitment to family and faith during his tenure as stake president. The Wright family is another one of those families with deep roots in Mesa. Mike's father served with distinction in the LDS Church and community; he was stake president for some twenty-three years. He also served on the Mesa City Council. "My father was an undercover liberal, very well-liked and respected," Mike said.

Mike and Pearce were classmates at Westwood High School, raised in the same stake, and they played football together. Mike also had the distinction of breaking Pearce's leg in a football game. After graduation, their paths diverged but their children grew up together, and Mike remained close with Pearce's relatives (Pearce's brother Richard became Mike's accountant). As a progressive Democrat, Mike had managed to do very well in Mesa, as a lawyer and small business owner. However, Pearce's views on immigration, his racist comments, and his passage of SB 1070 all signaled to Mike that Pearce had gone too far.

Mike could help thwart Pearce's sham candidate plan: he knew some of the people who collected signatures on Cortes's behalf were staunch Pearce supporters and members of Pearce's extended family. They all needed to be contacted, interviewed and, if necessary, subpoenaed. Mike told our attorney Tom Ryan he was prepared to help with that effort. As Mike and Tom pursued that strategy, we contacted thousands of voters to make sure they didn't waste their anti-Pearce vote on Cortes.

By the end of September and just two weeks before early ballots dropped, Citizens for a Better Arizona put out a door hanger hit piece to respond to the Cortes situation. At the top, it read, "Whose fingerprints are all over candidate Olivia Cortes?" The piece had a photo of Cortes with fingerprint marks and a magnifying glass to highlight the evidence of a "crime." In the middle, it read, "All evidence points to Russell Pearce. *A Vote for Olivia Cortes is a Vote for Russell Pearce.*"

This became our mantra until Election Night—a vote for Cortes is a vote for Pearce. Within the first week, we dropped more than 6,000 door hangers and made some 15,000 phone calls to inform voters not to be fooled by Cortes's sham candidacy.

Tom and Mike continued to build the legal case against Cortes. It was one thing for us to call Cortes a sham candidate but it would be better to have a court of law weigh in. Tom and Mike filed the petition on behalf of our local chairperson for the recall, Mary Lou Boettcher. Although Tom felt that pursuing a legal remedy to keep Cortes off the ballot would be a Hail Mary, he knew the process of holding a hearing on this matter would do more damage to Pearce and his campaign. And he was right.

The courtroom was packed, and the media were ready to drill Cortes about some of the comments she made and her undercover campaign. Tom finally got what he wanted—an opportunity to go after Olivia Cortes on the witness stand. Tom wanted to be respectful of Cortes but was not going to let her off without exposing what she was … a sham candidate.

Tom started with the basics of her campaign. Shortly after Western filed papers for Cortes's candidacy, "Sí Se Puede" signs popped up all over Mesa. Given the historical significance and symbolic meaning of the phrase, Tom started there.

"Sí Se Puede—that's an important phrase here in Arizona. Do you know what this means?"

"Yes. If you want to run for office here in Arizona, yes you can!"

"No. It is a slogan made popular by Cesar Chavez and the United Farm Workers Union. Who paid for the signatures to get your name on the ballot?"

"I don't know."

"Who designed the *Sí Se Puede* signs"? And who paid for them?"

"I don't know."

"How many signs did you put up?"

"I don't know."

"Who put up your signs?"

"I don't know."

"How much money have you raised?"

"I don't know."

"Do you have any endorsements?"

"No."

"Have you granted any interviews to the press?"

"No."

If anyone had any doubts about the purpose of Cortes's candidacy after Tom finished with Cortes, the testimony and tape recording provided by Susan Dreher left no room for Pearce and his supporters to distance themselves from this mess.

Dreher was hired to collect signatures for Cortes. Shortly before the hearing, a recording surfaced of Dreher's conversation with a voter she was trying to convince to sign Cortes' petition to be a candidate. Tom played the tape for everyone to hear.

"Are you registered to vote in Mesa?" Dreher tells a resident, a potential signee.

"Yes," the resident says.

"This is for Olivia Cortes for the state senate, to get her name on the ballot."

"Oh, is this about the Pearce recall? She wants to be one of the candidates? I don't think I want to sign because I support Russell Pearce."

"Then you will want to sign. The whole point of her running is to split the vote so Pearce does stay in office."

"Wouldn't it be better if there are only a couple of people running?"

"If there are only two people like there are right now running, Pearce and one other person, everybody that is against Pearce will vote for this person. But if there are two people and Pearce, then part of them are going to vote for one and the other, and Pearce will get a majority of the vote. But if this doesn't happen then Pearce won't probably get the majority of the vote."

"OK, I'll sign. If she is on the ballot, then who do you suggest we vote for?"

"Him (Pearce). People that don't want him will vote for both Jerry Lewis and her. Then Jerry Lewis will not get all of that vote and Russell should come out the winner. As it stands right now, with just one person, he is not probably going to win."

"Do you live in the district as well?"

"No. I am just helping."

"Are you a volunteer?"

"No. I am getting paid."

A few days later Judge Ed Burke, of the Maricopa County Superior Court, made the following ruling: "The court finds that Pearce supporters recruited Cortes, a political neophyte, to run in the recall election to siphon Hispanic votes from Lewis to advance Pearce's recall election bid."

Judge Burke also agreed that several Pearce supporters, including close family members of Senator Pearce, helped circulate petitions. Several people said they observed Pearce's brother Lester, a justice of the peace, driving around Mesa neighborhoods with Olivia Cortes signs in the back seat of his car. Lester's daughter, Pearce's niece, was also in the car and she was seen encouraging others to sign Cortes's candidate petition.

Pearce supporters found themselves doing double duty. In one week, a Pearce supporter might be circulating petitions to get Cortes on the ballot while passing out pro-Pearce literature at Republican Party meetings. Even Franklin Ross got in on the action. After his lawsuit to stop the recall failed, Ross signed up to collect signatures for Cortes.

Once the court adjourned, our legal team, Tom and Mike, held a press conference outside the courtroom. Still oblivious to the meltdown occurring within the Pearce campaign, Howie Fischer again questioned our tactics and purpose. He asked Tom with his condescending tone, "Do you really think you can pull this off?"

Unshaken by Fischer's skepticism, Tom responded, "You know, Howie your slavish devotion as the premiere political prognosticator has clouded your judgment. If I was you, I would take a deep breath about this and wait to see what happens."

Soon after the hearing, the *East Valley Tribune* editorial board echoed some of Judge Burke's findings and called out Cortes's sham candidacy more directly: "So in the fantasy world of Olivia Cortes, she wakes up one day and says, 'You know, I've never been involved in politics my whole life, but I'm going to enter the recall race against the most powerful Republican in the state. I don't plan to campaign or make myself available to voters or the media who might help spread my message. I don't need any volunteers to help with my campaign. And I'll be my own campaign committee chairwoman and treasurer. But gee, isn't it nice how this website and all these signs are miraculously appearing and being paid for by someone? And isn't it neat that the East Valley Tea Party, which worships at the throne of Russell Pearce, is now apparently behind my candidacy?' Please."

However, the very person at the center of this conspiracy refused to speak out against the Cortes "candidacy." Pearce, Mr. Rule of Law, saw nothing wrong with it. During an interview with ABC Channel 15 in Phoenix, he was asked if he felt her candidacy was a fraud. He quipped, "Are you talking about Jerry Lewis? He was put in by a left-wing community organizer. That's about as fraud as you get, in my opinion."

In the same interview, Pearce accused Jerry of coming "through the back door" by running against him in the special recall election. Instead of condemning the behavior of Western and his cohorts, Pearce chose to defend Cortes's campaign.

Pearce even attacked those who called on the court to remove Cortes from the ballot. Pearce ramped up his rhetoric, "Shame on them! Shame on them! At least Olivia is from inside our district."

Before our legal team could follow up with another evidentiary hearing, Cortes withdrew from the race. Although we had won the public relations battle on this one—one poll showing 85 percent of people supported pursuing criminal charges in the Cortes/Pearce scandal—the ballots had already been printed with Cortes's name included. Querard, Western, and other Pearce allies succeeded in getting one more name on the ballot to help their good friend Pearce beat back Jerry's challenge.

Shortly after Cortes's withdrawal, we met with Maricopa County Director of Elections Karen Osborne. We asked if she would be willing to consider some options to inform the voters in District 18 of this development. Her response was disappointing to say the least. She said,

"I am not required by law to do anything other than print the ballots. Cortes's name will stay, and it is up to the press and groups like yours to inform voters."

We appealed Osborne's decision to her boss, Maricopa County Recorder Helen Purcell. Given the historic nature of this special election and Purcell's discretion under the law (no provision prohibiting her from taking specific actions to inform voters), we asked that she take action to secure the fairness of this election. Furthermore, given Judge Burke's ruling that Cortes was a diversionary candidate, and given Cortes's withdrawal, voters had a right to receive some sort of official notice that she was no longer a candidate. By leaving Cortes's name on the ballot, the county became a participant in deceiving the voters about the election. This deception infringed on the constitutional standard for the purity of this election.

True to form, and in keeping with the tradition of supporting other Republican elected officials, Purcell took no action to address Cortes's withdrawal.

So, with the responsibility to educate voters dropped in our laps, we put out a second hit piece on the Pearce/Cortes scandal with a two-sided English/Spanish doorhanger. It had side-by-side headshots of Cortes and Pearce with the words WITHDRAWN in red across Cortes's face. At the top of the piece, it issued the warning, "A Vote for Cortes is a Vote for Pearce." Under the photos, it read, "Russell Pearce and the TEA Party want to Confuse and Divide the anti-Pearce vote. Cortes was put on the ballot by Pearce and TEA Party supporters." At the very bottom, we added a photo of Jerry with the clarification, "There is only one REAL choice—Vote for Jerry Lewis."

In addition to our efforts, the coalition of Latino organizations led by Promise Arizona in Action made Cortes's sham candidacy a central part of its message in an expanded door-to-door outreach campaign to thousands of Latino voters.

Our "A Vote for Cortes is a Vote for Pearce" campaign had a dramatic impact on the election. Prior to Election Day, Cortes received 252 votes by mail or early, in-person voting. On Election Day, after our final two-week blitz to inform the voters about Cortes's sham candidacy, only fifteen people voted for her—fewer than 0.3 votes per precinct.

And just like that, we restored and honored the true historical significance of those very special words—*Sí Se Puede!*

CHAPTER 24

Jesus, Wake Up!

It should be the power of our vote, not the size of our bank account, that drives our democracy.
~ Barack Obama

During the signature-gathering phase of the recall, we knew our campaign would benefit greatly from a focused Latino voter engagement strategy. So, when my initial conversation with Petra Falcon at Promise Arizona went nowhere, I called Rudy Lopez, a friend and someone who had extensive knowledge in building organizations and running campaigns—especially in the area of Latino politics.

Rudy Lopez grew up in East Chicago, Indiana—a place that exemplified plantation politics—where a White Irish mayor appointed minorities to high-profile positions but did nothing to improve the lives of ordinary Blacks and Latinos in poor communities. Rudy's first major encounter with injustice occurred when he returned home from high school one day to find his mother crying in the kitchen. Rudy's mother, an immigrant from Mexico and the only Latina who was part of the cleaning staff at a senior center, had been fired. Her White, English-speaking co-workers accused her of not cleaning certain rooms. It was a lie, but she was unable to speak English to defend herself.

Rudy realized in that moment he was a Latino of some privilege because he spoke English without an accent in an oppressed Latino community. That realization, coupled with a later experience—the Rodney King beating that occurred while he was in college—cemented Rudy's commitment to work on behalf of vulnerable communities.

Rudy worked for the Center for Community Change (CCC) in Washington, DC, a national organization that had helped Promise Arizona in 2009–2010 to generate grassroots support for immigration reform in communities like Phoenix. Given the failure by the federal government on immigration reform, groups such as the CCC ramped up efforts to cultivate local organizations to engage Latinos, especially Latino youth, to register, vote, and act collectively to build power. Rudy led their voter registration work and built a national political program. In short, his role at the CCC involved mobilizing the Latino vote to support a political agenda that served the interests of Latino families and their communities. When it came to electoral politics and mobilizing the Latino vote, Rudy was one of the best in the country.

To my surprise, Petra had not mentioned the Pearce recall to Rudy.

When I asked Rudy about his take on the Pearce recall, he paused for a few seconds—which felt like two minutes.

"Uh, what are you talking about, brother? What recall campaign?"

Three months had passed since our initial press conference and we were already two months into our signature-gathering campaign. I was a bit shocked: How had Rudy not heard of this? Everyone in the immigration rights field knew of Russell Pearce and Sheriff Arpaio. I had only assumed organizations such as Promise Arizona would share this information with their national network of organizations.

I shared a little more about the campaign.

Rudy chuckled. "So, you guys are doing what? Recalling Pearce? Do we even have a chance? Given his base of power, how is that even possible?"

I then ran down the numbers and shared our strategy. I could tell by the excitement in his voice he wanted to jump in right then and there.

"All right," he said, "you know how this goes. On a personal level, I am with you 100 percent. However, as you know, Promise Arizona is one of our affiliates and we cannot get involved on the ground in Arizona unless we hear from our leaders that this is something they want to do."

I asked Rudy to talk with Petra and see if he could persuade her to get involved now. "I am telling you, Rudy, this fight is not one you want to sit out. Imagine if we are successful while Promise Arizona *chose* to sit back and watch from the sidelines. This movement is now bigger than all of us. I cannot make any guarantees at this point, but I can guarantee you this—somehow, someway, we will get enough signatures to at the very least recall Pearce. And I feel once we do that, something good is going to come of this. I just did not want you to get blindsided by all this down the road."

Rudy thanked me for the heads-up and agreed to reach out to Petra. Rudy called Petra for her assessment of the recall campaign and asked some basic questions:

"Do we really have a shot?"

"What facts do you know that work in our favor?"

"What's your take on this? Should we get involved now?"

Petra's responses boiled down to, "We are going to wait and see."

Rudy tried a different track.

"Can we frame the work in such a way that even if Pearce prevails, we still win in some way?"

"Can we use this campaign to help build Promise Arizona's capacity— to identify, train, and develop new leaders? This could be our opportunity to target and recruit a whole new generation of Latino youth to reinvent Promise Arizona as a youth driven movement."

Rudy then made one final push: "Whether you get involved or not there is one thing I know for sure—Randy is not going to stop. If this campaign gets momentum something can really happen here. Is there anything we can do now to support what he is doing?"

Without making any hard commitments, Petra told Rudy she would "see what we can do."

To which Rudy replied, "We are ready when you are. Let's keep talking."

Despite the non-commitment, I was relieved the conversation had at least started. Petra was much more likely to take and receive feedback from Rudy and the CCC than from Citizens for a Better Arizona. Unlike Citizens for a Better Arizona that had been set up as a temporary recall committee, Promise Arizona's mission and vision extended well beyond this particular fight with Pearce. It was established to become a well-resourced institution that would be around for decades. Given that Promise Arizona was still a very young organization, a failed attempt to take out someone as powerful as Pearce could invite all sorts of unwanted attacks, scrutiny, and harassment. But it would take months for Promise Arizona to get involved.

Apart from Promise Arizona, and the Center for Community Change, I also met with Ben Monteroso, national director for Mi Familia Vota (MFV)—a network of organizations committed to expanding the Latino vote in states with large Latino populations. Ben and I knew each other from my days with the AFL-CIO, so it did not take long to figure out how MFV could help. Ben acknowledged the local chapter was not equipped to launch an all-out Latino voter engagement effort, but he committed to funding at least two major mailings targeting Latino voters during the election. Because MFV arrived so late in the campaign, Ben was less interested in receiving credit and more excited about removing Pearce from power and creating new opportunities to organize the Latino vote. As the campaign escalated, Ben directed his small team to do whatever it could in the field to support our campaign.

I then turned my attention to Raquel Terán (now a state representative) who had been working with Petra and Promise Arizona as an organizer and leader since 2010.

I met Raquel at a Somos America meeting in 2007. At the time I was the political director for the Laborers' International Union of North America (LiUNA) residential organizing campaign and Raquel was a junior organizer with UFCW Local 99.

In 2008 when Arpaio ramped up his worksite raids, we formed a new group called Maricopa Citizens for Safety and Accountability (MCSA) to hold Arpaio accountable. Although I could help guide the strategy and orchestrate the group's actions, I needed someone to do the daily work—making the calls, turning out volunteers, organizing meetings, preparing materials, and doing the follow-up after each action. For me, there was only one person at that time ready for such a challenge—and that was Raquel Terán.

Before offering Raquel the job, I had observed her at the weekly Somos America meetings. She would come in full of energy, always greeting everyone she knew with a hug and a smile. Raquel came from a bi-national Mexican immigrant family with roots in Aqua Prieta, Mexico, and Douglas, Arizona. Raquel disarmed people with her outgoing personality and welcoming demeanor. Where people seemed more guarded around me, they loved Raquel. Whatever Raquel lacked in organizing skills she made up for it with her *ganas*—her desire, passion, and drive to help people. Organizing skills are teachable, but drive, determination, and passion come from within.

As the signature-gathering phase of the recall effort picked up momentum, Petra's decision to keep Promise Arizona out of the recall fight frustrated Raquel. She explained, "I remember telling Petra, 'I am going to leave and go work with Randy. We have to go and do something. People are energized. I am leaving if we don't get into this fight.'"

Although Raquel made this threat more than once, each time Petra used the same excuses, "There's no candidate. There's no strategy."

Raquel saw things in a different way. "Petra wasn't driving it," she said. "She was not in the forefront. She had no control."

For Raquel, the recall was something concrete, something that could be done right now, something that would allow them to take on the very person responsible for causing so much pain in the Latino community. Unable to do anything through Promise Arizona, Raquel collected signatures on her own time.

Another organizer frustrated with Promise Arizona's decision to "wait and see" was Alejandra "Alex" Gomez (now co-executive director for Living United for Change in Arizona, LUChA). When Alex first heard about the Pearce recall, those in her circle were dismissive. They characterized the idea of removing Pearce from office as: "Randy's crazy." However, her interest in being part of the recall campaign grew every week, especially after we submitted the signatures.

Alex, too, unsuccessfully suggested to Petra that Promise Arizona needed to get involved in the recall. Each time she was told no. When Alex questioned Petra's decision, it had nothing to do with whether we had a candidate or a winning strategy. Petra's response, Alex said, became more personal: "I don't want to be cattle and just have bodies that go to support someone else's thing."

Despite the effort of young organizers to steer Promise Arizona in a different direction, the conversation did not translate into action. Alex felt the recall provided a sense of hope. "Wow, this could be something historic that we can actually do," she said. "Given all the bumps along the way and how heavy each failed fight felt, we needed something we could win now. The Pearce recall was a glimmer of hope. We had just been doing voter registration for registration's sake. We needed to show people now that they could make a difference."

After Jerry Lewis declared his candidacy, I reached out again to Petra in August, expecting to hear some long-awaited excitement and enthusiasm. She still refused to commit. Apparently, she and her leaders still needed to meet Jerry before making a final decision.

A bit frustrated, I told her, "Jerry is the candidate. I have never met Jerry and do not plan on meeting him until we win. We did not pick the candidate and neither will you. Our Republican allies have vetted Jerry already and we are all on board."

Jerry did not need or want our public endorsements, but he certainly wanted and needed our help—especially with the potentially decisive Latino vote.

Phil Austin, a respected Latino Republican lawyer in Mesa, arranged a meet and greet between Promise Arizona and Jerry at his law office. Raquel, impressed with Jerry's overall persona, remembered, "Jerry was just a good person. So honest, so kind. And Jerry had courage." She was a bit frustrated it had taken so long to get to this point.

Following that meeting, Promise Arizona began having conversations locally and with the CCC about what their role could be if they decided to get involved.

Those deliberations turned into action after September 9, when Pearce's allies launched the campaign of Olivia Cortes. Promise Arizona leaders knew they could no longer sit on the sidelines and watch a Pearce-loving Latina be used to confuse and divide the Latino vote.

"Olivia Cortes was another agitational moment for us," Raquel said. "We needed to be the organization out there reaching out to Latino voters, educating them about Cortes being a sham candidate and why they needed to vote for Jerry."

Another key member of the Latino engagement team was Reyna Montoya, a young Dreamer born in Tijuana, Mexico, who lived with her family in Pearce's district. The news of the Pearce recall affirmed her belief that she and her family were not alone. "Finally," she said, "there were good people out there doing something to fight back. This energized me and I watched and waited with much anticipation for an opportunity to get involved."

Reyna was a full-time student at Arizona State University. The defeat of the DREAM Act, the passage of Pearce's SB 1070, and the restrictions on financial support for undocumented college students deeply impacted Reyna and her peers. Something needed to be done to stop the avalanche of hate against immigrants.

Because she was undocumented, Reyna could not collect signatures. Only citizens eligible to vote could circulate recall petitions, but Reyna knew this would be the perfect opportunity to make a difference. As a leader with Youth in Education and Action, Reyna worked with Promise Arizona to recruit high school and college students to canvass neighborhoods in Mesa, especially Latino voters who were not registered or who rarely showed up to vote. Reyna's whole family got involved. "Because we lived in Mesa, we were able to help Promise Arizona connect with our network of grassroots leaders. When they needed an office for the campaign, my dad, through his contacts, got us free office space right there on the corner of Country Club and Southern."

Despite the long delay, and with only fifty days before the election, Promise Arizona agreed to spearhead the Latino engagement field operation and held their first training session for volunteers on September 19. Rudy invited me to speak to the young Latino activists about what we had done to get to this moment—a historic campaign to remove the author of SB 1070 from power. "It took us a few months," Rudy said, "to realize that the recall was real, that Promise Arizona needed to mobilize the Latino vote, and that by doing so we could also build and strengthen Promise Arizona."

Many of the volunteers who attended that session were Latino high school students eager to get involved. After I gave some remarks about the recall, Rudy immediately transitioned to what he does best—training. He introduced the group to the five Cs of voter outreach and community engagement—Connect, Context, Change, Commit, and Catapult. This would be their strategy as they knocked on doors and talked to Latino voters.

Promise Arizona was now committed to getting Jerry elected and activating a new generation of young Latino leaders. About halfway through the training, I slipped out and headed back to our office feeling confident that the campaign to reach some 5,000 to 7,000 Latino voters was in good hands. Citizens for a Better Arizona could now focus all of our resources on reaching the more than 10,000 Mesa voters that signed the recall petition and their household members, which pushed our voter universe to about 20,000.

Informed Latino voters—Latinos who followed the news of Arpaio's raids, SB 1070, and the rise of the Tea Party—knew Republicans were pushing the anti-immigrant agenda. They knew enough to express concern about Jerry's candidacy. At their doors, a typical response went something like this: "Let me get this straight ... After all the mess the Republicans got us in with the likes of Arpaio, Pearce, and SB 1070, you want us to now vote for a Republican? Aren't the Republicans the bad guys?"

"Our community was more sophisticated than we thought," Rudy observed. "We had to separate the greater Republican Party agenda from Jerry and remind them that this was an anti-Pearce vote, not a pro-Republican vote."

The reaction from Latino voters varied from "very informed" to "no clue" about the special recall election. As Raquel collected stories from the field she realized, "Because of SB 1070, people outside of the country knew about Pearce, yet people in his own district still had no idea who he was."

Alex, after leaving Promise Arizona, volunteered to knock on doors. She, too, was amazed at how disconnected Latino voters were from everyday politics. One voter told Alex, "No one has ever come to my house. I didn't know Pearce was the author of SB 1070 and president of the senate." But the visit had a profound impact: The woman completed her mail-in ballot right there in front of Alex and handed it to her. (Arizona's election rules at that time permitted citizens to vote by mail and allowed anyone to return completed, signed, and sealed ballots.) It was the first time this person had ever cast a ballot. These types of conversations were special—"crossover" moments—when a volunteer, through direct voter engagement, helps strangers cross over from being private residents to becoming public citizens by exercising their right to vote.

Promise Arizona's decision to get involved with the special recall election also helped unify the fragmented Latino political community. Each time Alex came out to volunteer she observed, "The split between Reform Immigration for America and Dreamer groups gradually dissolved as these groups came back together to focus their energy on the special election." By working in tight office spaces—phone banking every night, walking precincts, sharing rides—these groups became united in their efforts to take down the author of SB 1070.

Promise Arizona's presence provided the right platform and space for Latino youth of all backgrounds to contribute in a meaningful way. Volunteers came from as far away as New York, and others as close as Westwood High School in Mesa, to be part of the final push. Promise Arizona became a hub for young people to learn how to lead, how to conduct trainings, how to cut precinct walk packets, how to engage new and reluctant voters, and how to transform their personal stories into public power.

Volunteers such as Pedro Lopez drove vans from Phoenix to Mesa filled with students; Lydia Carrion cooked hot meals for the volunteers and "donated" two of her young adult children, Ruth and Jaro, to knock on doors. Promise Arizona became a place where young Latino activists and more established Latino political leaders could come together for the higher cause of defeating Pearce.

For these young emerging leaders, this fight was real. It was about protecting them and their families. One such leader was Yolanda "Yoly" Medina.[1]

Yoly, a student at Carl Hayden High School in west-central Phoenix, volunteered to be a team leader. A Dreamer from Durango, Mexico, Yoly came to the United States at the age of three with her mother. She was unaware of her undocumented status until she was asked for her social security number in high school as part of an application for a special leadership program. Undaunted by this discovery, Yoly plowed ahead and participated in other leadership programs that did not require a social security number. By the time she was a junior in high school—and following the passage of SB 1070 that resulted in her older brother self-deporting—Yoly was on fire to do something. She recruited more than thirty classmates to jump in a van a few times a week after school to knock on doors in Mesa, more than 20 miles east of their high school.

The impact of these young people's action was immediate and profound.

"I remember one woman could not find her ballot," Yoly said. "She invited me in to help her search for it and we found it in the *cajon* (drawer). Another person threw his ballot in the dumpster, so we went dumpster diving and found it. Both voters filled out their ballots right then and there and gave them to me to turn in."

This type of voter engagement cannot happen by spending millions of dollars on TV ads, radio spots, mailers, and other slick social media strategies. It only happens through face-to-face conversation—conversation that is intentional, agitational, and focused.

---

[1] In 2020 Yoly served as 2020 Census Coordinator for ONE Arizona—an organization committed to improve the lives of Arizonans, especially people of color and young people, by building a culture of civic participation.

Yoly's most memorable story occurred on election night, minutes before the polls closed. She knocked on a door, a woman answered, and Yoly asked if Jesus was home. The woman said, "*Sí como no, un momento* (Of course, one minute)," and went to get Jesus.

When she returned, she said, "*El está dormiendo* (He's sleeping)."

Still angry about how her brother's forced return to Mexico and how his absence took a tremendous emotional toll on their mother, Yoly was not about to be denied. With only ten minutes until the polls closed, she channeled the pain, anger, and frustration of all those who had suffered under SB 1070 and screamed, "Jeeessssuuusss! Despiertate! Ya es tiempo. Necesitamos tu voto! Jesssuusss, despiertate por favor! (Jesus! Wake up! The time has arrived. We need your vote! Jesus! Wake up! Please!)"

Yoly knew she had no time to move on to other homes. This was her last door-knock of the election. Yoly continued to scream out Jesus's name. Finally, the door opened, and there stood Jesus, half asleep but ready to go. "*A dónde Vamos?* (Where are we going?)" he asked.

"A votar! (To vote!)" Yoly shouted, pulling Jesus by his arm. They arrived two minutes before the poll closed—just in time to line up to cast a vote against Pearce.

Rudy and other experienced campaigners flew in to help with the effort. Rudy described it as, "The first time there was a convergence of different communities coming together, having solidarity, around the belief that things might be different this time. I hadn't seen something like this ever—a political campaign where unions, grassroots volunteers, Republicans and Democrats, Latino groups like Promise Arizona, and mostly White retirees were all aligned and working together."

For me, personally, I needed Promise Arizona all in because the Latino establishment needed someone they knew and trusted to facilitate their participation. And that person was not me. Latino politicians, such as United States House Representatives Ed Pastor and Raul Grijalva, never returned our calls for support, or reached out to me, or Citizens for a Better Arizona, during the recall campaign.

The only time I spoke to Congressman Pastor occurred unexpectedly in his Washington, DC, office, during the summer trip I took with my daughters. I stopped by Pastor's office to see my old friend, Laura Campos, who I had worked with on several projects in the late 1990s. She was now working as a senior advisor to Pastor and had arranged a special tour of the Capitol for my daughters.

When I was just about to leave, the door to Pastor's private office suddenly opened and Pastor invited me and my daughters into his office. Pastor was very welcoming and warm to all of us. As my daughters walked around his office, Pastor called me over to a table with maps spread out on them.

"Randy, take a look at these," Pastor said. "They are drafts of the redistricting maps for the new congressional districts in Arizona. You should consider running for this one (District 9) in 2012." I thanked Pastor for thinking of me, but I knew my brand of politics was much too progressive for that district—designed to be more of a swing district. The only congressional seat that best represented my strong progressive views was Pastor's seat—one of the safest Latino congressional seats in the country. And given that we were right in the middle of the recall fight, running for Congress was no longer on my to-do list.

Petra knew all the established Latino politicians personally and had worked with many of them. The three years I had spent in Arizona leading up to the recall were nothing compared to Petra's multigenerational ties. Her decision to join the campaign fifty days before Election Day attracted and unleashed volunteers, money, elected leaders, and donations of all sorts that probably would not have been utilized or available had Promise Arizona chosen to sit out this fight. Its entry into the fray resulted in the largest Latino volunteer effort to educate, engage, and mobilize the Latino vote in Mesa's history. For decades, Latinos in safe red Republican districts such as District 18 had been ignored or taken for granted. However, this election would be different.

For fifty straight days, Latino voters felt the love and attention of hundreds of volunteers who finally came to their neighborhoods, came to their *casas* (homes), knocked on their doors, and said, "We need your vote!"

Promise Arizona followed our lead and pursued a more aggressive approach at the doors with Latino voters by encouraging them to complete their mail-in ballots and offering to carry them to the election office. Each night, between Citizens for a Better Arizona's paid field campaign and Promise Arizona's volunteer operation, hundreds of ballots were completed and collected simply because we showed up and asked for their vote and their ballot. There was nothing so rewarding as seeing our canvassers and volunteers return to the office with four, five, eight, or ten ballots—from newly registered voters who supported Jerry.

Promise Arizona not only woke up Jesus, but its grassroots efforts woke up plenty of Marias, Joses, Jaimes, Lydias, Carmens, and Fidels—who, but for Promise Arizona's campaign, would have remained inactive, ignored or, even worse, invisible.

CHAPTER 25

The Perfect Alignment

When you see something that is not right, not just, not fair, you
have a moral obligation to say something. To do something.
~ John Lewis, US Congressman

As we headed into the final push of the election, there was an attempt to bring all the Latino groups together with Citizens for a Better Arizona to coordinate our field campaign. Despite the best efforts of well-established leaders like Tommie Espinoza from La Raza Development Fund to get us all on the same page, we agreed to work independently of one another. One deal-killer involved setting up an elaborate check-in system of conference calls and other meetings, which did not interest me. We had gotten this far without a single conference call and I was not about to jump on calls with folks who had just arrived. I was willing to meet as needed, but we all knew what had to be done in the final forty-five days—voter contact, voter contact, voter contact.

I also was reluctant to share our database of the more than 1,500 Latino voters who had signed the recall petition. We believed these voters needed to be touched as many times as possible. Our paid and volunteer canvassing teams had been in contact with these voters for more than eight months; their life experiences as teachers, nurses, school administrators, and retired professionals gave them a tremendous amount of credibility at the doors and on the phones. Outsourcing our universe of voters—Latinos, Whites, Democrats, Republicans, independents—to any other field operation was not going to happen.

When it came to our field campaign, Citizens for a Better Arizona had the basics covered—a fully-funded ground campaign with twenty-five paid canvassers and a database of more than three hundred volunteers to pull from for our nightly phone banking operation and daily door-to-door canvassing. Domingo Garcia, our main donor from Texas, suggested we run 30-second TV ads on local cable stations. No one expected us to have the resources for that, and the psychological impact alone on the Pearce team would be worth the investment.

Domingo offered to fund the entire media strategy, from ad production to ad placement. He connected me with Laura Barberena, owner of Viva Politics, a political consulting firm in San Antonio, Texas. I met Laura at the US Hispanic Leadership Conference back in the late 1990s, but we had never worked together on a campaign. Laura became our go-to person for opposition research and any other materials we needed, such as door hangers and other get-out-the-vote pieces. Laura, who worked on our response when the Olivia Cortes scandal broke, would now oversee all aspects of our paid media strategy.

Laura grew up in a household somewhat divorced from politics in San Antonio. Her father was Mexican immigrant and her mother had not finished high school. But Laura's parents believed strongly in education, which propelled her to obtain a doctorate in communication studies with an emphasis on political rhetoric and language at the University of Texas. She also studied film and worked in the ad agency of a former speechwriter for Jesse Jackson. Laura entered the business side of politics during the Clinton/Gore reelection campaign in 1996. As creative director, she produced all the TV, newspaper, and radio ads for Hispanic outreach.

Laura loved the idea of taking down Pearce but did not think much of our chances. "Arizona had not been known as the home of Latino politics—not necessarily a hub of Latino power," she said.

It stood in contrast to California, where Governor Pete Wilson in 1994 used an anti-immigrant statewide ballot initiative, Proposition 187, to resurrect his failing campaign. Although Wilson and Proposition 187 prevailed, that fight transformed Latino voter engagement in California and ushered in a new era of Democratic progressive politics. Today in California—a state that elected governors such as Richard Nixon and Ronald Reagan—it is nearly impossible for any Republican to win a statewide race due to the growth and activation of the Latino vote. Arizona, meanwhile, had yet to mobilize the political potential and power of its fastest-growing ethnic group—Latinos.

I argued that SB 1070 could do for Arizona's Latinos what Proposition 187 did for Latinos in California. However, it was not going to happen unless we relentlessly and unpredictably took on key anti-Latino leaders. Aware of how Pearce and Arpaio targeted Latinos, Laura enthusiastically responded to our call for help. She developed an ad aimed at Republicans that contrasted Pearce's extravagant lifestyle with his decision to cut funds and programs that benefitted children. Using the image of a gift box opening up with balloons and special gifts from lobbyists, Pearce was portrayed in the worst light possible for a far right, rule of law, Tea Party Republican.

The message said: "With all the gifts that Russell Pearce has received from lobbyists and special interest groups, you would think every day was his birthday: special football tickets, special trips, stays in luxury hotels, and even chauffeured car service. Meanwhile, back in Mesa, there was no party for our children. As the leader of the state senate, Pearce cut $450 million in education funding and he voted to eliminate children's health insurance, leaving 36,000 kids without access to affordable health care. Arizona, we deserve better. Let's tell Russell Pearce this party is over."

The stark contrast of Pearce riding in limousines with the harsh reality of children struggling in public schools and poor children being denied health care struck a nerve with a lot of mainstream Republican voters. We didn't need to convince them all. We only needed enough to divide the Republican base so Democrats, independents, and an energized base of Latino voters could swing the election. Laura's addition to our team provided us everything we needed for the final sprint to Election Day. We were firing on all cylinders: door-knocking, phones, TV, and social media ads working together to grow our anti-Pearce voting bloc.

At the doors, our strategy was about communicating our core message within seconds. "Can we count on you to vote Russell Pearce out of office?" If they said no, nothing else mattered. If they said yes, we then pivoted to, "Have you heard of Jerry Lewis? Jerry is the most viable candidate standing up to Pearce. Jerry cares about job creation and education. Can we count on you to vote for Jerry?" We ended with, "Have you heard of Olivia Cortes? She is a fake candidate; a vote for Cortes is a vote for Pearce."

We asked, more like instructed, our supporters to sign up for the Permanent Early Voter List, so ballots would be mailed to their homes. We could then come by later to pick them up. In a special election, with only one race on the ballot, most of the votes would be cast by mail. This process transformed the act of voting from a single Election Day event to a three-week experience of chasing, contacting, reminding, assisting, and encouraging our supporters to cast their ballots.

We simplified the message even more on the T-shirts our paid canvassing team wore in the field. Inside an outline of the state of Arizona was the message: "Citizens for a Better Arizona, Official Recall Ballot, Vote for One." We then listed each of the candidates as such:

- Russell Pearce – Mean Guy
- Olivia Cortes – Withdrawn
- Jerry Lewis – Nice Guy, Only Choice

We placed a check mark next to Jerry's name. I wanted the message so simple that if our canvassers forgot their rehearsed script, they could just show voters their T-shirts. Most of the voters we spoke to loved the shirts, and the message cut through all the deceptive tactics by Pearce and the misleading statements about Jerry.

Our full-time paid canvassing team consisted of individuals from eighteen to seventy-three years of age. What seventy-three-year-old would sign up for a job to knock on doors to defeat Pearce? Someone like Celia Arambula. As a child, Celia went to jail with her mother to stand up for mine workers in New Mexico. Celia's mother appeared in the movie *Salt of the Earth*. In the scene where the mine workers were informed of the injunction that prohibited the men from picketing the coal company, she replied, "That injunction may stop our men from picketing, but it says nothing about us women. We can take over the picket line."

Celia smiled at the memory. "As kids, we loved going to the picket line with our signs to march for justice. And when they finally arrested us and put us in jail, we had our little tin cups and we banged them against the bars." Celia's thirst for justice, her certain kind of fire, had been cultivated at an early age by her parents and the miners' strike.

Her fire burned bright again in 1972. At that time, Cesar Chavez, leader of the United Farm Workers of America started a fast in South Phoenix at Santa Rita Hall.

Celia stopped by to meet Chavez. Inspired by Chavez's fast, Celia quit her job and joined the union, earning $7 per week as a full-time organizer. "Cesar had so much respect and love for people," she said. "He had a magnetic presence." Celia spent over four years organizing support for the nationwide grape boycott. Eventually, family obligations forced her to return to a more stable line of work in hospital administration in the Phoenix area.

But even at seventy-three, her fire for justice still burned. When Celia heard about the recall, she had to get involved, "Here was a man that was racist. Someone had to light the match of justice. And it was you, Randy, the rabble-rouser. I really respected you and thought you were coming from a good place."

With her tiny frame, short hair, infectious energy, and flawless command of Spanish and English, Celia T-shirted up and hit the pavement. She refused to get caught up in anyone's anger, frustration, or hate, "When someone slammed the door, I would say, 'God bless you.' I always kept a peaceful presence no matter what they said. And I told myself, 'I am Shirley Temple *with* the dimples.'"

Because of people like Celia, thousands of voters requested mail-in ballots. Most importantly, we picked up close to 2,000 ballots at the doors—signed, sealed and ready for delivery. We referred to some of them as "garbage" ballots. We literally helped voters comb through their garbage or recycling bins to locate their ballots, which they sometimes tossed in the trash, because they were unaware of the importance of their vote. Once located, they'd fill them out, seal the envelopes, and give them to us to drop-off. But for our involvement, these citizens would not have voted.

On one occasion, volunteer Dan O'Neal called a voter in possession of three ballots waiting to be mailed. Dan asked if she and the other two people in her household had voted. Not yet, he was told. Dan repeated the pitch about the importance of the election and their votes. She told him to swing by the house in an hour to pick up her ballot. To Dan's surprise, when he arrived at the voter's home, he did not have to knock on the door. Not just one, but all three ballots were pinned to the door. And just like that, three more votes for Jerry.

Our field efforts also benefitted greatly from Pearce's mistakes and ill-advised strategies. For someone who bragged about being 16–0 when it came to elections, Pearce and his team continued to overestimate their support and underestimate our ability to mount a serious challenge to his base of power. His team continued to attack anyone and everyone—liberals, conservatives, Republicans and yes even Mormons in his own stake and ward—who supported Jerry. They even created a "Wall of Shame" website, where they posted photos of Jerry's supporters who volunteered with Citizens for a Better Arizona. Many of our volunteers, such as Amanda Zill and Julie Jorgensen, who had never been involved in politics, cringed at the thought of being at the center of any political attack. And yet there they were, being publicly shamed by the Pearce camp.

For Julie, the fight to recall and remove Pearce was personal. Julie moved to Mesa with her family in 1978 and attended Mesa High School. She became an English as a Second Language teacher in Mesa. As the mother of four daughters, Julie believed strongly in public schools and the importance of assisting those most in need. Before SB 1070, Julie and the leaders of Mesa public schools' Family Tree Program[2] invited Pearce to see their program. In need of additional funding, they thought a visit by the state senator would be helpful. However, Julie said, when Pearce walked in the door and saw all the Hispanic women participants, he said, "I don't like these people." From that moment forward, Pearce did anything he could to hurt the program, and once SB 1070 passed, students had to prove they were legal residents before they could enroll in the classes.

Julie heard Citizens for a Better Arizona was collecting signatures at the library. "When I arrived, I was so excited to see others who shared my dislike of Pearce and his policies. In the LDS Church we are taught to love our neighbor and follow Jesus. I knew the recall was David versus Goliath and clearly a long shot. I had no idea how mean and tough it could be, and the tricks people would play."

---

[2] The Family Tree Program provided classes to help parents learn English, acquire their GED, develop computer skills and learn how to help their child be successful in school. The program is now called The Family Literacy Program.

A lifelong Republican and devout Mormon, Julie was the target of undeserved criticism and personal attacks by other members of her church who believed strongly in Pearce and what he represented. One Sunday, a woman at church approached her, laughed in Julie's face and said, "How could you associate with someone like Randy Parraz, a communist?"

In the LDS Church, members must attend their neighborhood church and cannot just switch from one ward to another. Consequently, Julie had to face her detractors every weekend.

Julie remained steadfast in her commitment. "I am a person of faith and I honestly prayed a lot about it," she said. "I had a good feeling that somehow it was going to work out. That helped me too. I felt like what I was doing was right. I was not just some rebel trying to steer up trouble."

Pearce showed a propensity to bring trouble on himself. Only a few weeks before the election, he held a rally at Hohokam Stadium, the spring training facility for the Chicago Cubs baseball team that seated more than 10,000 people. Brenda Rascon, one of our volunteers and a proud "Wall of Shame" member, was sent to gather intelligence and take photos. "When I walked in, I was nervous, especially since my face had been posted on websites as a Jerry supporter," she said. "The stadium was empty—maybe 200 people sprinkled in behind home plate.

Sheriff Arpaio showed up and talked mostly about himself. His message, Brenda said, was that Pearce needed to win so Arpaio could continue his reign of profiling Latinos and harassing immigrants.

"The stadium had a feeling of death—like a sinking ship. The Tea Party was prominently displayed and Pearce's close ally and consultant, Constantine Querard, paced around the place waiting for more supporters to join them. It never happened."

The poorly attended event proved to be a turning point for all of us. Like pulling back the curtain on the Wizard of Oz to expose the deeds of a small, cowardly man using gimmicks to project a powerful and intimidating presence, the rally conveyed weakness, disorganization, and even desperation. It is always best to have a venue slightly smaller than the expected turnout, but 200 people in a stadium that seated over 10,000 was a complete and utter disaster. The mighty, powerful, and invincible senate president had just exposed publicly what only a few of us had believed since January—Pearce could be defeated in his backyard with the right strategy, message, and candidate.

While Pearce kept trying to explain away the Fiesta Bowl scandal, the poor showing at Hohokam Stadium, and the Cortes sham campaign, Jerry continued to put out a positive and straightforward message. In an email message titled "Stand up to Bullies," Jerry responded to the attacks and outlined the purpose of his candidacy: "As you know, I am NOT part of some carefully orchestrated left-wing plot! I have been recruited and supported by many conservative Republicans whom you probably know. I don't plan to make a career of politics."

Jerry promised, too, not to take a taxpayer-funded pension—nor even gifts, event tickets, meals, or trips. "Most of all," he concluded, "I will work each day to do what is right regardless of the consequences, and if I make a mistake, I will readily acknowledge it." Jerry made a point to reject the type of politician Pearce had become, and did so with grace, humility, and kindness.

Three weeks before the election, Chad Snow attended the final District 18 Republican precinct committee meeting at which Pearce was scheduled to speak. Chad had never attended a legislative district meeting and was reminded that he might be wading into hostile waters. When he pulled into the parking lot, news trucks were lined up to cover Pearce's remarks. Chad walked into a packed room with more than 200 people, most of them Pearce supporters. Chad stayed quiet for most of the meeting until Pearce went on a rant about how he had been called derogatory names by the recall supporters. Pearce claiming to be a victim was just too much for Chad to stomach.

He stood and claimed the floor, "Hello, my name is Chad Snow and I am chairman of Citizens for a Better Arizona. You have called us communists, fascists, open borders cartel members, anarchists, and thugs. So, by your own admission, you can't beat us on our arguments, so you just call us names."

Before Chad could continue, the crowd booed him down and yelled for the "outsider" to leave. Shaken by the nasty reception, Chad nonetheless stayed calm and remained seated until the meeting ended. Emotions ran high the entire meeting, and by the time Chad left, he was even more convinced of how tough Pearce and his ilk made it for even like-minded Republicans to be respectful to those with differing opinions.

Chad called me on his drive home. "We better win this thing."

"Why's that?"

"Because if we don't, based on what I saw tonight, all hell is going to break loose if Pearce survives this. These guys really do believe that we are being 'invaded' and Mexicans are to blame for all our problems. We need to end this now."

I assured Chad that our chances still looked good and reminded him that there was a lot of activity happening beyond the reach of Citizens for a Better Arizona's work. Promise Arizona was spearheading Latino outreach. Public Campaign, with a core strategy of limiting special interest money in politics, signed on, too, contributing more than ten mail pieces. The special recall election quickly evolved into the first competitive race of Pearce's career. And he could not have been more unprepared for it.

Almost every attack Pearce made against us exposed another weakness in his campaign. They accused us of being financially supported by national organizations, labor unions and billionaire liberals. But Citizens for a Better Arizona's official financial report filed at the end of October showed 997 individuals contributed more than $25 to our political committee. This figure did not include hundreds of others who contributed $25 or less and whose names did not have to be reported. More than 90 percent of our contributors lived in Arizona. In Mesa, more people donated to *recall* Pearce than those who donated to *elect* him in 2010.

With only five days to go, more than 11,000 citizens had returned their ballots. Meanwhile, we continued to expand our field campaign to reach thousands of voters who expressed their intention to remove Pearce from office.

On the weekend before Election Day, Don Stapley, a Republican and former county supervisor who endorsed Jerry on day one of his campaign, joined Chad to walk Pearce's neighborhood. Don had known Pearce for over thirty years, and he knew many of the voters in Pearce's neighborhood who had voted for Don many times. As they walked from house to house, Chad asked Don why he thought Pearce was the way he was.

Don said, "Guys like you and me who went on missions with the church had a chance to live among other cultures. We learned to love people different from ourselves. We learned to value other cultures and see that some cultures are superior to ours in some ways. A guy like Pearce did not do that. He's lived in this perfect, all-White, Norman-Rockwell community. So, when these brown people move in and become part of the community, he uses words and phrases such as 'being invaded' and being 'under attack.' Pearce really believes his way of life is threatened. He never really learned to appreciate those differences."

As they worked their way through the neighborhood, Chad was struck by how much this special election had divided the community. Some spouses were voting for different candidates and even some of Pearce's relatives were supporting Jerry. A few families showed off their divided households by placing campaign signs for both candidates in their yards.

And when the bishop for the Pearce family's ward posted a Jerry Lewis sign in his yard, Pearce's wife LuAnne, refused to speak to the bishop for the rest of the campaign—even though her role as president of a women's auxiliary for the church required that the two work together. The LDS Church took no position on the election, though members, regardless of their leadership position, were free to support either candidate or no candidate. Despite the divisiveness of the special election, it did not divide the LDS Church. It merely highlighted the diversity of beliefs that already existed around hot-button issues: immigration, public schools, and health care for the poor.

On Election Day, volunteers made calls, knocked on doors, and stood in front of most polling places. I stayed near our office to handle any last-second problems or breaking news. We asked our volunteers to be on the lookout for Pearce. Wherever Pearce showed up, we wanted our volunteers standing right next to him, battling for every vote. Chad took the day off and joined our get-out-the-vote push. He drove from one polling place to another, thanking and encouraging all our volunteers to hang in there for a few more hours. He passed one polling place with close to a hundred people in line, about 95 percent of them Latino. He thought, "How could Pearce represent these voters?"

Later in the day, Chad arrived at a polling location with our volunteers Saul Solis and his wife Lupe stationed out front. As Chad approached, Saul smiled and could not wait to share the news. "You arrived just in time. Pearce is over there, passing out his materials. We haven't said anything to him yet."

Chad, always the diplomat, walked up to Pearce and extended his hand. Pearce, unable to decline Chad's kind gesture, shook Chad's hand. Chad attempted to defuse the situation. "This is nothing personal against you or your family. We have tried to keep all the personal stuff out of it. I just disagree with your politics."

Pearce disagreed. "It is personal. You are trying to take me out of my job. I appreciate the gesture. But it was really Randy Parraz that brought this on."

Pearce's obsession with my role in the recall blinded him to the real truth as to why he was now standing in front of a polling place campaigning after just being elected a year ago. It was Pearce's own behavior, his own actions—not me—that brought this on. Had Pearce not authored SB 1070, the recall never would have happened. I will go even further and say that even with the passage of SB 1070, I probably would not have initiated the recall if Pearce had not become *my* senate president.

Pearce's career became personal to me the moment his Republican colleagues rewarded his extreme behavior by elevating him to the position of senate president. That title legitimized Pearce as a statewide leader and normalized many of his unconstitutional views about immigrants, guns, and law enforcement. For too many years, Republicans lacked the courage to challenge Pearce and Democrats lacked the vision to take him out.

From the moment we launched the recall, the right people and the necessary resources arrived just in time to accomplish the unthinkable. For us to have a chance, we needed a perfect alignment of strategy, message, and choice of candidate.

This snowballed into the largest and most aggressive field campaign Pearce had ever faced. Yet, on the eve of the election, he appeared confident that he would win thanks to his endorsements, large checks from lobbyists, loyal Tea Party followers, and, of course, a challenger who never ran for office. Soon, Pearce, Arpaio, and Brewer would find out that there is a certain kind of fire that no extremist like Pearce could ever put out.

CHAPTER 26

Joy Rising

My feets is tired but my soul is rested.
~ Mother Pollard, Montgomery Bus Boycott activist

"Joy rising." I first heard the phrase during *The Oprah Winfrey Show*. Oprah was describing how she felt when participating in one of the largest flash mobs ever in Chicago. Tens of thousands of people danced to "I Gotta Feeling," performed by the Black Eyed Peas. Although I had experienced joyful moments in my life, I had not felt the energy she talked about—a vibration that lifts you physically, emotionally, and spiritually into another dimension. On that transformative night—November 8, 2011—I, too, experienced the phenomena of *joy rising*.

I asked Mike Wright if we could use the Wright House again for what we hoped would be an election night victory party.

He responded, "If this party is anything like the one we had back on May 31 when we turned in the recall petitions, then let's party—again!"

I assured him that given all that we had done, this party would indeed be historic.

Polls and nightly field reports showed us slightly ahead, and the day before the election, I received calls from reporters, asking about our plans once the polls closed. After I confirmed that we would be gathering at the Wright House, at least three reporters asked me the same question:

"Do you know by chance where Pearce and his supporters are gathering to watch the election night returns?"

Fighting back my desire to laugh out loud, I remained calm and responded with, "Well, if by now you do not know where Pearce and his supporters are holding their election night party, then there won't be much for them to celebrate come tomorrow night."

I could not believe it. How could one of the most powerful politicians in the state not have some type of party planned? The Pearce campaign appeared to be admitting defeat before the polls opened on Election Day.

Our side, though, was planning for a victorious outcome. We invited Promise Arizona, the Arizona Dream Act Coalition, and other organizations that had focused exclusively on the Latino vote to join us. Soon after the polls closed, young people poured in to the Wright House and gathered on the back patio. As music played in the background, people walked in from all sides of the building, packed the main room, and waited for the results.

Meanwhile, I headed to a nearby hotel to shower and change before the party. Ignacio Hernandez (Nacho), my best friend and college room-mate, had just flown in from Sacramento for the final get-out-the-vote push. He had been following our recall campaign from California and wanted to join us for the final results. I called Chad and asked him to swing by the hotel with his wife Rachel so we could drive over to the Wright House together.

As Nacho drove the car to the hotel, I relaxed. I knew our movement to make Arizona better was not over, but this campaign was. Pearce's fate had been determined. The polls had closed.

When Chad arrived at the hotel, I told him, "If we win, if Pearce goes down tonight, our lives will not be the same."

"What do you mean?"

"When you go through a campaign like this, it changes both how you see the world and how the world sees you. Campaigns like this redefine what is possible and inspire others to dream even bigger," I said. "For the first time in my career as an organizer, I've witnessed citizens, immigrants, conservatives and liberals, diehard Republicans and Democrats and Christians of all faiths, especially Mormons, come together for a greater purpose.

"If we win tonight, we will alter the course of history for the entire state of Arizona. This will be a real-life example of what it means to put country, or in this case, state, before party."

My eyes welled up with tears. Nacho yelled out, "Let's go. The polls have been closed for over thirty minutes and we should be getting some preliminary numbers soon."

My Election Day challenges weren't over. I grabbed the keys from Nacho and we jumped in the car, with Chad and Rachel following. The City of Mesa's street repaving project was delaying traffic up and down Main Street. A drive that should have taken two minutes was now taking fifteen. I kept looking at my phone. I needed to be at the party when the results came in. The traffic inched forward a little more. Nacho checked the county recorder's website. Still, no results.

A bit desperate, I called Ken Chapman. As the executive director of the Maricopa County Democratic Party, Ken usually had access to election information at the county recorder's office moments before results became public.

Ken picked up the call immediately, and before I could say anything, he blurted out, "Motherfucker, Motherfucker! It's 52 to 48! It's 52 to 48!"

Ken was at the recorder's office and had just seen the initial results that showed Jerry ahead of Pearce. My call arrived at that instant.

"What? Repeat that again. What do you say—52 to 48?"

"Lewis is up, 52 to 48. And it doesn't look like this is going to get any better for Pearce. He is done. You did it!"

For an instant, time stopped. *He is done* echoed in my head. A few months ago, no one thought a newcomer like Jerry, someone who had never run for elected office, could defeat someone as powerful as Russell Pearce. And just eleven months earlier, no one thought a small band of committed activists, mostly retirees, could recall a sitting senate president, a Republican, in one of the reddest districts in Arizona. Now it was all but certain. Joy Rising!

"Ken, I love you, man! I am heading to the party now. Gotta go!"

Nacho heard the whole conversation, but he seemed more concerned than elated. "If Ken has this information, then the press will soon have it as well and it won't be long before they post the numbers on TV. We need to get to the party *now*. Let's go!"

I agreed, but I could not sit still. I slammed on the brakes, jumped out of the car, and ran back to Chad's car and banged on his window, yelling, "52 to 48! We are up 52 to 48!"

Traffic began to move, and drivers honked their horns, but I continued to stand there in the street leaning into Chad's window shouting, "Pearce is going down!"

I motioned for Chad to roll down his window and continued to shout, "I just got off the phone with Ken. Right now, we are up 52–48!"

It took a second for it to sink in. Chad then jumped out of his car and we hugged it out right there in the middle of the street. As I ran back to my car, I yelled again, "Pearce is going down!"

At this point, people were yelling at us. I jumped back into the driver's seat of my car and rushed to get us to the Wright House. By the time we pulled into the parking, close to 400 people were waiting for the results. When I entered the room from the back, and knowing we were already ahead, I felt as if I was floating as I made my way to the podium. The results had not been reported on the big screen yet. I arrived just in time.

I welcomed everyone to the party and thanked them for bringing us to this special moment in Arizona's history. Before I could finish my remarks, one of our volunteers, Fred Barlam, in his distinctively New

York accent, yelled out from the side of the room, "Pearce is losing 54 to 46!" The whole place erupted.

Joy rising!

People began to hug, cry, laugh, and chant "Sí Se Puede!" I had heard activists, musicians, poets, and, of course, Oprah use the phrase "joy rising" but I had never felt the purity and authenticity of that expression until this moment. I felt as if I were one with everyone in the room.

We all experienced *joy rising*.

As I stood at the podium, I looked past the lights from the TV cameras that had arrived by then and took in the faces in the audience. This fight brought together the most diverse group of people I had ever seen engaged in such a righteous cause. I saw children as young as four, Dreamers, and seniors pushing eighty and beyond. I saw Republicans and Democrats and those who rejected both political parties. I saw Latinos, Whites, Blacks, Asians, Native Americans—all beaming with pride. Come tomorrow morning, Arizona would be in the headlines for all the right reasons.

Our long-shot victory unleashed an emotional waterfall from the crowd. Within minutes of the news of Pearce's defeat, someone shouted out from the crowd, "Now let's go after Sheriff Arpaio!" The place erupted again.

I just smiled and stepped back from the podium. Once people experience the feeling of victory, once you help them expand their understanding of what is possible, you cannot ask them to dream smaller or to retreat from a larger fight.

When I arrived in Arizona in summer 2007, no one was talking seriously about going after Arpaio. As an organizer, to hear someone, no longer paralyzed by fear, shout "Let's go after Arpaio" represented the victory within the victory. I came back to the podium and looked in the direction of the comment and shouted back, "Let's just take this evening to enjoy and celebrate this historic outcome: the voters of District 18 have recalled and removed Russell Pearce from office."

I paused as the crowd cheered. I took in the moment, and then I shouted, "And, yes, Arpaio is next!"

The place erupted yet again with everyone hugging and high-fiving as the celebration took on a life of its own. Domingo Garcia, our main donor from Texas who flew in for the party, started popping bottles of champagne. As the champagne circulated, Tom Ryan (our lawyer), Petra Falcon and Raquel Teran from Promise Arizona, and John Loredo and Jeffry Robinson from Public Campaign joined me up front. If we could stop Pearce in Arizona, then we could come together to defeat copycat politicians and laws patterned after Pearce and SB 1070 across the country.

Tears of joy filled the room, and I remember a Latina grandmother crying as she held her granddaughter in her arms and shouted, "*Todo esto es para mi nieta. Sin Pearce, Arizona va a mejorar! Dios te bendiga!* (All this is for my granddaughter. Without Pearce, Arizona will be better! God bless you!)"

At last, the practice of rewarding politicians like Pearce for promoting mean-spirited, harmful, and racist laws had been challenged and defeated. Our movement was built on the idea that ordinary citizens *can* hold their elected officials accountable. When vulnerable communities are attacked, there must be swift consequences, so these laws do not spread to other states and cause other communities to suffer.

It felt surreal to see a dream realized—a dream that Lilia and I spoke of at the Colosseum in Rome. Because we did not have the resources to go after Arpaio in 2011, we needed a different strategy—one that would position us to take on Arpaio in 2012. We needed an adversary big enough to attract volunteers, earned media, and donations, and a campaign small enough to mobilize our collective frustration, anger, and disappointment in a real and meaningful way. Recalling Pearce provided the best strategy to accomplish both objectives. First, recall and remove Pearce, then redirect the power and organization that defeated him onto Arpaio in 2012.

The party continued well past midnight. As I moved through the crowd, a group of Dreamers approached me and asked me to come out back. They had a surprise. I walked with them outside where a large group of young Latino activists wearing bright yellow Promise Arizona T-shirts appeared to be standing in front of something. Citizens for a Better Arizona volunteer Julie Jorgensen then stepped forward, "On my way here to the party I picked up a little something that I thought you might appreciate," she said.

The crowd parted, revealing one of the red four-by-eight-foot anti-recall signs with my photo on it. For the past two hours, people had been signing it and leaving messages. The sign that once served to spread lies and half-truths about me and our recall movement had been transformed into an authentic piece of political liberation artwork. It captured the feelings in real time of those who struggled to make this happen.

Stunned, I pulled Julie aside and asked how she did this so quickly. "I was driving back towards the party after the polls closed. Those signs always made me mad because you were not even in the election. When I tried to take it down, I realized it was tied to the fence with wire."

So, Julie swung by the nearby home of a recall volunteer to borrow some wire cutters. "There I am," she said, "snipping the wires holding the sign to the fence with a police helicopter hovering above us. At this point, I am freaking out since I had never stolen anything in my life!" Julie finished the job and threw the sign in her car.

The police chopper took no action. Once Julie arrived at the party, she took the sign to the backyard for guests to sign. As more people signed, she worried less about stealing it. "I knew then I had done the right thing," she said.

Some of the messages read:

Thank you Union Boss
No More Profiling

No More Racial Prejudice
Future Senator
Brenda Rascon—Not an Outsider
ADAC was here

Someone even signed as "Matt Tolman," the architect of those signs and chairman of Pearce's anti-recall committee. But the best message was scribbled across my forehead in the picture: *"Sí Se Puede!* (Yes we can!)"

As we celebrated Jerry Lewis's victory, I still had not met the man. Tyler Montague, our liaison to Jerry, and I agreed to put that off until after the election. Any contact between us would likely be used by the Pearce campaign to bolster their false narrative that Jerry was merely a puppet of Citizens for a Better Arizona and the recall movement. As the crowd began to thin toward the end of the night, Chad approached me.

"Hey," he said, "Rachel and I are going by Jerry's victory party to say hello and congratulate him. Why don't you and Lilia follow us over there; it's only a few blocks from here." Eager to meet Jerry and curious to see how the other side celebrates, I agreed.

As we approached the front of the home hosting Jerry's party, news trucks were lined up doing live feeds. Cars were parked along the side of the road as far as you could see—some 300 people had turned out to support Jerry. We entered the backyard through the side gate. Other than Tyler, I did not know anyone else at the party.

Earlier in the evening, when the first results flashed up on the screen with Jerry up by eight points, NBC's Brahm Resnik turned to Tyler and said, "That's it. Your guy won."

At that moment, the crowd started chanting "Jerry … Jerry … Jerry," amazed that he emerged as the winner so early in the evening.

Tyler, not ready to declare victory, replied, "I don't know. Let's wait until the next dump of numbers." Tyler also wanted to wait for Pearce to concede.

When Pearce finally came out of his home to speak to the press, he appeared angry and upset. With Arpaio by his side, Pearce declared, "If being recalled is the price for keeping one's promises, then so be it."

Tyler's take: "He looked as if he had been crying. He was mad. He never called Jerry to concede or congratulate him. He was visibly upset and shaken."

New to election night theater, Jerry wasn't sure what to make of all this until reporters told him Pearce's deficit was too large to overcome. Afterward, Jerry said his immediate thought was, "What a great feeling to know that what I believed was right. The effort and sacrifices of many people from many walks of life from different political parties working together to accomplish something that unfortunately had to be accomplished. It was a feeling of relief. Then it really sunk in: 'What do we do now?'"

As I continued to look for Jerry, it felt as if I'd entered "The Twilight Zone" with people looking at me, them knowing who I was, and me looking at them, not knowing a soul in the crowd. I noticed a reporter from Univision asking one of the young Latina volunteers what this victory meant; when she spoke with such passion and conviction, a tear ran down the reporter's cheek. To see someone such as Pearce, who exhibited so much disdain and hate towards Mexican immigrants, fall so decisively had touched all those present—professionals, teachers, volunteers, grandparents and, yes, even reporters.

Finally, I saw Jerry. His back was to me, and he was shaking hands with one of his supporters. I touched him lightly on the shoulder, and when he turned around, I extended my hand. Instead of shaking my hand, Jerry threw his arms around me, gave me a big hug, and said, "Hermano, it is so good to finally meet you! Thank you for all that you did to make this happen. Without you, there is no recall and there definitely is no victory celebration like tonight."

Surprised by Jerry's warmth and brotherly embrace, I asked him how he felt.

Jerry paused for a moment and said, "It feels surreal. I did not realize how quickly things would move once the election was over. I just heard that I am supposed to go down to the Capitol for a meeting first thing tomorrow morning."

Still somewhat shocked that I was standing in the backyard of a Republican's home celebrating the victory of a conservative Republican who I just helped get elected to state senate, I shared one final thought with Jerry. "I cannot even imagine all that you have been through since you decided to run. Thank you, Jerry, for having the courage to run. This night does not happen without *you*."

Then a reporter grabbed Jerry by the arm. Before I left, we hugged again, and I told Jerry we would get together soon. He nodded, "Yes."

As I walked away, I heard the reporter ask, "So, is that the first time you met Randy Parraz?"

We returned to the Wright House to share more stories and to thank more of our volunteers. I did not want that extraordinary night to end.

When I finally got home, I tried but could not sleep so I went to the couch, grabbed my iPad, and scrolled through my Facebook feed. Soon, tears of immense joy rolled down my face as congratulatory messages poured in (shared as written except where English translation is added):

Vicki Evans: You and your intrepid band of above and beyond workers have shown us all that voters can change the course of government!!!!

Janet Higgins: So nice not to be the laughing stock of the nation for once.

Womyn Forward: Citizens for a Better AZ under Randy Parraz leadership were awesome. Despite Pearce's attempts to make this personal about one man, Mr. Parraz stayed on high ground and kept this about the ISSUES and the PEOPLE! Yay for values and integrity!

Linda Tórres: QUE PASA AZ ... "A NEW DAY in AZ," and District 18 ... a positive change for AZ. Thank You—Gracias.

Lisa Hoffman: All I can think of is when the wicked witch of the Wizard of Oz Died. How did that song go? Ding Dong Pearce concedes, Ding Dong the WICKED Pearce concedes. Ding dong Rustys gone ding dong the Wicked Pearce concedes.

Nadia Ramirez: Tonight is a big night. Tonight I'm proud to say my family and I were out there protesting for what is right. Tonight Pearce is the first sitting senate president in the NATION and the FIRST Arizona legislator EVER to lose a recall election. Tonight we must celebrate this victory.

Esther Duran Lumm: Thank you, God!!!! Good over evil ... finally!!

Alison McLeod: It's Russell Pearce Move Out Day!

Mohur Sarah Sidhwa: The elite said it could not be done. They said the ... man was too powerful. They said we were naïve to think it was possible. Yet when something truly evil is happening all good people can unite fight back if they have a leader who is truly excellent. In Randy we have such a leader. He united the right and the left with the center, leaving the cynics scratching their heads.

Eduardo Cadena Cid: si se pudo! si se pudo! gracias sr parraz lo felicito a usted y todo el gran equipo que lo acompana viva arizona!!!!! (yes we did! yes we did! I congratulate you, Mr. Parraz and your great team that worked with you Arizona lives!!!!!)

Sylvia Trujillo: Thank you and the leaders from AZ—when others scoffed that you all were tilting at windmills—you organized. When national figures twiddled their thumbs on the sidelines— you organized. When the rest of the country counted you out and wrote AZ off—you organized. It is a sobering reminder of our individual duty to keep going in the face of overwhelming odds when faced with injustice and a failure of those who control the body politic to pursue higher and nobler causes. I rise in the face of your collective strength.

Karyn Lathan: Thank you Randy for your vision and follow through. I also thank you for keeping the high ground. When the going got tough, you held on with integrity ... and WON! Congratulations. We all win.

Moira Carney: I wondered who that Wizard was, that day I sat in the Senate galley alongside Promise Arizona kids ... but it was Mr. Parraz saying "Look. He can't even get his fellow Republicans to vote with him." Over the last year, many of us were caught muttering to ourselves at the audacity of the multitude of horrible bills introduced by RP. Thankfully, Mr. Parraz, the Wizard, was able to coalesce the rest of us, and guided, prodded, and inspired us to see this Recall Pearce effort through. Some of us gave a little, others seemingly all of their spare time, money, and prayers. To all of us, but especially to Julie, Mary, Amanda, Saúl, Brian, Carolyn, Robert, Dennis, Steve, Lilia, and Randy un abrazo fraternal!

Linda Brown: The MANY triumphed over the MONEY. The people rejected a corrupt politician and said NO to government of, by and for Lobbyists. Randy Parraz, you are a gift.

Jeff DiGregorio: Salud! Your compassion and determination impressed us from the first day we met you, Randy. This is truly an accomplishment—not only one of human rights and dignity, but also of demonstrating to hateful ideologues that they have no place in Arizona leadership roles.

Hedy Trevino: What a wonderful statement. I share those feelings. I have a daughter and granddaughter and other family in Phoenix and I feel that as a result of this ouster the state of Arizona has a brighter future.

Genie Swanstrom: Hurrah!!! Imagine a future without those right-wing extremists in AZ. We need to take back AZ from them. We need humanity and justice and compassion in AZ again

Carlos Galindo-Elvira: Congratulations to Randy Parraz and the countless number of volunteers who knocked on doors, visited with voters, and placed signs in Mesa. Your efforts give new hope to all Arizonans that civility and dignity can and need to coexist in our political process. Let there be no doubt that every vote counts. The outcome clearly shows that every human counts. Thank you.

Laura Rivera: I'm still in awe ... Thx again to Mr. Randy Parraz and ALL of the people (especially all the students) who hit the pavement, going door-to-door, working HARD to get this on the ballot. I'm SOOO HaPpY! I hope Pearce moves to Alabama ...

Maria De La Luz Ortiz Castro: Que tiempos aquellos, creo que fue la unica vez que mire union de los diferentes grupos. Sin duda una noche especial. (I believe this is one of the few times where you see different groups coming together as one. Without doubt this is a special night.)

Reyna A Polanco: Maria dale las GRACIAS A RANDY POR AQUELLOS QUE NO TIENEN VOTO. DIOS LE BENDIGA POR SUS SACRIFICIOS PARA HACER JUSTICIA. (Let's give thanks to Randy and for those that do not have the right to vote. God bless them for their sacrifices to create justice.)

There, in the solitude of my living room, I felt the residue of Pearce's reign of power wash away. What a difference a year makes. In November 2010, I was sitting in this same room watching *Sunday Square Off* and seeing Pearce introduced as the new president of the senate. And now, almost a year later to the day, I was realizing a dream fulfilled.

Before I went to bed, I wiped away the tears and wrote one final thought on my Facebook page: "Last night was a historical night indeed. Thank you all for your comments and words of support. Like you, I am also inspired about what we accomplished. Today marks the beginning of a new era in Arizona politics. The reign of Senate President Russell Pearce has finally come to an end. Let us all lead by example and embrace this historic moment with dignity, humility and civility."

Now I could sleep—"feets tired" and "soul rested."

Photo Section

My father, John Parraz, died at the age of 37, when I was 11 years old. The tragedy shaped who I am today. He had just been appointed special assistant for minority affairs for the Sacramento County Sheriff's Department. *Photo credit: property of Randy Parraz.*

My mother, Inez Parraz. *Photo credit: property of Randy Parraz.*

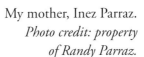

Me and my brothers, left to right, David and John Parraz, in 2005. *Photo credit: property of John Parraz.*

We announce the formation of Citizens for a Better Arizona on January 10, 2011, the first day of Arizona's Legislative Session. *Photo credit: Robert Hasch.*

State Senator Steve Gallardo welcomes Citizens for a Better Arizona to the Capitol, with Barbara Valencia by his side holding the "Stop the Hate" sign. *Photo credit: Robert Hasch.*

Chad Snow, chairman of Citizens for a Better Arizona, explains why
Republicans should be concerned about Russell Pearce's record.
Photo credit: Robert Hasch.

Saul Solis joins former State Senator Maria De La Luz Garcia as they serve
our 21-Day Notice to Senate President Pearce's secretary. Senate Sergeant at
Arms Joe Kubacki looks on in the background. *Photo credit: Robert Hasch.*

Mary Lou Boettcher, seated, Geoff Esposito, holding clipboard, and other volunteers collect signatures at the Mesa Public Library in March 2011. *Photo credit: Randy Parraz.*

Mary Lou Boettcher speaks to the press just before we submit our petitions. *Photo credit: Robert Hasch.*

Chad Snow at the podium, Mary Lou Boettcher, right, and Domingo Garcia, far right, as we gather before turning in the petitions. *Photo credit: Randy Parraz.*

On January 31, 2011, Citizens for a Better Arizona filed the official paperwork to recall Senate President Russell Pearce. Todd Selleck, a resident of Legislative District 18, signs the document to initiate the recall. *Photo credit: Randy Parraz.*

Reporter Howie Fischer, in blue short-sleeved shirt, attempts to interview Mary Lou Boettcher in the lobby of the Senate building on May 31, 2011—the last day to submit the recall petitions. *Photo credit: Robert Hasch.*

The unveiling of our resolution to recall Senate President Pearce in the lobby of the Senate building. *Photo credit: Robert Hasch.*

Saul Solis, holding the Arizona flag, and Paul Castaneda, holding the US flag, lead the march over to the secretary of state's office to file our petitions. *Photo credit: Robert Hasch.*

Many children of our supporters participated in the submission of the recall petitions. Although they could not vote nor sign the petition, their presence reminded everyone of the importance of our work. *Photo credit: Randy Parraz.*

Lilia Alvarez and Bob Unferth notarize the final recall petitions at the secretary of state's office. *Photo credit: Robert Hasch.*

Standing room only as Betsy Savino, followed by her husband Don Savino, line-up to turn in our recall petitions. *Photo credit: Robert Hasch.*

Todd Selleck with elections staff person after completing all the official paperwork related to our effort to recall Pearce. *Photo credit: Robert Hasch.*

The historic significance of citizens submitting more than 18,000 recall signatures drew media attention from across the state. *Photo credit: Robert Hasch.*

Candidate Jerry Lewis as he enters the race in July 2011. *Photo credit: Jerry Lewis.*

The chart that shows more citizens signed the petition to recall Pearce in 2011 than voted for voted for him in 2010. *Photo credit: Robert Hasch.*

Tyler Montague, my 'brother from another Mormon mother,' who worked behind the scenes to recruit candidates to defeat Russell Pearce. *Photo credit: Tyler Montague.*

Red Mountain Tea Party President Greg Western enters the secretary of state's office to submit candidate petitions for Olivia Cortes, whose candidacy was designed to draw votes away from Jerry Lewis. *Photo credit: Sara Ryan.*

The mysterious signs that showed up even though candidate
Cortes said she did not pay for them or know who did.
Photo credit: Robert Hasch.

Nancy Unferth, Gladys Angle, and Rachel Golubovich with mail-in
ballots collected by our volunteers during the final push to defeat
Pearce. *Photo credit: Robert Hasch.*

Left to right, Rosie Lopez, John Chiazza, Susie Rainish, Dan O'Neal, Nancy Unferth, and Fred Barlam as they get ready to make phone calls and canvass for Jerry Lewis. *Photo credit: Robert Hasch.*

Left to right, our office support team, Rachel Golubovich and Sara Ryan. *Photo credit: Robert Hasch.*

Failed rally for Russell Pearce at Hohokam Stadium. Fewer than 200 people showed up at a venue that seats 10,000. *Photo credit: Robert Hasch.*

Pearce's own signs were half the size of the ones featuring me. "Keep" is not much of a campaign slogan. *Photo credit: Robert Hasch.*

Left to right, Chad Snow, April Bojorquez, Nicole Macias, Randy Parraz, another volunteer and Carmen Guerrero with mail-in ballots collected the day before the election. *Photo credit: property of Robert Hasch.*

After confirming their support by phone, Dan O'Neal swings by a voter's home to pick up three more ballots for Jerry Lewis. *Photo credit: Robert Hasch.*

Top to bottom, Tom Ryan, Chad Snow, Randy Parraz, and Petra Falcon at the election night celebration. *Photo credit: Robert Hasch.*

Dreamers embracing one another shortly after hearing the news that Pearce had lost. *Photo credit: Robert Hasch.*

Tom Ryan and Domingo Garcia pouring champagne as the celebration continues. *Photo credit: Robert Hasch.*

Dreamers Maxima Guerrero, speaking at mic, and Reyna Montoya address the crowd on election night. Behind them, left to right, are Raquel Teran, John Loredo, Randy Parraz, and Jeff Robinson, representing Public Campaign. *Photo credit: Robert Hasch.*

Jackie Adams expressing how it feels to win. *Photo credit: Robert Hasch.*

Celia Arambula, our most "seasoned" canvasser,
gesturing triumphantly as she shouts, "Sí se
puede!" *Photo credit: Robert Hasch.*

Yolanda Medina, in the middle with scarf, surrounded by
Promise Arizona in Action's Latinx youth volunteers, celebrating
Pearce's defeat. *Photo credit: Robert Hasch.*

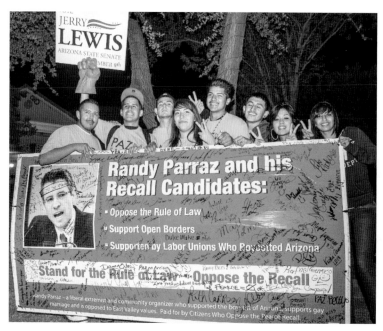

Hundreds of Latinx youth turned out to defeat Pearce and celebrate the victory. *Photo credit: Robert Hasch.*

Left to right, Raquel Terán, Sue Chinn, Petra Falcon, and Barbara Valencia at the Wright House on election night. *Photo credit: Robert Hasch.*

The recall opposition sign became a piece of liberation art.
Photo credit: Robert Hasch.

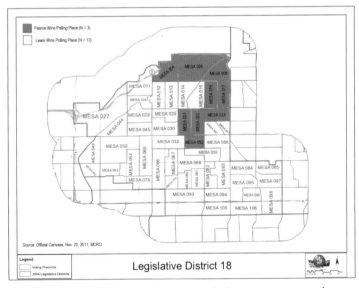

This District 18 map shows in red the precincts won by
Russell Pearce—Jerry Lewis won the remaining precincts.
Photo credit: property of Randy Parraz.

Volunteer Julie Kaye Jorgensen with the sign she "stole" on her way to the election night party. *Photo credit: Robert Hasch.*

Chad Snow addresses the media at the Capitol the morning after Pearce's defeat. *Photo credit: Robert Hasch.*

Brenda Rascon and April Bojorquez display the
Arizona Republic's front-page coverage of Pearce's
shocking defeat. *Photo credit: Robert Hasch.*

A week after our victory, the *Phoenix New Times* published an article about the recall. The original artwork had me holding a sword in one and an image of Pearce's head in the other. Given that I'd received numerous death threats, I asked the editor to consider using a different image than the one at left. The *Phoenix New Times* editors decided to use the image of a dragon instead. *Photo credit: Tim Gabor.*

Within hours of our victory, we were back at the Capitol for a press conference demanding a new era of respect and civility. *Photo credit: Robert Hasch. Used with permission*

Ken Chapman a couple of days after Pearce is dethroned pondering the question, "So, what's next?" *Photo credit: Leah Gillespie.*

Candidate Bob Worsley, founder of Skymall, as he entered his very first campaign to challenge Russell Pearce in the 2012 Republican primary. *Photo credit: Bob Worsley.*

Jon Hulburd presenting a check for $40,000 to Citizens for a
Better Arizona to fund our field campaign to defeat Pearce for the
second time in the 2012 Republican primary.
Photo credit: property of Johnny Lozoya.

Jon Hulburd stops by Moving Mesa Forward office to receive
a special gift from our team of canvassers—a t-shirt signed by
everyone—thanking Jon for his financial support. *Robert Hasch.*

Our canvassing team in August 2012 at the county recorder's office turning in ballots for Bob Worsley who challenged Russell Pearce in the 2012 Republican primary. *Photo credit: property of Randy Parraz.*

Our canvassing team moments before the final push on election day to defeat Pearce in the 2012 Republican primary. *Robert Hasch.*

Jaro Carreon out hustling on election day to pick up mail-in ballots to defeat Pearce in the August 2012 Republican primary. *Robert Hasch.*

Russell Pearce (in the hat) flanked by Matt Salmon standing outside a polling location on Election Day as I pass by him after dropping off eight ballots for Bob Worsley in the August 2012 Republican primary. This was the first and only time we ever had a face-to-face encounter. Pearce did not say a word. *Photo credit: Ramiro Luna-Hinojosa*

Left to right, a family affair—Mark Ryan, Sara Ryan, and Tom Ryan—celebrating Pearce's defeat a second time at the Wright House. *Robert Hasch.*

Following Bob Worsley's victory, we pivoted to our "Joe's Gotta Go" campaign to launch the largest paid field operation in Arizona's history that funded upwards of 100 canvassers knocking on doors six days a week. Because we collected thousands of mail-in ballots at the doors of Latino voters, in 2013, Republicans began the effort to criminalize this practice. *Photo credit: property of Randy Parraz.*

Ten years after the recall, this is the personalized license plate of "recalled and retired" Russell Pearce. "ARZ 1070" is short for the anti-immigrant bill Pearce authored in 2010—Arizona's Senate Bill 1070.
Photo credit: Steve Gallardo.

CHAPTER 27

ONE Vote Redemption

*Democracy is based upon the conviction that there are
extraordinary possibilities in ordinary people.*
~ Harry Emerson Fosdick, Pastor

After the cameras left and the victory party began to wind down, Jerry articulated his earlier uncertainty, "Now what?" he asked Tyler and his other close advisors.

They gathered at Tyler's house to strategize about the next day. Interviews with major networks, including CNN, were scheduled, with the first one only hours away at 5:30 a.m. Jerry also heard from some of his friends at the state Capitol that he was not going to be greeted warmly when he arrived for the first caucus of the Republican senators to elect a new president.

Unlike a typical election, Pearce's reign as senator and president of the senate ended the night of the election. Just like that, he was done and gone.

Early the next morning, I, too, was contacted by CNN. On the way to the interview, I picked up a copy of the *Arizona Republic*. The front page, above-the-fold headline read, "Pearce on Verge of Historic Loss" with a close-up photo of Pearce in front of his home and Sheriff Joe Arpaio standing next to him. They appeared tight-lipped and shocked, as they faced one of the worst nights of their careers. The photo was priceless.

No two individuals were more responsible for cultivating Arizona's extreme anti-immigrant and anti-Latino political landscape than Pearce and Arpaio. Both failed to understand the severity of the blow we had just inflicted on them. That night, Arpaio was already predicting Pearce would return to office in the next election. As for Pearce, he remained unwilling to admit a mistake, apologize for anything he did, or accept any blame for the first defeat of his political career.

Pearce did not know it then, but that night he lost more than an election. On November 8, 2011, *we ended his career as an elected official.*

I got out of my car for the CNN interview and saw a familiar face. "Two times in less than twenty-four hours," Jerry said as he walked towards me. He had just finished.

I reached back into my car and handed Jerry the paper. "Here I brought you a copy of today's *Arizona Republic*. You are going to love the cover."

Jerry's eyes lit up when he saw it—especially the photo of Pearce with Arpaio. Despite getting little sleep, Jerry still seemed full of energy and excitement. "I still cannot believe we won by double digits," he said. "I did not expect our victory to be so decisive so early in the evening."

"How did the concession call go with Pearce last night?" I asked.

With a smile on his face, Jerry responded, "What concession call?" We both laughed, knowing such a routine gesture of humility and decency from Pearce shouldn't have been expected.

Jerry then headed for the Capitol.

There, he did not expect a lovefest but he also did not plan to be so disrespected, even cursed at, by members of his party. Treating all people with civility and respect, whether you disagree with them or not, was second nature to Jerry. However, to many of the Pearce loyalists,

Jerry had crossed a line they deemed unforgivable; he would never be welcomed as a member of their team.

As Jerry entered the meeting room, he immediately felt the cold reception and his colleagues' disappointment. But he made his way around the room, extending his hand to each senator as he introduced himself. It was a historic occasion. For the first time in Arizona's 100-year history, a special meeting had to be called to elect a new senate president because the presiding one was recalled from office.

The successful recall emboldened a number of Republican senators to stay the course and govern as conservative Republicans, not anti-immigrant Tea Party loyalists. When Jerry walked into that room, the two factions were equally divided. Our decision to launch the recall in January was about to give us our first legislative victory two months before the opening day of Arizona's 2012 legislative session.

Jerry's meet and greet went surprisingly well until he came to Senator Al Melvin. Born in 1944, Melvin served in the navy and later settled in a conservative area just north of Tucson called Saddlebrook. As Arpaio and Pearce ramped up their war against immigrants, Melvin cheered them on, soon becoming one of their staunchest supporters.

As Jerry extended his hand to Melvin, he refused to stand. "I will never shake hands with you. As far as I am concerned, you do not exist."

A bit shaken by Melvin's decision to act like a two-year-old, Jerry made his way to where the more moderate senators were seated. Still, more hostility awaited. The Republican leaders facilitating the meeting decided it was better to let everyone express their anger, frustration, and dislike for their new colleague now rather than later.

Each senator at the table was allowed to speak directly to Jerry, who remained silent the whole time, never taking his eyes off of the person speaking. No matter how ugly the insult or degrading the comment, Jerry remained calm and steady.

Things heated up when Senator Frank Antenori stood to speak.

Antenori stared directly at Jerry across the table. His comments revealed the depth of the wound we inflicted the night before. "I will do whatever I can to make sure you do not pass any piece of legislation," he said. "I will do whatever I can to make you as ineffective as possible. You are a fucking traitor. A RINO (Republican in Name Only). And you are destroying good people just to make a name for yourself."

This vitriol went on for several minutes.

Senator Laurie Klein piled on. "You will never be elected again," she said, while others kept repeating, like a chorus to a song, "This is wrong. You don't recall our fellow members. That's just wrong."

Firmly anchored in his faith, Jerry refused to take the bait. At no time during this tidal wave of personal attacks did he attempt to defend his name, reputation, or explain his motives. Jerry knew this would pass, and at some point, the business of electing a new president of the senate would occur. His first vote as a senator would alter the future of Arizona's stance on immigration.

After about thirty minutes of the "Why We Hate Jerry Lewis" therapy session, Senator John Nelsen reminded the others that during their careers they had all sided with the opposition on various issues. And that what they were doing to Jerry was unfair. He brought them back to the main purpose of the meeting, "We are here to elect a new president of the senate. Let's move on."

For the first time, the focus moved away from Jerry and to the head of the table. Two candidates vied for the president's post: Senator Andy Biggs, an avid Pearce supporter, and the ironically named Senator Steve Pierce. The election of Biggs basically would be a vote to extend Pearce's agenda into the 2012 legislative session. However, Steve Pierce represented an opportunity for the senate to take a new direction.

Steve had grown up on a ranch in Prescott, a small town in northern Arizona some 200 miles from the nearest border crossing into Mexico. Steve's dad employed Mexican immigrants to help run the ranch. Steve even learned Spanish while working alongside one of his dad's most trusted workers, a Mexicano named Rigo. Steve considered Rigo and other workers his friends, part of their "ranch" family.

"When I was real young, my dad had *braceros* who came up and irrigated and cut cedar trees. I remember border patrol agents coming out to the ranch one time and they went through everything. I was very upset by what I saw. I wrote a letter to Senator Barry Goldwater and told him that what the border patrol agents did on our ranch was wrong."

Steve's commitment as a lifelong Republican did not mean he surrendered his ability to think, reflect, and make his own judgments about such hot-button issues as immigration. Early in his political career, Steve had to draw the line. "When I was first elected, I was active in the Tea Party and I went and spoke to them. But it got taken over by a radical wing and I didn't want to be involved with it anymore."

He discussed this with his wife, Joan, and they agreed it was the right thing to do.

Steve understood the bigger picture. With Mexico being Arizona's strongest trading partner, Arizona's need for immigration, and the negative impact of SB 1070 on families, Steve wanted to put an end to laws that attacked immigrants, especially Latinos. Steve, like most Republicans, advocated that people needed to immigrate legally, but he knew that a line had been crossed with SB 1070. The Latino community's reaction to it—the marches, protests, and calls to boycott Arizona—sent a loud and powerful message that the law struck a nerve and awakened a community to fight back like never before.

Steve believed too many Republicans had gone too far by using immigration in the worst possible way. He even went so far as to say, "A lot of them use race. There are a lot of them that are racists, but they won't say that. Frankly, I think Russell is a racist."

The recall had given individuals like Steve Pierce room to finally maneuver. Steve could now rally traditionally conservative and moderate

Republicans without Pearce breathing down their necks or threatening to "primary" them in the next election with a Tea Party loyalist. With Steve as president, Republicans would now be able to consider other bills and priorities that had nothing to do with immigration. Republicans could now engage in civil, respectful, and constructive conversations with the minority party.

In short, with Pierce as senate president, Arizona would go from *ground zero* on the fight against anti-immigrant legislation to *zero tolerance* for any bills attacking immigrants.

Steve knew the time was now to move away from Pearce's agenda and focus more on issues and concerns that impacted most Arizonans. He was determined "to cool things down" on the immigration front. Taking nothing for granted, Steve called Jerry before the meeting to secure his vote.

Unlike some politicians who like to lay it on thick, with big hugs, back slaps, and over-the-top compliments, Steve was direct. In his pitch to his colleagues, Steve got right to the point, "If you want more of the same, vote for Andy. If you want a change, vote for me. I will make you one promise. As long as I am president of the senate not one anti-immigrant bill will ever see the light of day. I don't believe in all that illegal stuff."

That was all the assurance Jerry needed.

The rules for this vote were simple: twenty-one senators would cast ballots, and the one with eleven or more votes would win. The senators wrote down their choices, and the votes were tallied. When the results were announced, the room gasped. A voice rang out, "Eleven votes for Senator Pierce. Ten votes for Senator Biggs. Congratulations, Senator Pierce, on being our next senate president."

Jerry's first vote shifted the balance of power within the Republican Caucus. He delivered the deciding vote to end the racist practice of using legislation to target, harass, and mistreat immigrants and Latino residents. Constructive conversations about health care, education, and the economy would now receive the attention each deserved.

While senate Republicans caucused inside, Citizens for a Better Arizona gathered in front of the Senate building to proclaim a new day for Arizona. My comments were brief and to the point, "When elected officials such as former and now-recalled Senate President Pearce push extreme pieces of legislation that attack immigrants, Latinos or any other group—there will be consequences. Last night, voters in one of the reddest districts in Arizona boldly declared that Pearce is too extreme for Arizona."

As the press conference broke up, I thought I'd have a little fun with one of my favorite journalists, Brahm Resnik, host of *Sunday Square Off.* I said, "Brahm, I just want to let you know that Oprah called and wants to interview me about last night's victory."

"Really? Oprah called you?"

"No, Brahm, I'm kidding. But please tell me what does a guy have to do around here to get on your Sunday show?" He smiled, then walked away. The next day I was invited to be a guest on *Sunday Square Off* which taped on Friday.

Towards the end of the interview, Brahm asked a question that spoke to the transactional nature of politics. "Now that you helped get Jerry elected, do you feel that he owes you anything?"

I do not recall all that I said, but it was something like, "The voters of LD 18 elected Jerry and they deserve someone who will listen to their concerns. I live in Scottsdale."

Looking back, I wish I had the wisdom and courage to say, "Jerry does not owe me anything. Anything he owed me, he paid back in full the moment he decided to run. In fact, I owe him a debt of gratitude for having the courage to run. Otherwise, Pearce would still be president of the senate."

The impact of the recall reverberated from Mesa all the way to the state Capitol building. Mesa City Councilmember Dennis Kavanaugh captured it all when he said, "I hadn't seen grassroots organizing like the recall in Mesa ever. That gave me hope: the huge quilt of a coalition that had been stitched together. We brought new people into the process. That night was one of the highlights of my life. I had never seen so many Democrats cry after electing a Republican to office."

Inside the Capitol, Senator Steve Gallardo snapped a photo of maintenance workers taking down Pearce's framed picture from the wall.

The morning after Pearce's defeat, young people poured into Ken's office asking, "Now what do we do?" and "What's next?" and "What about Arpaio?"

Ken said they represented "the New Hope—and it was beautiful."

But the Arizona Democratic Party overall did not quite understand the political impact of what had just taken place—especially for Latino immigrants and their families. Eager to raise money and desperate to maintain a house-on-fire mentality, the state Democratic party sent out a press release that said something along the lines of, "With the election of Steve Pierce to senate president, the only thing that has changed is the spelling of the name from an "e-a" to an "i-e."

Nothing could have been further from the truth. Unlike Russell Pearce, Steve Pierce spoke Spanish, grew up around and worked with immigrants, and was willing to meet with just about anyone. Much more of a pragmatist than an ideological purist, Steve steered clear of name-calling, fear-mongering, and he had a no-nonsense approach to getting things done. Most importantly, Steve's presidency meant an end to the assault on immigrants, Latinos, and their families.

There was an immediate change of tone—a change for the better. One of our volunteers observed, "After the recall election we went into the Capitol to hold another action. All of a sudden, the elevator doors opened and there stood Senate President Steve Pierce. He listened to our concerns and we reached a compromise. Pearce never came out and he always ignored us."

When Pierce heard some of his Democratic colleagues say they had never been invited to the president's office, Steve invited them over for a visit.

"The senate is supposed to be about people working for Arizona and not their own personal agenda," he said. "I represent my constituents but then I also represent the entire state and you are supposed to listen to everybody regardless of party."

Steve even dropped by a couple of times unannounced to the Democratic caucus meetings. "They said I was not supposed to be there. Before I left, I told them to let me know if I could help or work with them on any particular issue."

When it came to Steve being willing to meet with "extremists" like me, his Republican colleagues asked why and Steve replied, "Why not?" He was less concerned about appearances and more interested in getting things done.

For Rudy Lopez and Raquel Teran, it took a while for it to sink in that Arizona would no longer be a national platform and springboard for anti-immigrant legislation. Rudy returned to Washington, DC, emboldened and inspired by what he had witnessed. He told me, "This type of campaign—unions, grassroots, Republicans and Democrats, Promise Arizona, Latino youth, retirees—I hadn't seen something like this ever. People are still unable to capture the lessons from this victory. We had never won like this before."

Before the recall, to organizers such as Raquel, the campaigns meant taking on the likes of Arpaio, Brewer, and Pearce month after month, year after year, only to see them remain in power. This was different. "This was the first time we tasted a real victory, a *real* victory," she said. "I still remember thinking, 'So this is what victory feels like.' I didn't know it would take so long. It had been embarrassing to go back into our community time after time without a real win."

Jerry won 42 out of 51 precincts, capturing 55 percent of the vote to Pearce's 44 percent, or 12,812 votes to 10,121. It is always difficult to predict turnout for special elections, and even harder for an off-year special recall election with only one race on the ballot. The field campaigns of Citizens for a Better Arizona, Promise Arizona, and numerous other organizations fueled an intense door-to-door and phone banking operation that reached thousands of voters, resulting in an overall turnout of 33 percent. Latino voter participation surged just past 30 percent. This election showed that when Latino voters are treated like mainstream voters in terms of door knocks, phone calls, and mail pieces—they'll turnout at the same rate as White voters.

From a tactical perspective, former Democratic Minority Leader John Loredo, a seasoned political operative, applauded Citizens for a Better Arizona's innovative approach. Loredo appreciated the magnitude of our accomplishment. He said the recall was, "the first time you had the independent side driving the election. Usually, the party drives the election, or a particular candidate drives the election. This was the first time a nonprofit 501 (C) (4) social welfare organization drove the election—where we picked the fight and shaped the agenda. We had not done this before in Arizona."

I can take it a step further. We not only "drove" the election, but we forced the governor to call one. And by doing so, we upended the traditional paths to power by rejecting Pearce's anti-immigrant crusade on a timeline of our choosing. Pearce's defeat put Arizona on a completely different trajectory, one that meant a change in agenda, tone, civility, and direction.

Unable to understand and acknowledge the depth of his loss, Pearce refused to surrender. Come 2012, Pearce and the Republican establishment would deploy an array of tactics to do whatever it took to return him to power.

CHAPTER 28

Pearce's Last Stand

There is nothing more frightful than ignorance in action.
~ Johann Wolfgang von Goethe

We knew it was coming. Following his recall defeat, Russell Pearce boasted he would have won a traditional Republican primary. Now he had to make good on his boast.

In February 2012, the Arizona Redistricting Commission submitted new maps for legislative and congressional districts to the US Department of Justice. When the redrawn districts became public, we could not believe what they did to Pearce's old district—LD 18.

Pearce's allies on the redistricting commission created a new legislative district for him, Legislative District 25. This heavily Republican district cut incumbent Senator Jerry Lewis out by three blocks. Unless Jerry moved from his home of thirty years, there would be no Lewis–Pearce rematch. And to make good on their pledge that Jerry would never win another election, the new maps placed his home in a district that heavily favored Democrats. The redrawn district maps would all but guarantee Pearce's return to the senate, while ending any real chance for Jerry to get reelected.

Jerry was not about to move his family three blocks just to win an election. When that became known, Pearce and his supporters succeeded

294

in eliminating the only person who had ever defeated Pearce in an election. Despite Jerry's overwhelming victory in the recall election, Pearce's political comeback appeared almost a certainty. Surely no other sane or credible Republican candidate would dare enter the race once Pearce made his intentions clear.

Now, all the prep work necessary to guarantee Pearce's return to the senate had been done. Four months after the recall election, the Red Mountain Tea Party invited its strongest supporters to a March 19 gathering of prominent Republicans where Pearce was to make a special announcement. About a week before the event, Pearce emailed his fellow "Patriots," asking for their support and alluding to the recall: "As it goes, family can have disagreements, I hope as we do, we deal with them in a manner that keeps us close and united in our efforts to improve the quality of life for our families, taxpayers, and businesses, while protecting our God-given rights and our Constitutional liberties."

He was more specific regarding those of us who fought to remove him from office. "I am saddened by those who have invaded our state to go after Patriots doing their Constitutional duty and I am saddened by those who have joined them in this destructive behavior. I intend to stay in this fight for Constitutional liberties, families, and a secure America."

Once again, Pearce took the low road, knowing full well that everything we did was constitutional, legal, and legitimate.

On the day of Pearce's big announcement, I arrived about an hour early at the location in East Mesa and watched the cars pour in, many carrying four to five people. Almost all were White and grey-haired. Unlike the poorly attended rally at Hohokam Stadium, Pearce's team did a great job of turning out their anti-immigrant and anti-Latino base. News trucks lined up in front of the hall, and people waved signs for Pearce, patriots, and "God bless America." It was the perfect platform to make his case for another run.

Pearce's plans to run again caused Citizens for a Better Arizona to spring into action and gather as much information as we could.

We selected about ten supporters who could pass for Tea Partiers to go inside the hall, take notes, record video, and photograph Pearce and his supporters. One of our staunchest supporters, Carolyn Cooper, fit the part perfectly—White, over sixty, with glasses and white hair. We could count on Carolyn to take meticulous notes of the more alarming comments. Our volunteers were a bit disgusted to pay a $3 Tea Party entrance fee, but they were buying a ticket into a world they had never seen so up close and personal.

As our volunteers settled in for the meeting, the emcee issued a warning: "No one is allowed to take any pictures or videos except for the press and media in the back of the room! Anyone who came here tonight to protest will be arrested by the sheriff's men."

We had no desire to protest; you never want to interrupt your adversaries when they are about to give you a gift. It might not have been obvious to all, but Pearce running again actually was a gift.

It didn't take long for the emcee to rev up the Tea Party loyalists. Channeling Walter Cronkite himself and bringing them the evening news, he said, "Since Sheriff Arpaio's investigation into Obama's birth certificate was now complete, it was clear that there is a forgery in the social security number on Obama's birth certificate." The crowd booed and he continued with the predictable talking points of limited government and secure borders.

Then came the introductions, a who's who of Republican leaders: The State Republican Party Chairman Tom Morrisey; State Senators Andy Biggs, Don Shooter, Sylvia Allen, Judy Burges, Frank Antenori, and Ron Gould; State Representatives John Kavanaugh, David Gowan, Eddie Farnsworth, Justin Olson, Carl Seel, Steve Montenegro, Justin Pierce, and J.D. Mesnard; Sheriff Joe Arpaio; US Senate candidate Will Cardin; Phoenix City Councilman Sal DiCiccio; and, Gary Pierce, chairman of the Arizona Corporation Commission. The lineup sent a clear message to anyone planning to challenge Pearce in the primary—Arizona's Republican Party, top to bottom, stood with Pearce.

The emcee whipped up the crowd with attacks and jokes aimed at liberals. He repeated one often shared at Republican gatherings about how liberals solve problems: "If it moves, tax it. If it keeps moving, regulate it. If it stops moving, subsidize it!"

"But not to worry," he added, "Arizona is on its way back to prosperity in large part due to Russell Pearce!"

One of Pearce's closest allies, Senator Andy Biggs, took the mic. Yes, the same guy who lost to Steve Pierce by one vote to replace Russell Pearce as senate president. Biggs talked about how well Pearce knew the Constitution and how Arizona needed someone who understood states' rights. "Now, about this next election for Russell, it will be a fair fight this time. It won't be an election where another party comes in and affects the outcome. I've known Russell in the best of times ..."

Biggs paused and appeared to be on the verge of crying. He apologized for being overcome with emotion and continued, with his voice trembling, "… and I have known Russell in the worst of times." Whether the emotion was staged or not didn't matter. Biggs delivered the message to the faithful. Their friend and leader had been "unfairly" stripped of his power, and Arizona would suffer if they did not return Pearce to office.

State Rep. Kavanaugh revved up the crowd even more with his over-the-top condemnation of the recall, "I have seen a senate seat hijacked! SB 1070 transcends the United States. Because of Russell, SB 1070 is known worldwide!" Kavanaugh went on to characterize the "wrenching" of Pearce from office as a great loss for Arizona.

And if anyone still needed convincing, Rep. Eddie Farnsworth declared, "We are in a constitutional crisis now. Russell Pearce is a hero! He can lead us in the revolution."

What constitutional crisis? What revolution? By pursuing our constitutional right to recall elected officials, specifically granted by a hundred-year-old amendment in the Arizona Constitution, we simply replaced one Republican with another. No constitutional crisis. No revolution to fight.

The show would not have been complete without self-proclaimed world's toughest sheriff taking center stage. Arpaio aimed most of his vitriol at the media covering the event but also talked about how he needed Russell to do his job. "I can't enforce anti-illegal immigration law if there are no laws; so, Russell Pearce gets the credit for creating the laws." Arpaio closed by emphasizing how much they needed fighters like Pearce, and, of course, to "Never surrender! Never surrender!"

Finally, Pearce took to the stage with a thunderous standing ovation. He hit on the same old themes of obeying the rule of law. Pearce rambled on for about thirty minutes but failed to provide a coherent message. He talked about the Founding Fathers and how he cared more about freedom than security. He talked about a rogue government in Washington, DC, and how the Arizona Legislature was one of the best legislatures he had ever seen. Then he accused his opponents of name-calling. "No matter how nice you are, some people will still call you names, isn't that a shame?"

More unconnected thoughts rolled from Pearce's mouth, "Maybe my wife isn't so pleased to see me run again. But freedom isn't free! Sheriff Joe joined the army at the outbreak of the Korean War ... I'm having so much fun it would be easy to keep doing what I've been doing."

The rambling continued. Back to the Founding Fathers, whom he said prayed openly and asked God to, "smite their enemies—and now you wouldn't hear that today. It's about states' rights! Let's not apologize anymore."

Pearce then paused for a moment, took a breath, and shouted, "I am going to run!"

The crowd erupted.

Before exiting the stage, Pearce took a parting shot at President Obama. "Obama has done more to damage this country in his two and a half to three years than anyone else in the history of the country."

It was obvious that Pearce was not about to repackage himself as a kinder, gentler state senator. Instead, he doubled down. "I was Tea Party before Tea Party was cool! I love the Tea Party! The Tea Party doesn't want to go through a political party but sometimes you have to. I am a Republican. I am running for senate. I am running for you. I have taken on the left and won."

Much of this did not make sense. In his most recent race, Pearce had taken on the left and lost. Who other than Pearce would claim to be a winner four months after becoming the first legislator in Arizona's history to be recalled and removed from office by a movement sparked by the left?

When Pearce finished his remarks, I received a text that Pearce and Arpaio were making their way out to the back of the auditorium. Since Arpaio believed so strongly in Pearce's candidacy, I wanted to give him a gift, something to remind him of what was to come. Arpaio liked to collect signs and other political memorabilia. At the bottom of my trunk beneath a box of flyers I found a RECALL PEARCE sign. It was eleven-by-seventeen inches, bright yellow, and laminated—a real collector's piece. I wrote, "The result will be the same again," and signed it.

I stationed myself in the path Arpaio would take when he left the event. After a few minutes, he and his security detail exited the building as several supporters asked for a photo or autograph. Finally, he headed my way. I stepped up to him, put out my hand, and said, "Sheriff Arpaio, how are you? I am Randy Parraz and I hear you like to collect things. I have a gift for you." I then pulled out the sign to give it to him.

Things got a bit chaotic for a moment.

News cameras appeared quickly, and before Arpaio could respond, one of his supporters pointed at me and shouted, "Asshole Alert, Asshole Alert!"

Unfazed by the alert that he was under attack by an asshole, Arpaio replied in what I'd call an old Mafioso-style voice, "Randy, Randy, why don't you come visit me? Let's sit down and talk."

"Why meet now? You only have a few more months in office." As he walked away, I yelled out, "Thank you for endorsing Pearce again! The result will be the same."

Arpaio's security detail steered him in another direction. As he walked away, he said, "So, that is Randy Parraz. I had never met him before."

Despite all the excitement around Pearce's "surprise announcement," we planned to step all over it. Plans were already in motion to recruit our own candidate.

Later that evening, Pearce attacked us on Facebook. "It was a tough decision to jump back in knowing the evil media and the evil Randy Parraz bunch that have already declared war on me and other conservatives who respect the rule of law and love this Republic," he posted. "However, I know my duty to God, my Family, and this Republic … By the way I had a couple of very passionate Latinos speak tonight, I bet several a diet coke they won't be highlighted or even mentioned by the media?????"

Pearce had but one speed, full throttle. No one else talked in such extreme and rambling ways using words like "war," "duty," "God," "family," "the republic," "evil media," "rule of law," and "Diet Coke" as a lead up to an announcement to run for office.

Regardless, the time had come for the "evil Randy Parraz bunch" to get back together.

CHAPTER 29

Déjà Vu—Bob Who?

True heroism is remarkably sober, very undramatic.
It is not the urge to surpass all others at whatever cost,
but the urge to serve others at whatever costs.

~ Arthur Ashe

Well before Pearce's announcement, the same group of conservative Republican Mormons that we worked with during the recall election had already began the search for a Jerry Lewis-type candidate.

Our mission was to ensure that the primary would not be a cakewalk for Pearce, running unopposed and espousing the same unchallenged anti-immigrant rhetoric and anti-government policies.

State Sen. Rich Crandell was another Republican upended by redistricting. He lived in the newly created Legislative District 25. Crandell was hesitant to run against his seatmate Pearce and did not have the money and time to run a contentious campaign. Crandell let it be known that he was moving to East Mesa, an area that was part of his former district, where the competition would be easier. That left a big hole in terms of drafting a candidate to challenge Pearce.

Unlike the special recall election, in which everyone could vote, voters this time around would be primarily Republicans, with a small percentage of independents. Ideally, we needed a candidate who was White, male, Republican, Mormon, educated, intelligent, wealthy, articulate, Spanish-speaking bilingual, *and* moderate on immigration. As the search continued, one name kept climbing to the top of everyone's list—Bob Worsley.

Bob never had any interest in politics. He had not run even for student government in high school or college. He was a business guy, starting as a CPA at Pricewaterhouse. At thirty-five, he started SkyMall, the company that sold specialty products through its self-titled in-flight magazine. Bob later sold the multimillion-dollar business to media baron Rupert Murdoch. A Mormon and graduate of Brigham Young University, Bob and his wife Christi, moved to Arizona in summer 1980. Before the "Draft Bob" campaign reached him, his focus was on starting, running, and selling businesses while serving in various leadership roles in the Mormon Church.

Until SB 1070, Bob knew little about Pearce. However, during his tenure as president of a Hispanic congregation in the LDS Church, Bob started to see the real-life consequences of the anti-immigrant rhetoric and policies. As a young man, he learned Spanish on a mission to Uruguay and Paraguay. During this time abroad, Bob developed a profound respect and appreciation for different languages and cultures— especially the Latino community. As the Latino population blossomed in Mesa, Bob and his good friend Ken Smith helped establish two Spanish-speaking congregations.

"Ken had Valencia and I had Arboleda," Bob said. "We both had 150–200 families. Then all of a sudden, boom, they were leaving."

The shadow of SB 1070 was prompting immigrants to flee to Mexico. One of their members, a husband and father of three kids ages five and under, did not come home from work because he'd been stopped and later deported. Bob and Ken later learned that he had been found under a bush and near death on the Mexican side of the border.

"When he recovered, we took his wife and three kids to the border and crossed with them into Nogales to meet their father," Bob said. "We bought them bus tickets to their hometown and sent them off. We did this over and over again. We were living with the bloodshed, you might say, from SB 1070."

At the peak of the anti-immigrant fever, Bob and Ken lost a third of their congregations from worksite raids and deportations. Bob soon found out that one person was primarily responsible for causing all this pain and suffering: Russell Pearce.

"And here we were, two Mormon bishops trying to keep the congregation intact," Bob said, "and we have a fellow member of our church over here attacking immigrants. It was easy to support Jerry in the recall election. So, when Jerry got redistricted out, somebody else had to step up and run in the primary when Pearce said he was going to run again."

Bob had not known Jerry before he ran against Pearce, but he donated to Jerry's campaign. Still, supporting a candidate and being the candidate are two entirely different experiences demanding a different set of skills.

As the date for Pearce's announcement approached, Ken Smith, Tyler Montague, Jerry Lewis, and a couple of other guys decided it was time to have "the talk" with Bob. Ken pitched the meeting this way: "Hey, Bob, we are brothers losing our church members. We need to find someone to run against Pearce. Why don't you come to our special breakfast meeting and bring a list of names?"

Bob, a loyal and determined "any Republican but Pearce" supporter, agreed. He put together a list of names and showed up at the breakfast prepared to offer his limited perspective about electoral politics and write a check.

For Ken, the fight against Pearce was personal. Ken had served his LDS Church mission in Chile and became immersed in the Hispanic culture. As an attorney, he often represented Hispanic clients. "People who understood our relationship with the Latino community and the gospel knew this had to happen. In the LDS Church culture, Hispanics are special to us. We owe them. Our Book of Mormon came from prophets in Latin America. We were obligated to help them."

An article in the *Arizona Republic* pointed out this duality. How could Pearce worship as a Mormon on Sunday, then support deporting families the rest of the week? "I am left with crying mothers and crying children who no longer have a dad or financial support," Ken said. "It was devastating."

Ken asked Pearce in 2010 to not be so harsh. "Hey, Russell, why don't you take it easy on our Hispanic brothers and sisters?" Ken remembered.

Without hesitation, Pearce got in Ken's face, huffing and puffing with the same old rants of the "rule of law" and "illegal is illegal." According to Ken, as Pearce's anti-immigrant rhetoric intensified, many LDS Church members believed Pearce was no longer on the Lord's errand.

As the group discussed who would run, several mentioned how satisfying it would be to beat Pearce in the primary, especially since he boasted that he'd be unbeatable in such a race. As the breakfast was about to end, this issue of why they were there—to share their lists of potential candidates—had still not been raised.

Finally, Bob spoke up. "Look, I brought a list of names …"

Before he could finish, Jerry stood up, "Look, I have to go down to the Capitol to be on the senate floor. I can't stay any longer. Bob, we want you to run."

With that, Jerry walked out the door.

The conspirators had finally shown their cards. None of them, except Bob, brought a list of names to the breakfast. He was their choice—their only choice. Bob sat there, shocked. It took him a moment to collect his thoughts. "You are nuts" were his first words. "I am a business guy. My businesses have been up and down at times. I had to terminate people on multiple occasions. There are probably tons of people out there who do not like me. I am not your guy."

Bob explained there were much better candidates who should be considered. The group listened and allowed Bob to finish. But they all conveyed virtually the same message: "Think about it, Bob. Just think about it."

Bob left the restaurant thoroughly unconvinced that he should be the *one* to challenge Pearce.

Later that day, Bob and his wife, Christi, drove to Payson for a business meeting. During the 90-minute drive, they covered many topics but nothing about what Bob's friends had just asked him to do. But once they arrived, Christi asked about what happened at the breakfast meeting. "They want me to run against Russell Pearce in the Republican primary," Bob said.

"What? You?"

"Yes. I know it's ridiculous."

Well aware of her husband's limited political background, Christi initially agreed.

On the drive home, though, they kicked around the idea. "Are we the right people?" she asked. The Worsleys were not even precinct committee people. They were not involved in legislative district meetings. And they knew nothing about running a political campaign.

By the time the couple got home, they'd received several messages encouraging Bob to run. His breakfast companions had wasted little time getting others to weigh in.

The next evening, Bob and Christi went to Brent Ellsworth's home for dinner to discuss Bob's potential candidacy. About ten couples—prominent Mesa families such as the Montagues, Smiths, Wheelers, and Lewises—were there. The conversation lasted for hours. As 11:00 p.m. approached, Bob remained unsure and uncommitted. He needed to hear more from them. He needed to hear from their hearts.

"Look," he said. "It's getting late and we all have to go home. It is really flattering that you all think I can do this. I have no idea how to do this.

Before we leave and think about this some more, I want each of you to tell us why you are involved. Not why you think I should do this, but why you are here? Why are you involved? Why are you passionate about this?"

The ensuing conversation had a transformative impact on both Bob and Christi. Stories were told and tears were shed. So many tragic stories of people—good and hardworking people—whose lives had been upended and destroyed because of Pearce's anti-immigrant agenda: a husband who never came home from work; a daughter left at school; a mother forced to pack up everything and move; and children left without parents. With their hearts filled with compassion and purpose, Bob and Christi drove home.

On the way, they looked at each other and shared the same thought out loud, "Wow, we *really* have to think about this."

Bob woke up the next day inspired to give this opportunity the consideration it deserved. He called his stake president and shared the events of the past few days.

"I have had two meetings on this, and I kind of think we should do this," he said. "Christi and I think we should seriously consider placing my name on the ballot to challenge Pearce for state senate."

It was a good time for the Worsleys to take on this challenge. Bob's businesses were in a comfortable position. They had plenty of savings. Bob had the time to run, and if necessary, he could drop a million dollars of their own money on the race without hosting one fundraiser.

The stake president initially thought the needs of the church were more important. "No, Bob," he said. "Anybody can run for those political things. We need you to do this church work. We are going to get you on a mission. The mission is more important. Let someone else do the political work."

"OK. Well, we kind of felt there was a need here and there was no one else that could drop a million dollars on this race. Would you mind giving this some more thought?" Bob asked.

The stake president, being respectful of Bob's request, replied, "I am going to Temple tomorrow. I will think about it."

The next morning, the stake president called. "Bob, I am sorry about what I said yesterday, but I just got a really strong feeling that you need to do this."

"That's what I'm feeling too."

"We can find other people to serve in the church to do what we need."

Bob concluded that after the stake president prayed about it, he had a really strong feeling that this was important and that the LDS Church was being unfairly labeled as part of the problem than part of the solution. Christi and Bob considered it some more.

Just two days before Pearce's scheduled rally, Bob decided to say "Yes." His first call was to Tyler. "We're in."

That evening, the group began mapping a strategy to launch Bob's campaign.

Tyler then called me. With Pearce's announcement only days away, I had become restless and concerned about whether someone would be willing to run, again.

"Hermano Hernández," Tyler said. "You are not going to believe it."

"What do you mean?"

"We have a candidate to take on Pearce in the Republican Primary. His name is Bob Worsley."

"Bob who?"

"Worsley. Bob Worsley. If you thought Jerry Lewis was a great candidate, wait until you meet Bob. He is the former CEO of Sky Mall. He's Mormon. He speaks Spanish. He can self-finance his campaign. And he loves the Hispanic community. He can't stand what Pearce and Arpaio have been doing."

"Say no more, Tyler. We are in. And thank you for coming through with another candidate. If we do this election right, we will permanently retire Pearce from office. If we win this time, the former senate president will have lost a Republican primary in one of the reddest districts in Arizona."

"Since Bob has never ran a campaign," Tyler said, "we are going to need Citizens for a Better Arizona's field operation—especially when it comes to getting those independents who don't usually participate in primaries."

"No worries, Tyler. We are ready. You all do your part, and we will do ours. See you on election night!"

I hung up the phone again surprised by my Republican brother from another mother. There we were again—a conservative Republican and a liberal Democrat—collaborating to take down one of the most powerful Republican politicians in the state. And if Bob was good enough for Tyler, then Bob was good enough for Citizens for a Better Arizona.

Bob's team decided to leak word of his candidacy to the press on the morning of Pearce's evening rally. Soon, news vans and reporters staked out Bob's house, ready to pounce on the first opportunity to interview him. But instead of fielding questions, Bob asked the press to give him a week before he would go on the record and respond to questions. The damage to Pearce's announcement had already been done.

Bob's candidacy surprised the press, but no one was more dumb-founded than Pearce. He woke up that Monday, ready to announce that evening his plan to right the wrong of the special recall election. Instead of spending the day preparing his speech and talking to reporters about his political comeback, Pearce spent the day reaching out to his inner circle to ask them the same question reporters were asking him, "Who is Bob Worsley?"

Pearce had never seen Bob at any of the legislative district meetings, and except for Bob's views on immigration, he and Pearce shared many of the same positions on issues. Bob's bold declaration to challenge Pearce posed a real threat to his plan of creating a smooth and uncontested return to the senate.

The fight for a better Arizona was on again thanks to the courage and compassion of Bob and Christi Worsley. Talk about a dream candidate, Bob represented a kinder and softer approach to solving some of Arizona's most difficult problems. Bob, like Jerry, was pro–Dream Act and pro–immigration reform. But most importantly for us, he was *not* Russell Pearce.

CHAPTER 30

He's Done

Never doubt that a small group of thoughtful, committed citizens
can change the world. Indeed, it is the only thing that ever has.
~ Margaret Mead, Anthropologist

By April 2012, Citizens for a Better Arizona was gearing up to defeat Sheriff Arpaio in the November election—raising money, holding town hall meetings, and organizing public actions. Pearce's decision to run for state senate again forced us to rethink our strategy and resources. During the recall election it made sense to make our campaign a statewide fight. As senate president, Pearce controlled the legislative agenda that impacted all Arizonans. However, in this new race, that dynamic no longer existed. We could not just dust off our playbook from the special recall election and expect the same result. Primary elections usually attract voters at the extremes of the political spectrum, and in most cases, only voters of a particular party participate. Even though the Republican vote appeared to be leaning increasingly anti-Pearce, we could not sit back, watch from afar, and hope for the best.

Our database of anti-Pearce voters from the special recall election provided us the head start we needed to build a winning strategy. The newly created Legislative District 25 was more conservative-leaning than the former Legislative District 18, so whoever won the Republican primary would easily win the general election. We had to take out Pearce in the primary.

We had a four-pronged strategy: raise $40,000 to fund an intensive field campaign with more than twenty-five paid canvassers; create a new political committee called Moving Mesa Forward; target and identify independents, especially Latinos, who were anti-Pearce, to vote in the Republican primary; and, most controversial, persuade Democrats to reregister as independents so they could vote in the Republican primary.

With only a few months to go before the election, it became clear that none of the Latino organizations that were part of the final get-out-the-vote push to defeat Pearce in the recall election had any intention of getting involved in the Pearce–Worsley race. Other issues and priorities demanded their attention. Our new committee, Moving Mesa Forward, would have to go it alone from start to finish.

Within weeks of declaring our intention to take on this fight, I received a call from David Wade, one of the founding partners at Javelina Consulting in Phoenix. David had an extensive background in Democratic politics and served as the executive director and chairman of the Arizona Democratic Party. Knowing Citizens for a Better Arizona had spearheaded the Pearce recall, he suggested a meeting with one of his clients, Jon Hulburd, who was very interested in making a sizeable contribution.

Jon's name sounded familiar. A quick online search showed he ran as a Democrat for Congress in 2010 against Republican Ben Quayle. Jon, because this particular district leaned conservative, supported SB 1070 and opposed the DREAM Act as a stand-alone solution to the immigration crisis.

It had little impact. Jon lost by double digits, but more importantly, he regretted taking anti-immigrant positions. Early in his career, he worked for the liberal Democratic US Senator Gary Hart and he perceived himself as progressive. His run for Congress tarnished his reputation, especially in the Latino community. I also found out that Jon's wife, Carrie, was an heir to the SC Johnson & Son, Inc. family fortune. The couple had donated generously to candidates, causes, and organizations.

Before our lunch meeting, Jon had a heart-to-heart with State Representative Ruben Gallego (later a US Congressman). Following his loss in 2010, Jon remained interested in elective politics and had not ruled out running for statewide office or Congress. Jon wanted to make up for his pro–SB 1070 stance and anti–DREAM Act position. Ruben convinced Jon he could rehabilitate his reputation by investing in the effort to defeat Pearce.

When we sat down for our lunch meeting, the real work of preparing Jon to invest in Citizens for a Better Arizona already had been done by Ruben and David. I outlined, for Jon our plan to take on Pearce in the Republican primary. In Arizona politics, progressive groups hardly ever participated in Republican primaries, but the risk of Pearce returning to the senate mandated our involvement.

Jon didn't hesitate.

"I want to be helpful here," he said. "So, how much do you need to fund your field program?"

Hoping it wasn't too much, I asked for $40,000, which would allow us to have upwards of twenty-five canvassers for seven weeks.

"Done," he said. "Work out the details with David about payment. Now, let's enjoy our lunch."

There was no "let me think about it" moment. In 2010, Jon invested hundreds of thousands of dollars in voter registration efforts that fell far short of what was promised. He knew we had a well-oiled and disciplined machine with a proven track record of success. At the time of our meeting, $40,000 probably sounded like a bargain to him.

Just like that, we had enough money to fund our team and launch Moving Mesa Forward. And we used our "recall family" connections to make it happen. Our field campaign was anchored by Jaro Carreon, Michael Lyons (Mary Lou's grandson), Sara Ryan, and her brother, Mark Ryan. They infused a new level of energy, fun, and passion into the "rinse and repeat" routine of canvassing.

We recruited more than forty canvassers to ensure that we would have twenty-five canvassers knocking on doors every day. The team included high school students like Zari Chacon, working mothers like Rebecca Diaz and Rocio Patino, college students from around the state, and retirees. The diversity of our team enabled us to reach and connect with voters from all backgrounds. By July, Moving Mesa Forward was fully staffed, and our team was knocking on hundreds of doors each day.

Our public message steered clear of Bob's kinder, gentler approach on immigration. We intended to keep the message simple, emphasizing only Bob's business background. Our main talking points at the door and on the phones were: Bob founded SkyMall; he was endorsed by Mesa's mayor, the entire city council, and more than 300 local leaders and neighbors; and he created more than 1,000 jobs in Arizona.

For our anti-Pearce message, we continued to show a man so out of step with mainstream voters, so extreme, that he was the first senate president in the nation to be recalled. As senate president, Pearce worked to deny access to health care for poor people, advocated for guns on college campuses, led the effort to cut hundreds of millions of dollars for public education, and denied funding for sick Arizonans in need of organ transplants.

In some respects, our message did not even matter. We had made these points about Pearce during the recall, and it was less about persuasion and more about identifying voters and turnout. Eight months earlier, thousands of voters had signed the recall petition and voted against Pearce. We just needed to remind them to turn out again.

We created an even simpler message for our T-shirts: "No More Pearce … TOO EXTREME for Mesa!" followed by "ONLY CHOICE

Bob Worsley, State Senate, Republican Primary" with a checkmark next to Bob's name.

Bob's supporters, especially those whose lives he touched through his church service, responded to his core campaign message: "Elevate Mesa." They walked, made phone calls, and spoke to their networks of family and friends to expand Bob's base of support.

One respected leader on our side of the effort sent out an email with a campaign video that creatively depicted the most fundamental difference between Bob and Pearce.

It opened with Bob and Christi standing together, smiling, and sharing a warm embrace. The ad then moved to a person playing a piano, striking the same single note six times in a row, with the word "immigration" rising from the keyboard. After the sixth time, the screen went fuzzy. When the ad continued, the person at the piano stopped playing the single key of immigration. As he struck other keys, new words popped up: Lower Taxes, Jobs, Economy, Cut Spending, Education, Immigration (this time in very small font), and Family.

The music was soothing, calm, and soft. As the words swirled around in midair over the piano, the most prominent words in the ad were "Lower Taxes." When the music ended, the ad faded to black, and then the words "Strong on all Issues" appeared.

Without directly accusing Pearce of being a one-trick pony for his obsession over immigration, this ad reminded voters that there were other issues in need of attention. Bob was also a conservative Republican deserving of their vote. Like the Worsleys, the ad was classy, professional, and respectful, but most importantly, civil in tone.

With little name recognition, Bob used his resources to make up a lot of ground in a short time. Soon, Bob's campaign signs featuring his signature message, "Elevate Mesa," were all over the district. Bob adhered to the LDS Church teachings that encouraged followers to lead elevated lives. He knocked on doors and transformed a brand-new Prius into his campaign car with his name and image prominently displayed. As Bob talked to Republican voters, he was pleasantly surprised to hear that they didn't want their city associated with Pearce's radical anti-Hispanic rhetoric. Bob became even more convinced that he made the right decision as more conservative voters said of Pearce, "He has just gone too far. He is embarrassing us."

Bob used the campaign to *elevate* his conservative credentials. He served on the boards of very conservative and religious causes. However, when it came to anti-immigrant laws or policies, Bob would not go along. "I love my Hispanic friends. I love their culture," he said. "And saying these guys are all bad people and treating them this way is just wrong." Bob deployed his resources to highlight Pearce's offensive remarks and statements.

In July, Bob received a key endorsement from someone widely respected in conservative Republican circles, US Senator Jon Kyl.

Meanwhile, Pearce's campaign plateaued quickly and then spiraled downward. During the 2012 legislative session, he tried to get his buddies in the legislature to pass a bill to reimburse him $260,000 for his recall campaign expenses. In other words, Pearce wanted our tax dollars to reimburse him for the contributions he received from lobbyists, lawyers, business owners, and others who funded his unsuccessful campaign. We immediately turned it around, asking Pearce's buddies and Tea Party leaders such as Senators Biggs and Smith and Representative Montenegro to embrace their professed Tea Party values of fiscal responsibility and limited government. "At a time of competing priorities and limited tax revenue, to ask lawmakers to support a $260,000 welfare check to Pearce for losing his recall election was both immoral and illegal," we wrote.

The bill failed.

Pearce's campaign gave us another gift when it announced a fundraiser at Oaxaca's, a well-known Mexican restaurant near the Capitol. Given Pearce's views about Mexicans and immigrants, we were not about to let this go unchallenged. As soon as we informed Oaxaca's management of the optics of hosting the Pearce fundraiser at their restaurant, Oaxaca's canceled the event. Pearce's team then moved the event to Macayo's, another Mexican restaurant in Central Phoenix.

We contacted Macayo's and posted this on Facebook: "Russell Pearce is holding a fundraiser for his race for state senate. Let's send a powerful message that we will not allow his brand of extreme politics—a type of politics based on hate and fear—to return to the senate. Let his supporters know that they should be ashamed for contributing to Pearce's campaign."

Macayo's followed Oaxaca's lead and quickly canceled the event.

Still convinced that holding the fundraiser at any establishment that served Latinos was a good idea, Pearce's team moved the fundraiser to Central High School (in Phoenix), a school with a predominantly Latino student population. We called our allies and had them contact Dr. Kent Paredes Scribner, the superintendent of the Phoenix Union High School District. We asked that no public schools be used to host a fundraiser for any politician, especially someone like Pearce who led the effort to cut millions of dollars to public education. Within an hour, Paredes Scribner canceled the event.

From senate president to being unable to secure a location for a fundraiser, Pearce's hold on power deteriorated each day. In an attempt to soften his rough, tough-guy image, Pearce's nephew, Talmage Pearce, put together a flyer for an ice cream social. The flyer showed Pearce holding and feeding a baby with a bottle in his arms, while asking people to attend and meet his very special guest Sheriff Arpaio. No one would ever associate Pearce and Arpaio with ice cream, a baby, and a bottle. The initial enthusiasm and air of invincibility surrounding Pearce when he announced his campaign back in March had all but vanished. Now there was nothing inevitable about Pearce's chances of returning to the senate.

Mail-in ballots for the primary election were sent to voters the first week of August. No organization had developed a better system for collecting ballots than Citizens for a Better Arizona. Our canvassers were aggressive, persuasive, relentless, persistent, direct, and, of course, helpful.[1] Steve Lemons, from the *New Times*, observed us repeatedly dropping off hundreds of ballots at the county recorder's office. He referred to them as "election gold." During a seven-week canvassing operation, we knocked on more than 17,000 doors. We re-registered 544 Democrats as "other" so they could participate in the Republican primary and vote against Pearce. To increase our vote-by-mail universe, we signed up more than 2,000 independents to receive their ballots by mail. Most significantly, we tracked and collected more than 1,500 mail-in ballots for Bob. As the election neared, we were confident that our work provided Bob the boost he needed to win.

On Election Day, our team continued to call voters, knock on doors, pick up ballots, and push voters to the polls. Most of the day passed without incident. By 5:00 p.m., we were all in the field, me as well, making our final push. In less than two hours, my precinct walking partner Ramiro Luna-Hinojosa and I picked up eight ballots.

Born in Monterrey, Mexico, Ramiro was seven when he came to the US with his parents. Ramiro's father, unable to find a job in Mexico, came to Texas in search of a better life.

I met Ramiro, a Dreamer, earlier in 2012 in Dallas, when I did some work for Domingo Garcia's Congressional campaign. Before I returned to Phoenix, I invited Ramiro to join our "Joe's Gotta Go" campaign in the fall to take out Sheriff Arpaio. A few months later, Ramiro was on his way with two other volunteers, Lorena and Victoria. They arrived early enough to join us for the final week of our campaign to defeat Pearce in the Republican primary.

---

[1] Because of our effectiveness in collecting ballots, the Republican–controlled legislature later made it a crime to pick up and return someone else's ballot.

After living undocumented in the US for more than twenty years, Ramiro was now part of the campaign to defeat one of the most anti-immigrant and anti–Dreamer politicians in the country. It was a new experience for Ramiro. "I had always been part of campaigns to help people get elected into office," he said. "This was about taking someone out. I had never gone to a White man's house to ask a Republican to vote for another Republican. This changed my own view of who the bad guy was."

Nothing prepared Ramiro for what happened next. With only ten minutes to go until the polls closed, I asked Ramiro to take us to the nearest polling location. Within minutes we arrived, and I jumped out of the car to drop-off our final batch of ballots for Bob. As I neared the building entrance, two men were passing out campaign literature. One had on a gardening hat with a wide brim to block out the sun. I peered closer and about tripped over the curb.

Standing right in front of me was Russell Pearce.

As I passed him, our eyes met and I shouted, "Eight more votes for Bob Worsley!" I held up the ballots so Pearce could see them. He did not say a word as I walked by. His companion, Matt Salmon, a candidate for Congress, said something like, "We're going to sue you."

I ignored his comment, dropped off the ballots, and was about to pass by Pearce a second time. On my way out, I noticed Ramiro had stayed in the parking lot. Initially shocked by seeing Pearce, Ramiro soon embraced the moment. "It felt like my heart dropped," he said. "Is it really him? I felt a sense of power and strength. We were going to topple him over." When Ramiro saw me say something to Pearce on my way in, he realized he should take a photo when I came out.

This time when I looked at Pearce, he appeared much smaller than the image he projected. The loud-mouthed, anti-immigrant and anti-Latino recalled senate president still had nothing to say. I did not attempt to engage him this time. He just stood there red-faced and tight-lipped. When I passed Pearce and turned back for one final look, Ramiro snapped the photo. As we jumped in the car, Ramiro asked in complete amazement, "Did that really just happen?"

"Yes," I said, "and that is a sign that we are going to win! You just witnessed what losing looks like—standing in front of a polling place ten minutes before it closes, passing out campaign literature, and begging people for their vote. Let it sink in a minute; we may have just dropped off the very ballots that will decide this race. From what I could tell, Pearce's head was about to blow when he saw us walk up with those ballots for Bob. Now, let's go eat!"

A much smaller group of supporters than the recall election party gathered again at the Wright House. This time, Mike set us up in the sunken garden, which had the feel of a small Tuscan village. Stone walls, statues, beautiful flower arrangements, and special lighting set the mood for a celebration. Mariachi musicians, featuring one of our very own canvassers, Jaro, played as we waited for the returns. Our wait did not last long.

While we gathered at the Wright House, Pearce had invited his supporters to join him at the Rockin' R Ranch, an Old West-themed dinner theater in the heart of his district. However, he banned all reporters from attending—a sign he knew his time was up—again. As the returns came in, Pearce refused to leave the room and speak to reporters waiting outside.

Shortly after the polls closed, the results for the first batch of vote-by-mail ballots were announced, 52 percent to 48 percent, with Bob leading Pearce by a narrow margin.

With each new update, the lead widened. By the time the last vote was counted, our team had defeated Pearce again by double digits, 56 percent to 44 percent.

This night deeply impacted Ramiro's view of politics. "I could not stop smiling," he said. "As an immigrant, politics was always about being attacked. That night I felt big and experienced firsthand what it took to move the people, energy, and resources to bring down someone as powerful as Pearce."

As the party wound down, it was hard to separate the Democrats from the Republicans in our crowd. We felt more like citizens simply doing what needed to be done for a better Arizona.

Afterward, my daughter Natalia, then twelve, and I drove to Bob's home to meet him for the first time and congratulate him on his victory. Natalia was more excited to meet the founder of SkyMall than the new state senator-elect from LD 25.

By the time we arrived, large media satellite trucks were lined up in front of the house and the party was well underway. I was greeted at the door and told Bob would be out shortly. Following a brief wait, Bob came out, and we shook hands. I thanked him and his wife Christi for having the courage to take on Pearce and running such a disciplined and focused campaign—especially for someone who had never done this before. He agreed to meet with me in the coming weeks after things had calmed down. Natalia, impressed by the amazing spread of food, grabbed some of the treats as we walked out.

The day after the election, I sent out a thank you email to our supporters, reminding them once again what we had achieved. In less than one year, Russell Pearce went from senate president and one of the most powerful politicians in Arizona to being effectively dismissed from holding office by the very voters who knew him best.

By working together, we established a new normal for LD 25, where a safe Republican seat would now be represented by a senator who was conservative *but* pro–DREAM Act and pro-immigration reform. For that district—and Arizona—this was the best outcome imaginable.

Bob's 12 percentage-point victory margin slammed the door on Pearce's career in politics as an elected leader. Bob was definitely the better candidate, but the better candidate does not always win. This double-digit landslide victory happened because we were strategic, disciplined, and tenacious with our field campaign for seven weeks in over 105-plus-degree heat.

A reporter from the *Arizona Republic* asked me about Pearce's future in politics. I said, "This is the same Russell Pearce who said he'd never lose a primary. He misjudged the fact that he was no longer a conservative Republican—he was an extreme Tea Party Republican. There's no comeback for Russell Pearce. He's done."

And a decade later, that statement still holds true for Pearce and his anti-immigrant machine—*done* in Arizona.

CHAPTER 31

A New Hope

*Most of the things worth doing in the world had been
declared impossible before they were done.*
~ Louis Brandeis, U.S. Supreme Court Justice

Although I had no power to stop Pearce from running for office
again, my words "he's done" foreshadowed his decade-long absence
from office. His Republican primary defeat in a notoriously conservative
district silenced those progressive skeptics once and for all. In January
2011, many of them believed that even if we beat Pearce in a special recall
election, he would get reelected in the next Republican primary—and
that our recall was just a waste of time.

Our decision to recall Pearce at the height of his power was widely
ridiculed as tilting at windmills. However, at that moment in Arizona's
history, the decision to recall Pearce was the only realistic, pragmatic,
and sensible response to the crisis confronting immigrants and their
families. To their credit, many of the pundits that initially dismissed
the recall as an impossibility, later described it as the most significant
political event in Arizona over the past twenty-five years.

The Pearce recall provided the necessary space for decent, civil,
kind, and good-hearted Republicans to join Democrats and say, "No

more. Our values, our beliefs, and our issues will no longer be defined and represented by this man." And once they experienced Jerry Lewis's victory and witnessed what a true servant leader looks like, these very same Republicans rejected Pearce again when he attempted to return to the senate nine months later.

Surprisingly, Pearce received thirty-four more votes in the special recall election than he did in the Republican primary. Both Jerry and Bob, citizens who had never before run for office, defeated Pearce by double-digit percentage points—something we call a "landslide" in politics. Two different elections; amazingly similar results:

2011 Special Recall Election
    Lewis: 12,812
    Pearce: 10,121

2012 Republican Primary Election
    Worsley: 12,789
    Pearce: 10,087

On the first day of the 2013 legislative session, Bob approached Andy Biggs, the new senate president, and drew a clear line in the sand. "Andy, you know I am a very conservative guy, and I will be a good member of your caucus unless you bring more immigration bills to the floor. If you do, I will be a Tasmanian Devil. I will be the worst nightmare you have ever had. I will do whatever I can to stop you."

Biggs, a Pearce loyalist, heard Bob's message and replied, "I understand. You don't agree with us on immigration." Biggs, to his credit, did not call Bob any names or make any threats. Further, he did not bring any draconian anti-immigrant bills to the floor for a vote. Following Bob's victory, the entire Republican establishment—Republican-controlled senate and house, and governors, Jan Brewer (2010–14) and Doug Ducey (2014–22)—all heeded Bob's warning.

By the time Bob arrived in the senate, even Senator Al Melvin, the fierce Pearce loyalist who refused to shake Jerry's hand after his defeat of Pearce, recognized the shift. Early on, Bob, who sat right in front of Melvin, could all but feel Melvin's disdain. Bob still shook Melvin's hand

and they served together on some committees. By midsession, Melvin approached Bob and said, "I need to tell you something. I really like you. I didn't think I would. Last night I went to Russell Pearce's home."

Melvin shared that during his visit with Pearce, he asked the deposed senate president if he would be upset with Melvin if he pursued a friendship with Bob. Melvin liked Bob's ideas, his business savvy, and wanted to learn from him.

Pearce did not stand in the way. The next day Melvin walked up to Bob and said Pearce "released" him to be Bob's friend and work with him.

But Pearce wasn't done meddling in the business of the legislature. He pushed his former colleagues to support a bill to reform and "fix" the recall process with a constitutional amendment requiring all future recalls to be decided by a primary election instead of a special election in which all voters could participate.

When the bill failed, Pearce refused to walk away quietly. In an email to his loyal supporters, he continued to push a narrative that bordered on lunacy. He wrote, "For Republicans to join hands with the likes of Randy Parraz, the extreme left and the open border crowd is more than disappointing. We know we have huge election fraud going on all over this nation, investigations, indictments, hundreds of thousands of registrations that appear to be fraudulent … If they can't get you out in a legitimate election, then they will use voter fraud, recall or any means possible. It is nothing less than voter fraud disguised as an election!" Without any facts or evidence, Pearce pressed forward and poisoned the political discourse with one lie after another.

Republicans did not "join hands with the likes of Randy Parraz"; they simply felt the framers of the Arizona Constitution got it right the first time. In more than a century, the recall provision had been utilized scarcely, and only once successfully—hardly a situation needing a legislative remedy to stamp out voter fraud or other illegal activity. Yet the lies continued.

During the recall and special election, the constant attacks and alarmist language directed at Chad and me resulted in death threats by phone and mail at our businesses and homes. One letter directed at me said, "People like you end up buried in the desert." I reported the death threat to the Phoenix police. The next morning, a reporter at Fox News called, saying they were running a story about it and wanted a comment. I learned quickly that such conversations with law enforcement do not necessarily remain confidential. Feeling compelled to defend our work and not wanting the threat of violence to silence me or anyone else, I consented to be interviewed for the story. I also wanted to expose the depth of the hate we faced.

The death threat came a week after the *Phoenix New Times* ran a cover story with the word "Headhunter" right below an animated depiction of a dragon's head in my hand with a bloodied sword in the other. The original artwork had me holding Pearce's decapitated head, a gruesome image for even the most anti-Pearce crowd. I asked the New Times to reconsider using such a provocative image. I reminded them of all the hate mail, obscene phone calls, and online harassment we had received during the recall; such an image would only further antagonize Pearce and his supporters—especially so soon after his defeat. Thankfully, the final copy swapped out Pearce's head with that of a dragon.

Pearce's persistence, though, in portraying those aligned against him as unpatriotic, evil, and lawbreakers made it easier for his supporters to demonize and dehumanize Chad, myself, and many others who followed the law.

Reflecting today on what Pearce's removal meant, Tyler Montague said, "We stopped the state from continuing down the path of tribalism. Governor Ducey is down in Mexico trying to cut deals. He is not interested in anti-immigrant legislation. The governor will not allow the state to become an Alabama (which passed a more extreme version of SB 1070) on this topic anymore. They all lived by the xenophobic nationalist sword, and they died by it."

Despite Pearce's fall, Arizona did not become a model of bipartisan unity. Republicans and Democrats still pushed opposing agendas, but the barrage of bills, laws, and policies against immigrants, their families, and those who enabled "illegals" in any way finally ended. The Pearce recall movement gave Arizona a fresh start, an opportunity to move in a different direction.

Just four months after Bob took office, the change of tone and civility led to a different outcome when it came to expanding Medicaid. With Governor Brewer's support, a minority of Republican senators joined the Democrats to provide more than 300,000 low-income Arizonans health care insurance. Under a Pearce-controlled senate, such an initiative would never have happened.

Senator Steve Gallardo characterized Pearce's defeat as a breath of fresh air, and even the lobbyists knew it was going to be a new day at the Capitol. For Gallardo, "It was a weight off a lot of people's shoulders. This was a turning point for Arizona."

On the first day of the 2013 legislative session, when Bob was sworn in, I was at the Capitol with Citizens for a Better Arizona for our "Let Dreamers Drive" action. We wanted Governor Brewer to allow Dreamers to obtain a driver's license in the state of Arizona. Before our action started, I bumped into Gallardo, who asked, "How does it feel to be the most hated Democrat in the state?" Despite this post-Pearce era of civility, there were plenty of Republicans still enraged over what we did to Pearce.

I paused for a moment, then smiled. "If being one of the most hated Democrats in the state by this group of Republicans is the price I must pay for helping to elect two conservative, pro-immigrant, Republican state senators, then so be it."

We both laughed.

I tended to use laughter to deflect and dismiss all the personal attacks, hate, and threats that came my way. Unlike our recall chairman, Chad Snow, I knew what I was getting into the moment I said "yes" to taking on this challenge back at the Colosseum in Rome. For Chad, though, the fighting, name-calling, and all-out attacks against him and his business took a toll. The Pearce recall was the beginning and end of Chad's involvement with politics.

"The hate and vitriol were thick," Chad recalled. "There were death threats called into our office, and some of our clients fired us. And each week, more and more negative comments about me, my law firm, and those I cared about popped up on all sorts of websites."

The recall and ouster of Pearce in two elections proved that no one is beyond the reach of accountability by voters who are educated, agitated, and engaged. The recall provision in Arizona remains one of the most powerful and underutilized laws in Arizona to rein in and moderate politicians who abuse their power through lies, fear, and intimidation. The strategy proved that in the safest of districts, red or blue, Democrats, Republicans, and independents could coalesce and remove politicians who were unworthy of holding office. Such work must be initiated by citizen groups or organizations, not political parties.

When I asked Domingo Garcia why he chose to show up and invest in this fight, he said, "Why? It was a historic moment. For the first time, people in Arizona had hope when it came to fighting back against those that attacked immigrants. When you had all those volunteers and people who had been working in the hot Arizona sun, gathering signatures, and we had enough signatures to recall the first state senate president in American history—the person who had passed SB 1070—that sent a message of hope to people who lived in Arizona that cared about American values, that cared about what the Statue of Liberty represented."

From the moment we launched Citizens for a Better Arizona, Pearce and many others on the progressive side failed to understand that recall campaigns are never about finding the right candidate or a disgruntled outside group looking to overthrow an election. Recalls are about incumbents—what they say and do—and whether they deserve to remain in office. Pearce did nothing to change who he was, what he did, or what he said. Instead, he chose to amplify the very qualities we believed made him unfit to serve.

In an article in 2020, marking the tenth anniversary of SB 1070, Pearce expressed no regrets for authoring SB 1070. When asked if it was rooted in bigotry, he replied, "Lies, lies and more lies." According to Pearce, he lost because his opponents "lied and cheated and spent a lot of money ... it was inappropriate and wrong."

Pearce's anti-immigrant crusade was not a gimmick, a ploy, or stunt by a politician looking to grab headlines. This is who he was and remains today. He even personalized his license plate to read "ARZ1070," a reminder of his notorious law every time he drives.

Those on the outside looking in—reporters, political pundits, and other elected officials—still mistakenly simplify the recall as a move by the LDS Church to punish Pearce for his extremist views on immigration. Most LDS Church members, including Tyler Montague, Jerry Lewis, and Bob Worsley, never signed the recall petition. The LDS Church took no official position on the recall, the special recall election, or the Republican primary where Pearce was ultimately retired from elected office.

When asked by a reporter if he used the LDS Church to go after Pearce, Tyler responded, "No. We had conversations in the church, but the church didn't do this." The LDS Church never told members how to vote nor endorsed any candidates. Despite the recall, and all the work we did in the field, Pearce still received votes from some Mormons—just not enough to win.

At the end of our petition turn-in celebration at the Wright House on May 31, 2011, Mike Wright came to the front of the room and handed me a thank you gift. When I opened the package, the word "Radical" in bright red stood out. It was the book titled, *Radical, a Portrait of Saul Alinsky.*

Inside the cover, Mike wrote, "To Randy Parraz—the Saul Alinsky of his generation—for his work on the Recall Pearce campaign."

As an organizer, to be compared to someone like Alinsky, whose teachings I studied, admired, and applied, was the highest compliment. I felt my journey as an organizer had come full circle—beginning in Dallas as a community organizer with a national organizing network founded by Alinsky—and culminating with the historic recall campaign.[2]

In Latin, the word *radical* comes from *radix,* which translates to "root." In organizing, that means getting to the root of the problem in any given struggle or confrontation. In 2011, the root cause of every anti-immigrant bill, law, or policy in Arizona could be traced back to one man—Russell Pearce. To end the relentless assault against immigrants we had to end Pearce's career as a politician.

Establishment leaders, those embracers of the status quo, find it difficult to appreciate the role of the radical organizer. I think that's because too often, the work of a radical organizer is perceived as an indictment against the status quo—offending even those good-hearted liberals who have spent decades working to make their communities better. With a fresh set of eyes and a framework for building power, the radical organizer, unencumbered by local relationships and their shared historical experiences, sees things differently. A skilled organizer, using the same resources available to everyone else, can reorganize, reframe and reshape the discussion, the issue, or the fight. Our idea to recall Pearce

---

[2] Given that my great grandparents, Ynes Navarrette and Katarina Hernandez, were married on December 29, 1905 in Jeff Davis County, Texas, a county named after Jefferson Davis, the President of the Confederacy, this victory in some small way 106 years later served as a belated wedding gift for all the indignities they most likely had to endure.

the moment he reached the pinnacle of power as senate president was bold, crazy, and, yes, radical.

Since the 2011 special recall election, there has not been one—repeat, not one—anti-immigrant bill passed into law. In less than twenty months, Arizona went from being *ground zero* in the fight to defeat racist laws like SB 1070 to *zero tolerance* for any anti-immigrant bills.

As with the struggles that came before ours, the fire for social justice continued to burn brightly and intensely inside so many of the individual leaders and volunteers who chose to join our movement.

We did not let Sheriff Arpaio, his illegal raids, and racial profiling of our immigrant families and Latino residents put out that fire.

We did not let SB 1070 and all the other anti-immigrant and anti-Latino bills, laws, and policies put out that fire.

And we did not let the author of SB 1070, Senate President Russell Pearce, put out that fire.

That fire burning inside each of us must become an inferno for justice, capable of consuming every last ounce of hatred and racism that pierces our politics in the form of words, actions, and unjust laws. My father, John Parraz, could not be there physically on the night of the historical special recall election, but his spirit was. After all, it was him who ignited my fire and inspired me to be a force to help others—a force capable of withstanding whatever obstacles stand in the doorway of justice.

With a little bit of vision, provision, agitation, conflict, and heat, our collective fire ignited a movement—one that cut across party affiliations, religions, generations, genders, races, ethnicities, and ideologies. A movement where private *individuals*—regardless of their legal status—became public *citizens* in their pursuit of creating a better Arizona. And a movement that ultimately shutdown Arizona's anti-immigrant legislative machine and transformed the debate about how immigrants should be viewed and treated—with dignity and respect for all.

Afterword

The vision Lilia and I verbalized in Rome—to use the Pearce recall to build the power necessary to take on Sheriff Arpaio in 2012—came to pass. Immediately after we defeated Pearce in the 2012 Republican primary, we focused all our attention, efforts, and resources on defeating Arpaio. The Pearce recall made it possible for Citizens for a Better Arizona to raise upwards of $800,000 to launch the largest paid field canvassing operation ever to take on any one elected official in Arizona's history.

Our "Joe's Gotta Go" campaign funded a team of one hundred canvassers six days a week to knock on doors, register voters, stage public actions, make phone calls, and chase down vote-by-mail ballots. Our efforts, combined with Promise Arizona's and UNITEHERE's "Adios Arpaio" campaign that focused on turning out low-performing Latino voters, came within eight-tenths of one percent of surpassing the 50 percent mark for the anti-Arpaio vote. After Arpaio spent more than $6 million—the most for any sheriff's race in Arizona's history—he won with 50.7 percent of the vote. Four years later, Arpaio, like Pearce, was defeated by another political newcomer, Paul Penzone, by double digits.

Before the Pearce recall, no one talked about a multilayered million-dollar strategy to go right at Arpaio in a county where Republicans outnumbered Democrats by more than 200,000 voters. The recall's success caused us to dream bigger and bolder and attracted the resources we needed to fight a more powerful adversary.

Our effectiveness in getting Latinos and other low-propensity voters to participate so outraged Pearce, Arpaio, and their Republican allies that Republican legislators spent the next few years crafting a bill to criminalize the act of picking up mail-in ballots. It is now a felony punishable for up to eighteen months in jail. Under this law, citizens can be punished not for stealing or destroying ballots but for *successfully* turning them in (with the expressed consent of the voter). The ban on collecting ballots took effect in 2016. Although the law was challenged in court and momentarily struck down, the conflicting legal decisions and appeals elevated this case to our nation's highest court. It July 2021, the U.S. Supreme Court, in a partisan 6-3 decision, upheld Arizona's ban on the collection of ballots by organizations like Citizens for a Better Arizona with a proven record of helping citizens—especially Latinos—to register and vote. Such acts will now be criminal.

Like the tactics Trump and his allies deployed after the 2020 election about widespread voter fraud, illegal activity, and the ultimate lie that the election had been stolen, Republicans in Arizona used some of the same arguments to justify banning the practice of picking up mail-in ballots. Without evidence of ballot tampering, voter fraud, illegal voting activity, or reports of stolen ballots, Republicans marched forward to ban one of the most effective methods we deployed to get citizens to vote. The visual of us dropping off thousands of mail-in ballots of voters with the last names of Rodriguez, Gomez, Garcia, Hernandez, and many other Spanish surnamed voters—many of them first-time voters—threatened Republican leaders so much that they changed the rules. Instead of trying to beat us in the field by doing the hard work of engaging voters in their homes, they pivoted to changing the rules of the game.

During the nine years I lived in Arizona (2007–2016), many of my friends who lived outside the state were shocked by the stories I shared about Arpaio, Pearce, and former Governor Jan Brewer. "How could they get away with some of the things they did and said?" many asked, thinking such behavior was somehow unique to Arizona. Unfortunately, they did not have to wait long to experience on a national level what we had been dealing with in Arizona for years.

Trump's ride down the escalators of Trump Tower in 2015 would spread the pain of what we had been experiencing in Arizona to a national audience. Before Trump's divisive and hard-hitting candidacy, we already were dealing with politicians who characterized Latino immigrants as "invaders," engaged in racial profiling, ridiculed their opponents through name-calling, and made wild, unfounded claims about voter fraud and the legitimacy of elections. Trump borrowed a page from the Pearce, Arpaio, and Brewer political playbook and took it to the next level.

On January 6, 2021, we all witnessed the destructive and deadly consequences of allowing figures such as Trump to occupy *our* White House when his supporters attacked our nation's Capitol in an attempt to reverse the outcome of the 2020 presidential election. Lies repeatedly told by our elected leaders—bold, outrageous lies—can get ordinary people to act out in an outrageous, illegal, and violent manner.

Pearce's rise to power exposed the fragility of our democracy in Arizona and the fundamental belief in the rule of law. When politicians use their power to pass discriminatory laws or to racially profile citizens, and their hold on power is legitimized with each re-election, people *learn* over time that their vote does not matter. Sometimes their act of not voting is not even a conscious choice because no one is speaking to them—no one is telling them that their vote *matters* and that their vote is *needed*.

The main reason why thousands of Latino voters gave us their mail-in ballot is because we *asked* them to! We *asked* them to register to vote. And they did. We *asked* them to sign up to receive their ballot by mail. And they did. We *asked* them to vote for our candidate. And they did. And we *asked* them to give us their mail-in ballot, so we could turn it in for them. And they did. Our canvassers were practitioners of democracy—not criminals attempting to steal an election.

In *Democracy in America*, Alexis de Tocqueville wrote, "The further electoral rights are extended, the greater is the need for extending them: for after each concession the strength of democracy increases and its demands increase with its strength." Our collective strength as a democracy comes from expanding the right to vote and embracing those who have been traditionally disenfranchised. De Tocqueville reached this conclusion in the 1830s, and here we are in 2021, witnessing some of the most partisan, restrictive, and retaliatory attacks against the rules that govern how, when, and where we vote—rules that will disproportionately harm people of color. However, nowhere in history does it say that progress is inevitable or that victories once achieved can never be undone. When it comes to rebuilding, revitalizing, and preserving our democracy, the difficult work must continue of removing every barrier—every racist law, policy, or practice—that undermines and subverts the compelling ideal of one person, one vote.

Book proceeds will go to the Organizing Institute for Democracy to promote and expand the right to vote for all individuals who own businesses, work, pay taxes, raise their families, and make our communities thrive. As hundreds of bills are being considered to limit, restrict and change how we register and vote, we need to draw from our history and enfranchise those who contribute to the vitality of thousands of communities around the country.

Author's note: The quotes cited in this book came from television transcripts, videos, personal interviews I conducted, emails, newspaper articles, Facebook posts, government documents, personal recollection, and original materials produced by Citizens for a Better Arizona. To the best of my knowledge, each conversation shared in the book is a fair and accurate representation of what took place some ten years ago.

Where Are They Now?

Russell Pearce, state legislator, 2001–2011: After losing to Jerry Lewis in the 2011 special recall election, Pearce never recovered to run successfully for office. Despite being recalled and removed from office, he remained a powerful voice within the Arizona Republican Party until his comments supporting forced sterilization for poor women on Medicaid forced him to resign in 2014 as vice-chairman of the state Republican Party. After his final election loss, Pearce did not remain unemployed for long. His GOP allies secured him a job at the Maricopa County Treasurer's office, which resulted in a significant raise, job security, and a pension. Ten years after the recall, Pearce still refuses to return my calls or meet with me in person.

Joe Arpaio, Maricopa County Sheriff, 1993–2017: In 2012, Arpaio spent more than $6 million to survive the closest election of his career, winning just 50.7 percent of the vote. In 2013, a federal judge found Arpaio and his department guilty of racially profiling Latino residents during raids and traffic stops. By 2016, Arpaio's record of corruption and abuse of power sparked a countywide rejection by Democrats, Republicans and independents. Despite Donald Trump winning Maricopa County by over 44,000 votes, Arpaio lost to Democrat Paul Penzone by over 196,000 votes—a 56 to 43 percent embarrassment. In 2017, President Trump pardoned Arpaio after being found guilty of criminal contempt for continuing to direct his deputies to target immigrants.

At the age of eighty-six, Arpaio attempted to stay relevant. Bids for US Senate in 2018 and for sheriff again in 2020 failed miserably—like Pearce, he was too toxic to win even a Republican primary.

Chad Snow, Chairman, Citizens for a Better Arizona: After the recall, Chad returned to his law practice and continued to support our efforts to defeat Sheriff Arpaio. The Republican Party's shift to the far right, culminating with the election of Donald Trump as President in 2016, caused Chad to reregister as an independent. Chad, his wife, Rachel, and their family reside in Peoria. For the past few years, Chad has been battling a life-threatening form of cancer, but he continues to touch people's lives with his kindness, generosity, and humor. He and Rachel spend as much time as possible enjoying their children and grandchildren and traveling the world with their friends and family—especially to Hawaii and Costa Rica.

Domingo Garcia, the main donor from Texas: Domingo continues to manage a successful and expanding law practice in Dallas, Texas. In 2018, he was elected president of the League of United Latin American Citizens—the largest and oldest Hispanic civil rights organization in the US. He is one of the most influential Latino leaders in the country and one of the most prominent Latino donors to the Democratic Party and Latino candidates running for Congress.

Jerry Lewis, state senator, 2011–2012: After defeating Pearce in the recall election, Jerry ran unsuccessfully in 2012 in a newly drawn Democratic-leaning legislative district. The 2011 special recall election was the first and only election Jerry won. Jerry is assistant superintendent for Edkey Inc.—Sequoia Schools—and he remains involved as a servant leader in the Mormon Church and community.

Bob Worsley, state senator, 2013–2019: After defeating Pearce in 2012 in the newly created Legislative District 25, Bob won reelection three more times. Before returning to the private sector, Bob made sure his replacement shared his opposition to anti-immigrant legislation.

Tyler Montague, LD 18 Republican precinct committee person: Tyler continues to work as a business analyst at a prominent financial institution. He remains engaged in politics as a common-sense Republican consultant who endorses traditional Republican values while rejecting anti-immigrant extremists such as Pearce, Arpaio, and Trump. He recently played a major role in getting a minority of Republicans to support a legislative initiative that would reverse the statewide ban on Dreamers to qualify for in-state tuition for college. A statewide initiative will be on the ballot in 2022.

Kyrsten Sinema, state senator, 2011–2012: In 2012, she was elected to represent Arizona's 9th congressional district. Her voting record was one of the most conservative among her Democratic colleagues during her six years in the House. In 2018, she was elected to the US Senate. With the Senate split 50/50 Sinema is a swing vote for President Biden's agenda on health care, immigration, voting rights, infrastructure, racial justice, and raising the minimum wage.

Ken Chapman, executive director, Maricopa County Democratic Party: Ken left the party leadership in 2013 and co-founded Poder in Action, a community-based organization committed to dismantling systems of oppression. As a strategic advisor, Ken played a pivotal role in the defeat of Sheriff Joe Arpaio in 2016. In 2019, Ken co-founded The Prometheus Conspiracy, a Black-led organization focused on abolishing the criminal legal system and dismantling Arizona's far right-wing movements. Ken is also a core member of Drinking Gourd Farms, a Black food sovereignty organization led by Muslim refugee moms who grow and maintain an autonomous and sustainable food system.

Tom Ryan, lawyer: Tom continues to work for injured parties as a personal injury and wrongful death attorney. In 2012, he received the Outstanding Trial Lawyer of the Year award by the Arizona Association for Justice, which also gave Tom a lifetime achievement award in 2019 for his efforts as an advocate. Numerous local radio and television news outlets invite Tom to share his expertise as a contributor or consultant on issues related to election integrity.

Sara Ryan, office manager, Citizens for a Better Arizona: Sara graduated from Arizona State University Magna Cum Laude in 2012. She then attended the University of Arizona Law School and graduated in 2016. Sara received a Diploma in Human Rights and Humanitarian Law from American University in Washington, DC. Sara works with her father, Tom Ryan, in personal injury and wrongful death cases and assists in pro bono election-law cases.

Mike Wright, lawyer and owner of the Wright House: In 2012, Mike was elected president of the Arizona Association for Justice (formerly the Arizona Trial Lawyers Association). As a partner with Udall Shumway, Mike represents personal injury plaintiffs and shares his expertise in medical and safety matters. He and his wife, Peggy, still manage the Wright House and host an array of events.

Mary Lou Boettcher, chairperson, Citizens for a Better Arizona: Mary Lou continued to advocate for improvements in public education. In 2012, she joined our "Joe's Gotta Go" campaign to defeat Arpaio, and she was a spokesperson for our "Respect Arizona" campaign in 2013 to recall Arpaio. Mary Lou was later diagnosed with dementia and passed away in 2020.

Raquel Teran, deputy director, Promise Arizona (2010–12): Raquel continued her work as an organizer and community leader. She lost a

2012 race for Arizona State Senate but captured a seat in the state house of representatives in 2018. She was reelected in 2020, and was elected to serve as the chairperson of the Arizona Democratic Party in 2021.

Rudy Lopez, political and field director, Center for Community Change (2007-14): Rudy lives in southern California and works for the office of professional development at the California Department of Justice. He creates leadership curriculum and trains DOJ managers and supervisors. Prior to this, he served as director of organizational and community outreach at Urban Strategies—an organization that improves the health, education, social, and economic conditions of marginalized populations.

Alejandra (Alex) Gomez, organizer, Promise Arizona (2010–11): Alex currently serves as the co-director of LUChA—a statewide organization in Arizona committed to building power for working families in the areas of racial, social, and economic justice.

Petra Falcon, executive director, Promise Arizona (2010–present): Petra continues to serve as the executive director of Promise Arizona.

Steve Gallardo, state senator: Steve served until 2014. He then won a seat on the Maricopa County Board of Supervisors and remains its only Democrat. He also serves as the governing board president of the Cartwright Elementary School District.

Lilia Alvarez, co-founder, Citizens for a Better Arizona (law student): Lilia completed law school, started an immigration law practice, and was appointed to serve as the presiding judge of Guadalupe Municipal Court (a small town situated between Phoenix and Tempe). She served as the legal director for the Central American Resource Center in Washington, DC, and then was selected as a US Supreme Court Fellow. She now works as a senior advisor and law clerk to the chief judge of the US District Court for the Eastern District of California.

Randy Parraz, co-founder and president, Citizens for a Better Arizona: Randy led Citizens for a Better Arizona's fight against Arpaio in the 2012 election and the 2013 Arpaio recall effort. He then returned to the national AFL-CIO in the area of governance and organizational leadership. Later, he served as national director for the Making Change at Walmart campaign for the United Food and Commercial Workers International Union. In 2019, Randy joined Domingo Garcia at the League of United Latin American Citizens as a senior advisor. In 2020, Randy, Lilia, and their son, Leonel, relocated to Sacramento, California, to pursue Lilia's work in the federal judicial system. Today, Randy is co-founder and president of the Organizing Institute for Democracy.

Acknowledgements

The idea of this book originated in 2012, but the real writing didn't begin until the summer of 2018. Along the way, many people had a hand in making it happen. With the support of my partner Lilia, I was able to step back from my professional responsibilities and write. Thank you, Lilia, for having the courage, conviction, and integrity to join me in this fight from the very beginning. You are an inspiration to our son Leonel and me: your life's work continues to serve as an example of what it means to be a force for good.

Once I decided to write, I spent many hours in the Jefferson Building of the Library of Congress piecing together the narrative of my journey through Arizona and the unfolding of events that led to the Pearce recall. Each time I entered the main reading area, I checked my backpack at the counter, and the attendant gave me a small chip with a number. About a month into my routine, I received a chip with the number 1070. I knew then I was on the right path.

This book would not have been possible without the financial support of the Organizing Institute for Democracy, the International Association of Machinists and Aerospace Workers, and Domingo Garcia. Thank you, International President Robert Martinez, General Vice President Gary R. Allen (Western Territory), and Chief of Staff Bobby Martinez (Western Territory), for believing in me and responding to my request for support without hesitation. I especially want to thank Bobby Martinez for his friendship of more than twenty years. His daily commitment to his family, his union, and his community embodies the characteristics of a true servant leader. Thank you, Domingo, for showing up again and again in my life to support the work of social justice and for the financial support you provided to write this book. When it comes to Latino politics, your generosity and willingness to invest in fights and people you believe in are unmatched. You are in a class of your own. *Como tu dijiste* (like you said), *"Hasta la Victoria* (onwards towards victory)!"

I also want to thank President Jim McLaughlin and the United Food and Commercial Workers International Union Local 99 for their continued support of the Organizing Institute for Democracy. For the past two decades, Jim, you have been someone I could count on for support, especially when it came to supporting Latino immigrants and their families in Arizona.

I want to thank my editors, Jim Davis, from TypeRight Editing and Mary Holden, a freelance editor and friend in Phoenix, for the thousands of suggestions, comments, and corrections to improve the book. Jim, I did not fully understand what it meant to "tighten" my chapters until I reviewed the editorial magic you did that resulted in the loss of over 15,000 words from the original manuscript—while keeping the story intact. I appreciate immensely all the hours you devoted and expertise you applied to polish, scrub, and perfect the final manuscript. Mary, you provided a fresh set of eyes and expertise at the time when I most needed it. Thank you for your stylistic suggestions, words of encouragement, and friendship. This book does not happen without the two of you by my side. Thank you!

Many stories in this book are shared for the first time. This would not be possible without all those who agreed to share their perspective about the recall. Thank you all for your willingness to go on the record:

Lilia Alvarez, Joe Arpaio, Brian Barabe, Laura Barberena, Fred Barlam, Sandra Boettcher, Paul Castaneda, Ken Chapman, Carolyn Cooper, Molly Duran, Steve Gallardo, Domingo Garcia, Alejandra Gomez, Virginia Hauflaire, Jon Hulburd, Julie Jorgensen, Dennis Kavanaugh, Jerry Lewis, Rudy Lopez, John Loredo, Ramiro Luna-Hinojosa, Amy McMullen, Yolanda Medina, Tyler Montague, Reyna Montoya, Carolyn O'Conner, Dan O'Neal, Steve Pierce, Brenda Rascon, Roberto Reveles, Sara Ryan, Tom Ryan, Don and Betsy Savino, Todd and Diane Selleck, Kenny Smith, Chad Snow, Saul Solis, Raquel Teran, Bob Unferth, Bob Worsley, and Amanda Zill.

Chad and Rachel Snow, thank you for being a part of this journey from the very beginning, despite the risks to you and your family. Chad, when others rejected the idea of recalling Pearce, you said yes, when it was not popular to do so. Thank you for your courage, unwavering commitment to our cause, and friendship. And, yes, you are better looking than me!

Ken Chapman, thank you for believing that the Pearce recall could be the "New Hope" for Arizona. Your fingerprints are all over this victory, and now people will know just how much of a hero you really are.

Todd, Diane, Stephanie, and Jamie Selleck, thank you for joining us on our first walk and for your family's commitment to the recall. Todd, thank you for being our "John Hancock," the first signature on the original petition to initiate the recall process.

Paul Castaneda, thank you for your leadership and for opening the doors of the Communication Workers of America to Citizens for a Better Arizona.

Tyler Montague, my other brother from a Mormon mother, thank you for providing the bridge to victory. Without you and your friends, things may have turned out differently.

Tom and Anita Ryan, thank you for serving as our legal team throughout the entire fight. With your daughter, Sara, and later your son, Mark, this was indeed a Ryan family affair. Tom, your tenacious defense of our cause and pursuit of the truth is deeply appreciated.

Mike Wright, thank you for your support early on in the recall and for opening up the Wright House for us to celebrate our victories. Your willingness to join Tom and our legal team to expose the sham candidacy of Olivia Cortes was extremely helpful.

Jerry and Janet Lewis, thank you for reconsidering your "no politics" marital pledge and for listening to your divinely inspired premonition to run. And, Jerry, thank you for being an example for all married men of what it means to serve your community while honoring and respecting your wife.

Bob and Christi Worsley, thank you for being brave enough to do something that you both felt so unqualified to do—run for office. Bob, your passion and love for Latino immigrants and your presence in the legislature for six years helped dismantle Arizona's legislative anti-immigrant machine.

Jon and Carrie Hulburd, thank you for providing the financial support we needed to challenge Pearce's return to power. It was a game changer.

Diana Loken, thank you for taking on the challenge of serving as the treasurer for Citizens for a Better Arizona. You did an amazing job—especially given all the financial components needed for our success.

Bonita Burks, thank you for the consistency and professionalism Sign Here Petitions provided during the signature-gathering phase of the recall. You delivered on everything promised and then some.

Randy Keating, thank you for setting up our voter database for walking precincts, validating signatures, and multiple donations. I much appreciated your technical expertise.

Lyle Dillie and Victor Ahumada, thank you for creating our website and getting us online in less than five days! You worked around the clock to make it happen.

Jim Parker, the number one canvasser when it came to collecting signatures, thank you for being relentless in your pursuit of signatures to recall Pearce. Your efforts inspired others to do more.

Geoff Esposito, thank you for coordinating our volunteer signature-gathering operation and making sure our teams had what they needed to get the job done.

Sara Ryan, thank you for providing the stability we needed in our office for our final push towards victory. You were an invaluable member of our leadership team as you trained the volunteers, tracked our progress and oversaw the day-to-day operations of our field campaigns for both Jerry Lewis and Bob Worsley. And thank you, Rachel Golubovich, for joining our team and doing whatever was asked of you by Sara and Lilia as we ramped up our field campaign.

Dennis Kavanaugh, Beth Coons, and Mary Lou Boettcher, thank you for guidance, inspiration, and leadership in January 2011 when no one thought this was possible.

Don and Betsy Savino, thank you both for showing up at our very first town hall in Pearce's district and for your consistent support (money, office supplies, snacks, etc.,) throughout the campaign. I think Don logged in the most hours as our in-house notary by signing off on hundreds of recall petitions.

Thank you, Citizens for a Better Arizona's dedicated team of canvassers and volunteers, for turning out thousands of votes for Jerry Lewis. You all made it happen: Jacqueline Adams (deceased), Carolina Alvarez, Frank Alvarez, Gladys Angle, Sal and Nona Baldenegro, Celia Arambula, Doug Arnold, Vickie Aronson, Ana Maria Ayala, Brian Barabe, Fred Barlam, Dina Bayardo, Brandon Bass, Wendy Bergsmen, Mary Lou Boettcher (deceased), April Bojorquez, Maritza Broce, David Cleaveland, Mike Conway, Carolyn and Howard Cooper, Laura Copple, Paloma Cordova, Jean Devine, Patricia Drake, Buddy Duran, Molly Duran, Craig Falasco, Sandra Fischer, Lydia Garcia, Krystal Foster,

Preet Ghuman, Carmen and Zarco Guerrero, Virginia Hauflaire, Ed Hermes, Beth Hoffman, Lorena Parra Howard, Dominique Hunter, Don Johnson, Julie Jorgensen, Dana Marie Kennedy, Lauren Kuby, Olivia Kuby, Todd Landfried, Robert Langoni, Rosie Lopez, Carla Mannes, Wayne Manske, Dan and Lilian Martinez, Craig McDermott, John McDonald, Amy and Bob McMullen, Adam Mortemer, Barb Njos, Carolyn O'Connor, Barbara Ann Olbinski, Dan and Isa O'Neal, John O'Neal, Jason Odhner, Danny Ortega, Jim Parker, Tania Perez, Alison Porter, Wayne Porter, Susie Ranish, Brenda Rascon, Emilio and Lida Roman, Ruben Romero, Gina Rose, Sheila Ryan, Ester Sanchez, Norbeto Saenz, Ariana Sauer, Antonia and William Schnebly, Amanda Shelley, Christina Shelley, Eric Shelley, Lupe Solis, Saul Solis, Lucy Sheehan, Suzanne Taylor, Julie and Jildard Tenorio, Bob and Nancy Unferth, Cecilia Valdez, Barbara Valencia, Cristal Villa, Jordan Weiner, and David Williams. And a special thank you to my longtime *compadre en la lucha* Ignacio "Nacho" Hernandez for joining us for the final push of the campaign and providing me the support I needed to finish strong.

Thank you, canvassing team for Moving Mesa Forward, for helping elect Bob Worsley. You did an amazing job in 100 degree-plus weather: Cristina Aguilar, Marty Boozer, Jairo Carreon, Reggie Carrillo, Zari Chacon, Denis Chavez, Carolyn Cooper, Howard Cooper, Rebeca Diaz, Eric Dill, Victoria Frayre, Ashley Glass, Raquel Guerrero, Corey Harbison, Chimene Hawes, David Heward, Ramiro Luna-Hinojosa, Michael Lyons, Benjamin Marin, Colin Marston, Mario Miranda, Mayra Miranda, Leslie Mitchell, Ricardo Moreno, Alexis Morgan, Rocio Patino, Lisa Perez, Joshua Potter, Chris Russell, Mark Ryan, Patrick Ryan, Ulises Sanchez, Theresa Scott, Tyler Sherwood, Michael Speshock, Shannon Spechock, David Talenfield, Omar Torres, Lorena Tule-Romain, Bob Unferth, Nancy Unferth, and Richard Vaughn.

Thank you Promise Arizona and all those who were part of the Latino outreach campaign—Petra Falcon, Raquel Teran, Yolanda Medina, Pedro

Lopez, Shuya Ohno, Alex Gomez, Rudy Lopez, Sue Chinn, Ed and Jan Booth, Chris Torres, Lucy Piñon, Erika Andiola, Reyna Montaya, Maxima Guerrero, Lidia Carreon, Ruth Carreon, and the hundreds of others who volunteered.

Finally, thank you to the hundreds of Democratic grassroots leaders and volunteers from legislative districts across the state that helped drive our field campaign. I especially want to thank the leadership of LD 18—Andrew Sherwood, Wayne Mansky, Michael Conway, and the rest of the LD 18 precinct committee members—for embracing our anti-Pearce strategy and supporting Jerry Lewis. And when Pearce ran again in the newly created LD 25, I want to thank David Butler and his team for helping us elect Bob Worsley—thereby permanently retiring Pearce from elected office.

The success of our efforts also depended on hundreds of other individuals whose names go unmentioned. To all the unsung heroes and sheroes—volunteers, phone bankers, canvassers, donors, and allies who showed up for one hour, one day, or for the entire campaign—thank you for answering the call to action.

Photo Gallery: All the photos included in the photo gallery have been generously donated for the purposes of this project. I especially want to thank photographer Robert Hasch for providing most of the photos in the book and for working with me to develop the photos on the front and back cover. Robert, I appreciate your talent and patience as we worked together within a very tight time frame to get this done.

About the Author

Randy Parraz is co-founder and president of the Organizing Institute for Democracy—a nonprofit organization committed to civic engagement and expanding the fundamental principle of one person one vote. Since 1995, Randy's vocation as an organizer has been devoted to helping people build power to solve problems. From church-based organizing, to working with the National AFL-CIO and other labor organizations, to sparking grassroots efforts to hold extremist politicians accountable, Randy has extensive experience with multiple approaches to social change. He has also taught college courses on social change and enjoys facilitating workshops on leadership, power, and organizing.

Randy is a graduate of U.C. Berkeley, Berkeley Law, and the John F. Kennedy School of Government at Harvard University.

To learn more about the Organizing Institute for Democracy please go to: OIDemocracy.org. Speaking engagement requests for Randy Parraz can be submitted online at Dignitybyfire.com.

Appendix

APPLICATION FOR RECALL PETITION SERIAL NUMBER

Secretary of State
1700 W. Washington, 7th Floor
Phoenix, AZ 85007

RECEIVED
SECRETARY OF STATE

The undersigned intends to circulate and file a recall petition demanding the recall of:

2011 JAN 31 PM 12: 21

Russell Pearce
(Name)

State Senate - District 18
(Title of Office Held)

The grounds of the recall are as follows: (State in not more than 200 words the grounds of the demand.)

We, Citizens for a Better Arizona and residents of District 18, submit this petition to recall State Senator Russell Pearce for his failure to focus on issues and concerns that affect all Arizonans. Mesa and Arizona need a leader who will pass laws to create jobs, protect public education and ensure access to health care for our children and those most in need. We deserve a representative that reflects our values, beliefs and vision for Mesa and all of Arizona. By signing this petition we publicly withdraw our support for Russell Pearce and what he represents.

I hereby make application for the issuance of an official serial number to be printed on each side of each signature sheet of the petition (please affix to lower right-hand corner).

Todd A. Selleck
Signature of Applicant

Todd A. Selleck
Printed Name of Applicant

P.O. Box 41232
Address

Mesa   AZ   85274
City   State   Zip

(480) 748-8991   info@recallpearce.com
Telephone Number   Email Address

Citizens For A Better Arizona
Name of Organization (if any)

P.O. Box 41232
Address

Mesa   AZ   85274
City   State   Zip

(480) 748-8991   info@recallpearce.com
Telephone Number   Email Address

Chad Snow, Chairman
Name of Officer and Title

P.O. Box 41232
Address

Mesa   AZ   85274
City   State   Zip

(480) 748-8991   info@recallpearce.com
Telephone Number   Email Address

Diana Loken, Treasurer
Name of Officer and Title

P.O. Box 41232
Address

Mesa   AZ   85274
City   State   Zip

(480) 748-8991   info@recallpearce.com
Telephone Number   Email Address

Date of Application   January 31, 2011

Signatures Required   7,756

Deadline for Filing   May 31, 2011

Serial Number Issued   RC-04-2011

FOR OFFICE USE ONLY

CF ID# 201200056

Office revision 04/2005

351

Recall Petition

We, the qualified electors of the electoral district from which **State Senator Russell Pearce, District 18** was elected, demand his recall. The grounds of this demand for recall are as follows: (Name and title of office)

We, Citizens for a Better Arizona and residents of District 18, submit this petition to recall State Senator Russell Pearce for his failure to focus on issues and concerns that affect all Arizonans. Mesa and Arizona need a leader who will pass laws to create jobs, protect public education and ensure access to health care for our children and those most in need. We deserve a representative that reflects our values, beliefs and vision for Mesa and all of Arizona. By signing this petition we publicly withdraw our support for Russell Pearce and what he represents.

	Signature	Name (first and last name printed)	Actual address (street & no. and if no street address, describe residence location)	Arizona post office address & zip code	City or town (if any)	Date signed
1.						
2.						
3.						
4.						
5.						
6.						
7.						
8.						
9.						
10.						
11.						
12.						
13.						
14.						
15.						

Secretary of State
Revised 6/18/2003

The validity of signatures on this sheet must be sworn to by the circulator before a notary public on the form appearing on the back of this sheet.

Number RC-04-2011

KEN BENNETT
SECRETARY OF STATE
STATE OF ARIZONA

TO: Chad Snow
Citizens for a Better Arizona
P.O. Box 41232
Mesa, AZ 85274
(480) 748-8991

Having completed the requirements of A.R.S. § 19-208.03, I, Ken Bennett, Secretary of State, hereby certify that:

63 signature pages bearing 633 signatures for recall petition serial number RC-04-2011 have been refused for filing in this office because they did not meet the requirements set forth in A.R.S. §§ 19-121.01(A)(1) & (2). A total of 494 signatures included on the remaining petition sheets were found to be ineligible pursuant to A.R.S. § 19-121.01(A)(3). A total of 6,569 signatures were invalidated by the county recorder resulting in a failure rate of 38.79 per cent. [A.R.S. § 19-121.02(A)] The actual number of remaining signatures for such recall petition number RC-04-2011 is equal to or in excess of the 7,756 minimum required for state senate, legislative district 18, by the constitution. The petition therefore qualifies to be placed on the ballot at the next following consolidated election date pursuant to A.R.S. § 16-204 that is ninety days or more after the order calling the election.

IN WITNESS WHEREOF, I have hereunto set my hand and affixed the Great Seal of the State of Arizona. Done at the Capitol in Phoenix, this 8th day of July, 2011.

KEN BENNETT
Secretary of State

1700 W. Washington Street, 7th Floor
Phoenix, Arizona 85007-2888
Telephone (602) 542-4285 Fax (602) 542-1575
www.azsos.gov

KEN BENNETT
SECRETARY OF STATE
STATE OF ARIZONA

July 8, 2011

The Honorable Jan Brewer
Office of the Governor
1700 West Washington Street
Phoenix, Arizona 85007

Dear Governor Brewer:

Pursuant to Arizona Revised Statutes § 19-208.03(A)(1), this letter serves as notice that the recall committee, Citizens for a Better Arizona, has met the signature requirements for placement of RC-04-2011 on the ballot at the next following consolidated election date pursuant to A.R.S. § 16-204 that is ninety days or more after the order calling the election.

Enclosed are the final tabulation of the signature verification and a copy of the official receipt.

Sincerely,

KEN BENNETT
Secretary of State

Enclosures

1700 W. Washington Street, 7th Floor
Phoenix, Arizona 85007-2888
Telephone (602) 542-4285 Fax (602) 542-1575
www.azsos.gov

354

KEN BENNETT
SECRETARY OF STATE
STATE OF ARIZONA

NOTICE OF RECALL

RECEIVED

July 8, 2011

JUL 0 8 2011

OFFICE OF THE PRESIDENT

The Honorable Russell Pearce
Arizona State Senate
1700 West Washington Street
Room 205
Phoenix, Arizona 85007

Dear Senator Pearce:

Pursuant to Arizona Revised Statute (A.R.S.) § 19-207, this letter serves as written notification that the recall petitions circulated by Citizens for a Better Arizona have been certified to contain more than the minimum number of signatures to qualify for placement of the recall on the ballot.

The petition RC-04-2011 filed by Citizens for a Better Arizona states the following grounds for recall:

> "We, Citizens for a Better Arizona and residents of District 18, submit this petition to recall State Senator Russell Pearce for his failure to focus on issues and concerns that affect all Arizonans. Mesa and Arizona need a leader who will pass laws to create jobs, protect public education and ensure access to health care for our children and those most in need. We deserve a representative that reflects our values, beliefs and vision for Mesa and all of Arizona. By signing this petition we publicly withdraw our support for Russell Pearce and what he represents."

You have the right to prepare and have printed on the ballot a statement containing not more than 200 words defending your official conduct. The defensive statement must be received by our office within ten days. If you fail to submit a defensive statement, only your name will be printed on the ballot. You also have the right to resign by filing a written notice within five days, excluding Saturdays, Sundays and other legal holidays, with our office, in which case there will be no election and the vacancy will be filled as provided for by law. [A.R.S. § 19-208]

Should you have any questions or need additional information, please feel free to contact me at (602) 542-8683.

Sincerely,

Amy Bjelland
State Election Director

xc: Citizens for a Better Arizona
    Recall file

1700 W. Washington Street, 7th Floor
Phoenix, Arizona 85007-2888
Telephone (602) 542-4285 Fax (602) 542-1575
www.azsos.gov

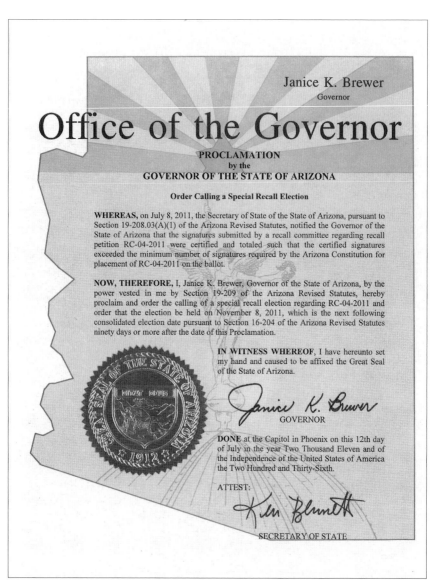

Janice K. Brewer
Governor

Office of the Governor

PROCLAMATION
by the
GOVERNOR OF THE STATE OF ARIZONA

Order Calling a Special Recall Election

WHEREAS, on July 8, 2011, the Secretary of State of the State of Arizona, pursuant to Section 19-208.03(A)(1) of the Arizona Revised Statutes, notified the Governor of the State of Arizona that the signatures submitted by a recall committee regarding recall petition RC-04-2011 were certified and totaled such that the certified signatures exceeded the minimum number of signatures required by the Arizona Constitution for placement of RC-04-2011 on the ballot.

NOW, THEREFORE, I, Janice K. Brewer, Governor of the State of Arizona, by the power vested in me by Section 19-209 of the Arizona Revised Statutes, hereby proclaim and order the calling of a special recall election regarding RC-04-2011 and order that the election be held on November 8, 2011, which is the next following consolidated election date pursuant to Section 16-204 of the Arizona Revised Statutes ninety days or more after the date of this Proclamation.

IN WITNESS WHEREOF, I have hereunto set my hand and caused to be affixed the Great Seal of the State of Arizona.

Janice K. Brewer
GOVERNOR

DONE at the Capitol in Phoenix on this 12th day of July in the year Two Thousand Eleven and of the Independence of the United States of America the Two Hundred and Thirty-Sixth.

ATTEST:

Ken Bennett
SECRETARY OF STATE

Citizens for a Better Arizona   Confidential   Recall Signer Demographics

Gender:	Women	4395	% of Category	% of Category
	Dem	2614	0.59476678	0.595
	Rep	748	0.170193402	0.170
	Green	8	0.00182025	0.002
	Lib	14	0.003185438	0.003
	Other	1011	0.23003413	0.230
	Total	**4395**	**1.000000**	**1.000**
	Men	3300	% of Category	% of Category
	Dem	1772	0.536969697	0.537
	Rep	556	0.168484848	0.168
	Green	14	0.004242424	0.004
	Lib	33	0.01	0.010
	Other	925	0.28030303	0.280
	Total	**3300**	**1.000000**	**1.000**
	Unknown Gender	**1416**		
	Total by Gender	**9111**		
Age:	Range	9111	% of Category	% of Category
	18-34	2465	0.27055208	0.271
	35-49	2232	0.244978597	0.245
	50-64	2652	0.29107672	0.291
	65+	1762	0.193392602	0.193
	All Ages	**9111**	**1.000000**	**1.000**
Party:	All	9111	% of Category	% of Category
	Dem	4953	0.543628581	0.544
	Rep	1449	0.159038525	0.159
	Green	24	0.002634178	0.003
	Lib	54	0.005926902	0.006
	Other	2631	0.288771814	0.289
	Total	**9111**	**1.000000**	**1.000**

6/28/11 12:53 PM

357

March 14, 2011

Senator Russell Pearce, Senate President
Arizona State Senate
1700 W Washington, Room S-205
Phoenix, AZ 85007

Dear President Pearce,

Thank you for your willingness to serve Arizona as a Member of the Arizona State Senate. We, like you, are concerned about the challenges facing our State, particularly the need to address our structural deficit and insure an economic environment that attracts and retains high quality jobs.

While we recognize the desire for states like Arizona to fill the leadership vacuum left by federal inaction on immigration, we strongly believe it is unwise for the Legislature to pass any additional immigration legislation, including any measures leaving the determination of citizenship to the state.

We agree with you that our borders must be protected first, and now. We also believe that market-driven immigration policies can and should be developed by the federal government that will sustain America's status as a magnet for the world's most talented and hard-working people and preserve our ability to compete in the global economy.

If the Legislature believes it is worthwhile to debate the question of citizenship, we believe that debate is best held in the U.S. Congress. Already, Senators David Vitter of Louisiana and Rand Paul of Kentucky have introduced legislation aimed at amending the 14th Amendment to deny "birthright citizenship" to those born to individuals living in the U.S. illegally. Iowa Rep. Steve King has introduced similar legislation in the U.S. House.

Arizona's lawmakers and citizens are right to be concerned about illegal immigration. But we must acknowledge that when Arizona goes it alone on this issue, unintended consequences inevitably occur. Last year, boycotts were called against our state's business community, adversely impacting our already-struggling economy and costing us jobs. Arizona-based businesses saw contracts cancelled or were turned away from bidding. Sales outside of the state declined. Even a business which merely had "Arizona" in its name felt the effects of the boycotts, compelling them to launch an educational campaign about their company's roots in Brooklyn. It is an undeniable fact that each of our companies and our employees were impacted by the boycotts and the coincident negative image.

Tourism, one of our state's largest industries and employment centers, also suffered from negative perceptions after the passage of SB 1070. The fact Governor Brewer directed $250,000 to repairing Arizona's reputation strongly suggests these efforts – whether fair or unfair - are harmful to our image.

Let us be clear: our dissension with legislative action on the state level does not translate to our being "pro-illegal immigration." To the contrary, we believe Congress must address border security, identity theft, sound and implementable employment verification systems and policies and the creation of a meaningful guest worker program. Therefore, we urge the Legislature to redirect its energy by joining us in pressing the federal government for meaningful immigration reform. Together, we can get results.

Respectfully,

Drew Brown
Managing Director
DMB Associates, Inc.

Philip Francis
Executive Chairman, PetSmart
Chairman, GPL

Ronald Butler
Arizona Managing Partner
Ernst & Young

W. Douglas Parker
Chairman, President/CEO
U.S. Airways Group

Ronald Brown
President
Atrium Holding Company

Richard Dozer
Chairman
GenSpring Family Offices

Stephen Rizley
Sr. Vice President/General Mgr.
Cox Communications, Inc.

Daniel Connor
President/CEO
Blood Systems

John Graham
President
Sunbelt Holdings

Peter Fine
President/CEO
Banner Health

Craig Phelps
Provost
A.T. Still University

Jeff Whiteman
President/CEO
Empire Southwest LLC

Thomas Sadvary
President/CEO
Scottsdale Healthcare

William Coats
Chief Executive Officer
The Leona Group

Herman Chanen
Chairman/CEO
The Chanen Corporation

Lee Hanley
Chairman/CEO
Vestar Development Company

William Schubert
Chairman
Kitchell Corporation

Jon Pettibone
Managing Partner
Quarles & Brady LLP

Paul Dykstra
Chairman, President/CEO
Viad Corporation

David Bruno
Vice Chairman, Managing Director
DHR International, Inc.

Marty Laurel
Vice President
Blue Cross Blue Shield of AZ

359

James Gentile
President/CEO
Research Corp for Science Adv.

Roger Vogel
Chairman, President/CEO
Vante Medical Technologies

Michael Duran
Vice President, Chief Dev. Off.
TMC Healthcare/TMC Found.

F. Michael Geddes
Chairman, President
Geddes and Company

Bruce Beach
CEO, BeachFleischman PC
Chairman, SALC

J. Doug Pruitt
Chairman/CEO
Sundt Construction, Inc.

Brian Johnson
Managing Director
Loews Ventana Canyon

Peter Likins
President Emeritus
University of Arizona

Robert Delgado
President/CEO
Hensley Beverage Company

Michael Kennedy
President
Gallagher & Kennedy P.A.

Bruce Dusenberry
President
Horizon Moving Systems, Inc.

Robert Underwood
Chief Executive Officer
Under wood Brothers, Inc.

Shelly Esque
Vice President, Legal/Corp Affairs
Intel Corporation

Denise Resnik
President
Denise Resnik & Associates

Vince Roig
Chairman/CEO
Helios Foundation

Constance Perez
Chief Executive Officer
Adreima

Susan Williams
President/Founder
HR Choice

Kevin Sandler
President/CEO
ExhibitOne Corporation

Debbie Johnson
President/CEO
Arizona Hotel & Lodging Assoc

Jim Click, Jr.
President
Jim Click Automotive Team

David Cohen
Executive Vice President
BeachFleishman PC

Donald Pitt
President
Campus Research Corporation

Alan Klein
Board Chair
So. Arizona Lodging & Resort Ass.

Michael Kasser
President
Holualoa Companies

Linda Hunt
Area President, CHW Arizona
President/CEO, St. Joseph's Hosp

John Zidich
CEO/Publisher
Arizona Republic

Howard Fleischmann
Owner
Community Tire & Auto Repair

Nancy Stone
President
ILX Resorts, Inc.

Janice Cox
Retired CEO
Carondelet Foundation

Don Budinger
Chairman/Founding Director
The Rodel Foundations

David Anderson
President
Off Madison Avenue

Steven Wheeler
Chairman
Greater Phoenix Chamber

Bill Calloway
Plant Manager
Nestle-Purina, Flagstaff

J.R. Murray
Chairman
Flagstaff Forty

Kenneth Lamneck

Frances Merryman

The following inclusion of names is authorized, but signatures were not available at the time of printing.

Reginald Ballantyne III, Senior Corporate Officer, Vanguard Health Systems, Inc.
Gerrit van Huisstede, Regional President, Wells Fargo Bank
Earl Petznick, Jr., President/CEO, Northside Hay Company